Suspended Lives

CRITICAL REFUGEE STUDIES

Edited by the Critical Refugee Studies Collective

Suspended Lives

NAVIGATING EVERYDAY VIOLENCE
IN THE US ASYLUM SYSTEM

Bridget M. Haas

UNIVERSITY OF CALIFORNIA PRESS

University of California Press
Oakland, California

© 2023 by Bridget M. Haas

Library of Congress Cataloging-in-Publication Data

Names: Haas, Bridget M., author.
Title: Suspended lives : navigating everyday violence in the US asylum
    system / Bridget M. Haas.
Other titles: Critical refugee studies ; 4.
Description: Oakland, California : University of California Press, [2023] |
    Series: Critical refugee studies; 4 | Includes bibliographical references
    and index.
Identifiers: LCCN 2022041036 (print) | LCCN 2022041037 (ebook) |
    ISBN 9780520385108 (cloth) | ISBN 9780520385122 (paperback) |
    ISBN 9780520385139 (ebook)
Subjects: LCSH: Political refugees—Violence against—United States. |
    Asylum, Right of—United States.
Classification: LCC JV6601 .H33 2023 (print) | LCC JV6601 (ebook) |
    DDC 323.6/310973—dc23/eng/20221108
LC record available at https://lccn.loc.gov/2022041036
LC ebook record available at https://lccn.loc.gov/2022041037

Manufactured in the United States of America

32 31 30 29 28 27 26 25 24 23
10 9 8 7 6 5 4 3 2 1

To Kirk, Casper, and Thea
And for asylum seekers everywhere

Contents

Acknowledgments

So many people have helped to bring this book to fruition and the project has benefitted greatly from their guidance, support, and feedback. First and foremost, I am immeasurably grateful to the asylum seekers who shared their lives, their time, and their stories with me to make this research possible. I am honored and humbled to have learned so much from them and I treasure the friendships I have developed with them over the many years of this project. It is my sincere hope that this book reflects their kindness, courage, and unwavering pursuit of dignity and justice.

In addition to the asylum claimants in Minnesota who so graciously welcomed me, I am grateful to the many asylum advocates and attorneys who took the time to talk to me and to let me observe immigration proceedings. In particular, before and during my initial fieldwork, Emily Good, then at the Advocates for Human Rights, was instrumental in facilitating my connection to local asylum claimants and helping me understand the institutional landscape of immigration in the area. Thanks to Kenneth Madsen, of US Citizenship and Immigration Services, and the asylum officers who agreed to be interviewed and willingly shared their perspectives on what is undoubtedly a challenging and important job.

The research for this book would not be possible without the generous funding of the National Science Foundation (grant #SES 0921535) and the Wenner-Gren Foundation for Anthropological Research (grant #8026).

Numerous people at the University of California, San Diego, where I completed my PhD in anthropology, were instrumental in shaping and giving life to this project. Above all, Janis Jenkins has been an extraordinary mentor. Her sustained, insightful, and thorough feedback on this project, during and long past its dissertation form, has enriched this project and book in so many ways. I have been fortunate to also have Tom Csordas and Steve Parish as mentors and thank them both for their support, insights, and intellectual exchange over the years. Material in this book has also been enriched by presentations at the UCSD department colloquia and the UCSD Seminar in Psychological and Medical Anthropology.

Many people at Case Western Reserve University, where I first began my anthropology training and then returned as a post-doctoral fellow and eventually teacher, have supported my work and shaped my thinking. I have been very fortunate to have Jill Korbin as a mentor and colleague. As my faculty advisor during my T32 NIH postdoctoral fellowship at CWRU, Jill offered sage commentary and guidance, not only about this project and other research, but about academic and professional life more broadly. In addition, Jim Spilsbury has been an important mentor and colleague at CWRU. Sana Loue was an excellent fellowship director who provided meaningful feedback and critique. I have benefitted from the interdisciplinary perspectives of Kristi Westphaln, HaeNim Lee, and Eunlye Lee. Thank you to Talia Weiner and Allison Schlosser for their friendship and intellectual conversations about anthropology and beyond.

I am appreciative of the intellectual relationships with many other anthropology friends and colleagues over the years, including Stephanie McClure, Elizabeth Carpenter-Song, Sarah Rubin, Leah Retherford, and Ilil Benjamin. Whitney Duncan has been a dear friend and colleague since our time together at UCSD, and her powerful work as an engaged anthropologist of migration inspires me. I thank her for her thoughtful feedback on earlier iterations of several chapters in this book. A very special thanks to Nadia El-Shaarawi. I am grateful for our friendship and writing partnership. Nadia's close reading of nearly every sentence of this book, her keen ethnographic sensibility, and her incisive feedback have greatly strengthened this project and facilitated its full development.

I am grateful to Amy Shuman for her mentorship, collaboration, and friendship. Her vital work on asylum and her intellectual legacy has informed this project. I appreciate her review and support of this book. Conversations with Amy about asylum, suspicion, and deservingness led to our co-organization of a Wenner-Gren-funded workshop in 2015, during which I cultivated and received feedback on larger ideas that I developed further in this book. I am grateful to additional, valuable comments and exchanges during that time with John Haviland, Charles Watters, Marco Jacquemet, and Rachel Lewis.

At the University of California Press, I extend my gratitude to the editors of the Critical Refugee Studies Book Series—Yến Lê Espiritu and fellow members of the Critical Refugee Studies Collective—for taking on this project. Thank you to Naomi Schneider and Summer Farah for ushering this book through its many stages. Thanks also to Emily Park and Teresa Iafolla at UC Press. I am very grateful to Catherine Osborne for her detailed work in copyediting this manuscript and to Amron Lehte for her hard work at creating the book's index.

The book was significantly improved by the detailed and incisive reviews of two anonymous reviewers. Their keen and attentive feedback helped to sharpen key arguments and numerous aspects of the book. I am also grateful to Beatriz Reyes-Foster, who reviewed this book and offered valuable suggestions for revision.

Finally, to my family, my gratitude exceeds words. My mother and father, Margo and Len Haas, have always nurtured my curiosity about the world and instilled in me the importance of social justice. Their steadfast support of me and this project has taken many forms, from countless hours of childcare to reading and discussing chapter drafts. The book has especially benefitted from my mother's sharp editorial eye and thoughtful feedback. My amazing sister, Gretchen, has always believed in and supported me and I am grateful for her love and companionship. Her generosity and her ability to always make me laugh are gifts I cherish. Thank you to Gabrielle, Keli, Julie, Heidi, and Meghan for their love and support.

Above all, the unwavering support, love, and patience of Kirk, Casper, and Thea grounds and inspires me, and have helped me through every stage of this project. Thank you, Kirk, for your optimism, humor, and for challenging my thinking. To Casper and Thea, thank you for the joy you bring to each day. I am so lucky to share my life with the three of you.

List of Acronyms

ATD	Alternatives to Detention
BI	Behavioral Interventions Incorporated
BIA	Board of Immigration Appeals
CHR	Center for Human Rights
CPDM	Cameroon People's Democratic Movement
DHS	Department of Homeland Security
DOJ	Department of Justice
EAD	Employment Authorization Document
EOIR	Executive Office for Immigration Review
ICE	US Immigration and Customs Enforcement
IJ	Immigration Judge
ISAP	Intensive Supervision and Appearance Program
PLR	Permanent Legal Resident
SCNC	Southern Cameroons National Council
USCIS	United States Citizenship and Immigration Services

Introduction

It was early 2010 and I had known Louise, an asylum claimant from Cameroon, for many months.[1] Louise was in her early forties and had a warm demeanor and an easy laugh, which I found remarkable given all that she had been through. She had quickly become one of my closest collaborators in the field. Late one evening, long after dusk, Louise called me, asking if I could come to her home. She was upset and wanted to talk in person. I made my way to her St. Paul, Minnesota neighborhood, to the building where she rented a small room in an apartment owned by an elderly woman with physical disabilities. In exchange for her full-time work as this woman's caretaker, Louise was provided the room and a small weekly pay. Usually not one to complain, Louise would, in her more despondent moments, confide in me that her inability to afford her own living space felt demoralizing. When I arrived at the apartment complex, Louise was waiting for me in the lobby. "So, Immigration thinks we are liars!" she said to me in a near-shout before I could even offer a greeting. Louise was waving a piece of paper in the air. "They say that Cameroonians lie! That Cameroon is good and that we come here and lie just to live in America." As we rode the elevator up to the sixth floor, I read the letter, sent by the lawyer—a patent attorney—who had been representing Louise *pro bono* during her asylum case as part of his volunteerism with a local human rights organization, which I refer to in this book as the Center for Human Rights (CHR). The letter included a copy of a communication from the US Department of Homeland Security (DHS) indicating that DHS attorneys had filed a motion to put Louise's asylum case on hold and begin an overseas investigation in Cameroon in order to verify documents and aspects of Louise's testimony that she had submitted as part of her asylum claim. No projected timeline was given.

This was a huge blow. Louise had been in the United States since 2005. She had been embedded in the US asylum system for years, having already had an asylum interview and an initial immigration court hearing, neither of which resulted in a decision on her case. Louise had anticipated receiving a final decision on her claim at her long-awaited second immigration court hearing scheduled for that spring, just months away. DHS's investigation would not only cause additional delays, exacerbating her uncertainty about the future and prolonging her separation from her husband and four children still in Cameroon. It was also, according to Louise, rather absurd. "So they will go and then tell me my country is corrupt. Of course Cameroon is corrupt!," Louise said, now ushering me into her small room in the apartment. "That's why I'm here in the first place! But why are they treating me like a criminal? It's very, very painful." She sighed heavily. "You know my story. I have suffered so much as a political supporter [in Cameroon]. My family has suffered a lot. And now I'm suffering here. I need this country to help me, to be a secure place for me." I did know Louise's story. Or part of it, as her story—at least the story of her displacement and search for refuge, as she told it—was still unfolding. But let me pause here and take us back a bit, to the preface, so to speak, of that day in 2010.

Before fleeing to the United States, Louise had lived her entire life in Bamenda, a city in the northwest region of Cameroon—one of the two English-speaking regions in the country. In Bamenda, Louise had been involved in oppositional political movements that protested the systematic oppression and economic, political, and cultural marginalization of Anglophone Cameroonians at the hands of the Francophone government, the Cameroon People's Democratic Movement (CPDM), led by President Paul Biya since 1982. Her decision to join the Southern Cameroons National Council (SCNC), a nonviolent oppositional party that advocates for the secession of the English-speaking (northwest and southwest) regions of the country from the rest of Cameroon, was driven by a sense of moral imperative. "It was like Cameroon was a prison and the prisoners are the Bamenda people," Louise described, adding, "so I was thinking 'what future is there for my children? Why should we be made to live like this, like second-class citizens by the French in our country?' It was a like wake-up call, and I realized I had to join [the SCNC], to fight for our freedom." In the early 2000s, Louise, like other SCNC activists, was subjected to threats and harassment by members of Biya's ruling government. Even after being physically assaulted by CPDM *gendarmes* (military police), Louise kept up her political activity, alongside her regular job of running a small café, despite her feelings of unease. Her greatest fear was realized, however, when she was abducted from her café by CPDM forces and taken to a government detention facility where she endured daily interrogations and beatings for several months. Upon her release, which was ordered only after Louise agreed to indefinite weekly check-ins at the detention facility, Louise knew that staying in Cameroon put not only her own life, but also those of her family, in grave danger. Over a series of months, with Louise in hiding, the local SCNC chapter raised enough money for a plane ticket and a visa for Louise, plus additional money for the many bribes to government officials that were necessary to obtain them. Someone in the local SCNC chapter found acquaintances, a married couple in Minnesota, who agreed to house Louise upon her arrival to the United States.

Louise had not heard of "asylum" before coming to the United States, but the couple with whom she was staying told her she would need to have this to stay beyond the few months covered by her visitor visa. Through word of mouth, Louise found an attorney who advertised quick and cheap assistance filing asylum applications, and she submitted her claim with their help. Shortly after that, the couple with whom she was staying informed Louise that they regrettably could no longer host her, as the wife was pregnant and expecting twins. For the next couple of years, Louise, with no work permit, was able to cobble together barely enough money to sustain herself through informal sewing and house-cleaning jobs. She shuffled from house to house, as various community and church members were able to take her in for only relatively short periods. Louise recalled what a difficult time this was for her: "I was feeling homeless, I had no money, missing my family so much. I was suffering and was not knowing what was going on with my asylum [case]." One afternoon in 2008, Louise offhandedly mentioned to a friend from her church that she had been waiting three years for a response about her asylum application. Louise's friend told her that this was too long, suggesting something was likely amiss, and subsequently referred Louise to the Center for Human Rights. CHR staff discovered that Louise's file was not registered with the US Citizenship and Immigration Services (USCIS), the division of government responsible for handling asylum applications. Louise's file had either been lost by the state or had never been filed by the lawyer she had paid to do so. In any case, Louise would need to file another asylum application, placing her at the beginning of the queue and facing an additional year before she would have an asylum interview. Louise described how she felt during this time:

> It was very bad, very bad. I left my country because of problems. For three years [in the United States], if I were to die, then no one would even know. When I came to the US, I thought this is where my problems can be solved. But then I realized that they didn't even know I existed, you know. It was a horrible situation. It weighed me down because I felt like if I died, then nobody would even know. Nobody would even recognize me. But I thought that I was doing the right thing, going through the proper paperwork.

Louise was happy and grateful for the legal representation and assistance with her asylum application provided by CHR. To be sure, asylum seekers in the United States without legal representation for their asylum cases face an astoundingly higher rate of denial: almost 90 percent of asylum claimants without legal representation are denied, as opposed to 60 percent of those with legal representation. But the hope that Louise had about her case was constantly being tempered by the painful waiting and uncertainty she was forced to endure, the onerous and disorientating asylum bureaucracy, and the economic and structural precarity she faced. Though the asylum officer who interviewed Louise referred her to immigration court because of concerns surrounding Louise's perceived credibility, Louise tried to maintain an optimistic attitude about her case. She believed that the US government would ultimately recognize what Louise knew to be true: she was deserving of asylum status. Yet it became clear that her assertion of deservingness—what Louise understood to be her *right* to protection—would be contested in complex, protracted, and often painful ways. This brings us, then, to the evening in 2010 when the letter informing her of the overseas investigation brought into stark relief Louise's ambiguous and tenuous status in the United States.

It is notable that when Louise referred to her "story" of displacement, she included both her past struggles as a political activist in Cameroon and her current sense of suffering in the United States. Indeed, throughout my longitudinal ethnographic fieldwork on the lived experiences of those seeking asylum in the midwestern United States, I was most struck by the ways in which the US asylum system not only exacerbated asylum claimants' past trauma, but also inflicted new forms of suffering, with effects that often outlived the resolution of their asylum claims. My focus in this research is on asylum seekers like Louise who had filed what is termed an "affirmative" asylum application. Unlike asylum seekers who are apprehended at the US border or at a port of entry and are immediately put into deportation proceedings, affirmative asylum applicants are already within the United States when they file their asylum claims. Affirmative asylum applicants start their process in a non-courtroom setting and are not (initially, at least) charged with defending themselves against removal from the country. Yet, as Louise's story reveals, the US asylum system simultaneously animates both hope and fear for affirmative asylum applicants.

Asylum claimants occupy a transitory space, as those who have asserted their need of protection but have not yet—and may never—be recognized as in need of it (Coutin 2003; Cabot 2014). The asylum system is simultaneously exclusionary and inclusionary. Caught in a system that will produce them as either deserving/legitimate or undeserving/illegitimate, asylum seekers inhabit a dual positionality while their claims are being adjudicated: they are at once "citizens-in-waiting" and "deportees-in-waiting" (Haas 2017). This paradoxical lived positionality is codified in legal language, as asylum claimants are both "persons living under the color of the law" *and* "deportable aliens."

If an asylum decision, which often takes years to be reached, has perceived life-and-death per CMOS and latter instances in text consequences, the asylum process itself also shapes everyday life in profound ways. Because asylum claimants have not yet proven their deservingness of protection, they are confronted with a host of bureaucratic policies and procedures that treat them as morally ambiguous subjects. When Louise declared that the letter from DHS about the overseas investigation communicated that "Immigration thinks we are liars ... that we come here and lie just to live in America," she was, of course, not reflecting the verbatim language of the letter. Yet, her interpretation of DHS's actions was accurately reflective of what I term an institutional *ethos of suspicion* that undergirds the US asylum regime. While Louise knew she was telling the truth in her testimony and that she deserved a secure place in the United States, she could not evade the state's mistrustful and punitive gaze. And she was ever aware that it was the state, and not her, that would be the ultimate arbiter of her appeal for protection.

A CONTINUUM OF VIOLENCE WITHIN THE US ASYLUM SYSTEM

An institutional ethos of suspicion, which positions asylum seekers as potential threats or malingerers, informs a range of technologies of "managing" and policing asylum claimants. In this book, I examine the lived consequences of these bureaucratic policies and practices. How do the institutional techniques of governing associated with the US asylum system shape the subjective, affective, and social lives of those embedded in it? To ethnographically explore this, I begin with the claim that the numerous institutional techniques of governing and disciplining asylum claimants constitute a "continuum of violence" (Scheper-Hughes and Bourgois 2004a, 1). In their response to Paul Farmer's (2004) elaboration of "an anthropology of structural violence" as a critical theoretical intervention, Scheper-Hughes and Bourgois (2004b) argue that "structural violence," while having analytic value in understanding life experiences, is nonetheless too broad and undefined a term and thus risks collapsing qualitatively different forms and experiences of violence into a singular concept. To avoid the conflation of various forms of violence, Scheper-Hughes and Bourgois (2004a) suggest the framework of a "continuum of violence" which accounts for—but differentiates—forms of violence ranging from torture and genocide to the violence of poverty and social exclusion. As they argue: "Violence can never be understood solely in terms of its physicality—force, assault, or the infliction of pain—alone. Violence also includes assaults on personhood, dignity, sense of worth or value of the victim. The social and cultural dimensions of violence are what gives violence its power and meaning" (1).

We can see a continuum of violence stretching from asylum seekers' countries of origin to the United States. Attention to asylum seekers' past experiences is important not only because they shape how claimants experience the asylum process but also because it provides a basis for understanding how the US asylum system both serves as a potential refuge from past violence *and* creates new forms of violence. If reaching the United States meant an end to forms of violence like the torture Louise endured in military prison, asylum claimants were nonetheless met "with further displays of state power and violence, even if the latter takes on only bureaucratic and juridical forms" (Daniel and Knudsen 1995, 7). Yet, the extension of violence from past to present is but one iteration of a violence continuum. The idea of a violence continuum is also instructive to our understanding of the US asylum system itself. Indeed, this is my primary focus and guiding conceptual framework for my analyses of asylum seeking in this book. By positing that the US asylum system comprises a continuum of violence, my goal is to a) expose the bureaucratic forms of governing within the asylum system—often normalized and/or invisible—*as forms of violence*, and b) ethnographically elucidate the often-deleterious subjective effects of these myriad technologies of governing, which are interrelated but also distinct in terms of their contours and lived consequences.

The routinization of policies and practices that comprise the asylum system's violence continuum is integral to the operation and effectiveness of the system. In other words, these bureaucratic practices work as technologies of power in part because of their normalization and, often, their invisibility. Scheper-Hughes and Bourgois's (2004a) framework of a violence continuum is theoretically rooted in a significant line of scholarship over the past several decades that has troubled the idea of violence as primarily overt and visible (Das et al. 2000; Farmer 1996, 2004; Holmes 2007; Jenkins 1998; Scheper-Hughes 1992). Important to this conceptual expansion of violence is Bourdieu's concept of "symbolic violence," or "the gentle, hidden form which violence takes when overt violence is impossible," and his related concept of "misrecognition," whereby violence becomes naturalized as a routine part of experience and social life (1977, 196). Thus, symbolic violence is powerful in its pernicious ability to dominate, though not be recognized as such.

My exploration of the violences of the US asylum system is inspired by recent scholarship that has made violence central to analyses of immigration bureaucracies and regimes. Wendy Vogt's (2018) moving and richly theorized account of Central American migrants in transit draws on concepts of "poststructural violence" and intersectionality to understand the multiple forms of violence inflicted upon (and by) migrants, attending to their "ripple effects" (5). In their work with refugees and asylum seekers in Canada, Rousseau et al. (2004) argue that those seeking political asylum "are subjected to forms of 'clean violence,' a form of violence associated with technocratic organizations that is more subtle but as damaging as other forms of organizational violence" (1095). Menjívar and Abrego (2012) introduce the concept of "legal violence," an analytic category used to "capture the normalized but cumulative injurious effects of the law" (1380). Finally, in their research on the everyday lives of asylum seekers in the United Kingdom, Lucy Mayblin and colleagues (Mayblin 2020; Mayblin, Wake, and Kazemi 2020) propose a conceptual framework that puts necropolitics (Mbembe 2003) and "slow violence" (Nixon 2011) into dialogue. Critical to their postcolonial intervention, Mayblin, Wake, and Kazemi argue that necropolitics, the subjugation of some populations to conditions of harm or death, is integrally linked to colonial racial hierarchies. In turn, for asylum seekers, these underlying conceptions of differential human worth produce the everyday as a site of "slow violence," which Nixon (2011) defines as "a violence that occurs gradually and out of sight ... an attritional violence that is typically not viewed as violence at all" (2).

These concepts draw important attention to the misrecognition of institutional violence and its everyday effects. Certainly, the overarching theoretical frames of "legal violence," "clean violence," and/or "slow violence" would aptly describe the everyday lived effects of the US asylum system, and I do draw on these. Yet, I find the framework of a violence continuum to be the most productive of a deeper understanding of the harms generated by the US asylum system. As an analytic framework, the violence continuum allows for an appreciation of the cumulative and interrelated effects of the asylum process while still accounting for important distinctions inherent in different mechanisms of power. Thus, by engaging the concept of a violence continuum to understand the lived experiences of asylum seeking, we can account for a range of violences including—but not limited to—forms of clean, slow, and legal violence. While many of the routinized and normalized violences associated with the asylum system are hidden, others are not. My interlocutors contended with myriad forms of violence, from less overt or symbolic forms of harm and dignity assaults to more direct, physical, and/or structural forms. The frame of a violence continuum captures how these multiple forms of violence had their own subjective and affective consequences for asylum claimants, as well as having cumulative and synergistic effects.

So, what does the violence continuum associated with the US asylum system look like? The brief snapshot of Louise's story that opened this chapter begins to bring this into view. As we trace Louise's experience of seeking asylum in the United States, many different and intersecting forms of bureaucratic violence can be uncovered. These are taken up in the chapters that follow, but I briefly outline them here to provide a preliminary ethnographic anchor to my conceptual framework and a road map of the book itself. First, Louise was confronted with institutional technologies of visibility and opacity, which I frame as the *violence of in/visibility* (chapter 1). A key aspect of asylum seekers' subjective experience of the asylum process relates to what I label a *paradox of visibility*. By lodging an asylum claim with the US government, asylum seekers are, in effect, seeking to be visible. Their goal is to be recognized as refugees under international and domestic law, and thereby granted legal status. Indeed, Louise articulated her non-presence (her invisibility) to the US government—when she learned that she was not in the USCIS system—as an existential threat. After learning about the need to apply for asylum, my interlocutors, with few exceptions, willingly filed their claims as quickly as possible.[2] By engaging with the asylum system, asylum claimants become both liminal subjects—noncitizens whose legal status is to be determined—and (hyper)visible figures (see Tyler 2006, 193). Asylum seekers' visibility expresses the desire and hope for security. Yet, that same visibility is often experienced as a profound source of *in*security. As asylum claimants are subjected to the scrutiny of a new state power, they find themselves visible in terms not of their own making, evidenced by the putative criminality thrust upon Louise (see also Abarca and Coutin 2018). At the same time, the opacity and illegibility of asylum bureaucracies are fundamental to state power. Louise's struggle to know the proper channels for submitting her asylum claim, for example, speaks to the political force of such illegibility.

Second, Louise's story highlights the *violence of waiting* as a salient dimension of the asylum process (chapter 2). Though there were moments in which time and waiting was foregrounded and more palpably present, it was also the case that temporal violence was an overarching and pervasive facet of asylum claimants' lived experiences. The asylum claimants I knew waited, on average, two and a half years for a final decision on their cases, but many of them waited for over five years. In my analyses, I approach waiting as both an institutional technology of power and a phenomenological state. Louise's story exposes these dual dimensions. DHS's ability to indefinitely pause her case was an expression of state power. Here, Louise was *made* to wait. At the same time, her narrative illustrates the lived effects of waiting, as she framed this as a form of suffering, prolonging her insecurity and separation from her family. The title of this book, *Suspended Lives,* calls attention to asylum seekers' descriptions of their lives within a space of uncertain and ambivalent refuge. Asylum claimants described their experiences of the asylum process in terms of immobility: as life "stuck," "hanging," "suspended," "on hold," and "frozen." This is not to suggest, however, that asylum seekers were passive. Indeed, they were constantly engaged in maneuvering through a complex and oftentimes oppressive institutional landscape. They actively endured the asylum process. Thus, while the techniques of governing to which asylum seekers were subjected powerfully shaped their lived experience, they were not determinative of it. Asylum seekers' experiences involved "a dual process of self-making and being-made within webs of power" (Ong 1996, 738). In this way, asylum claimants' positions of "stuckedness" (Hage 2009) provide an opening for exploring agency and experience in sites of confinement and (hyper)regulation. Using this position of suspended life as my point of departure does not reduce asylum seekers to passivity, but rather allows for an investigation into how they forged lives in a space they themselves defined in terms of immobility.

Third, there are many places in Louise's story where her *socioeconomic marginalization* is evident, from her earlier experiences with housing and financial insecurity to her meager salary and social isolation even after being granted work authorization. The institutional production of Louise's economic and social-structural precarity constitutes an additional form of violence associated with the US asylum bureaucracies (chapter 3). As they engaged in their often-protracted quest for legal protection in the United States, my interlocutors found themselves lacking material resources, exacerbating their sense of vulnerability. Legally and politically categorized as "noncitizens," asylum claimants do not qualify for any housing assistance that relies on federal or state aid. Under federal law, non-pregnant adult asylum seekers who do not have children living with them also do not qualify for any federal or most state cash assistance programs. In addition, asylum claimants are not immediately authorized to work—the law requires a mandatory wait period after an asylum application is filed before an asylum seeker can even apply for a work permit. Though not representative of all asylum applicants, most of my interlocutors did not arrive in the United States with savings or consistent access to financial support. Asylum claimants in Minnesota did have access to state-funded health care coverage,[3] though lack of information about this program along with fears about their tenuous legal status proved to be barriers to its utilization.

Finally, though outside of the asylum interview room or immigration court, Louise's story reveals the *epistemic violence* of the asylum system and of asylum adjudication more specifically (chapter 4). Louise's sense that "Immigration" or "they"—the nameless and often faceless asylum bureaucrats—interpreted her as a liar was not merely a logistical headache or misunderstanding. Rather, it highlights the profound struggle over the meaning of one's story that asylum adjudication entails. Again and again, I witnessed a profound disconnect between the meaning that asylum claimants assigned to their experiences and the bureaucratic logic and grammar of the legal bodies that assessed them. The struggle over meaning was, for asylum claimants, an existential issue. The perceived life-and-death stakes of an asylum determination and the inequitable field of power in which these decisions unfolded made these struggles both urgent and fraught.

Just as these forms of violence outlined above were normalized as routine aspects of the asylum process, the profound distress of my interlocutors was largely rendered invisible. This point was driven home when at an immigration conference in 2019, I attended a panel on legal representation for detained asylum seekers—those who have been apprehended by DHS and put into removal proceedings, having filed "defensive claims." The attorney leading the panel described to the audience the grim circumstances of his detained clients: they are imprisoned, unable to visit with family and friends, have limited information and access to legal assistance, and often have no idea when they will be released. The attorney then contrasted the lived realities of his clients with affirmative asylum claimants, who, he declared, "have it so much easier." Affirmative asylum claimants, the attorney told the audience, are not in detention, and after a period of waiting, they are able to work and, as he put it, "live a normal life" while their claims are pending. I was taken aback by this relatively rosy picture. Having spent a good part of the previous decade working with affirmative asylum claimants, I had learned something very different. Indeed, as Louise's story keenly illustrates, life as an affirmative asylum seeker was hardly "easy" or "normal," given the multiple forms of violence to which she was subjected. Yet, this attorney's claim reinforces my argument that it is the routinization of these violences that enable their reproduction.[4]

Additionally, what this attorney failed to clarify is the fact that many affirmative asylum applicants are not successful at the affirmative (interview) level and their cases are referred to immigration court, at which point they are, in fact, in "defensive" proceedings (see figure 1). Though affirmative asylum applicants do have materially different experiences than defensive claimants, these categories are more fluid than discrete. These different paths are also part of the same governmental apparatus, part of a larger shared continuum of violence. To be clear, I am not suggesting that life in detention is the same as life outside it. The policy of detaining asylum applicants—those who are legally pursuing a right to protection—is an appalling violation of human rights and an abdication of the state's ethical and legal obligations. My interlocutors, who filed affirmative asylum claims in a non-border, or "interior," location, were, for the most part, not subjected to these egregious forms of violence, epitomized by the "spectacular" violence of the US-Mexico border (Chavez 2008; De

Genova 2013). Moreover, unlike the situation of my interlocutors, for newly arrived asylum seekers at the border, recent policies have made the defensive asylum system significantly more complicated and unjust (see Erfani 2022). Yet, it is critical that attention to the "hyperviolence" of detention and deportation not render other forms and other migrants' experiences of violence invisible (Lopez 2019, 158).

SITUATING ASYLUM AND ASYLUM SEEKERS

Asylum is a humanitarian protection granted to foreign nationals already in the United States or at the border who meet the international definition of a refugee. In the United States, the same criteria are used to define refugees and asylees. The legal difference is that refugees are granted status prior to their admittance to the United States, while asylum status is granted to those who ask for protection after arriving. The definition of "refugee" in US law is taken from two international law treaties, the 1951 Geneva Convention and the 1967 Protocol Relating to the Status of Refugees. It was incorporated into domestic (US) law through the 1952 Immigration and Nationality Act (INA), and amended in the 1980 Refugee Act, which defines a refugee as:

> Any person who is outside any country of such person's nationality, or in the case of a person having no nationality, is outside any country in which such person last habitually resided, and who is unable or unwilling to return to, and is unable and unwilling to avail himself or herself of the protection of, that country because of persecution or a well-founded fear of persecution on account of race, religion, nationality, membership in a particular social group, or political opinion.

As noted, this book focuses specifically on those persons who have lodged a formal claim with the US government to seek asylum status—to be legally recognized as meeting the criteria of a "refugee." Throughout, I use the terms "asylum claimant," "asylum applicant," and "asylum seeker" interchangeably. I recognize that categories such as "asylum seeker," "refugee," and "migrant" are socially and historically constructed and derive from specific policy agendas (Hathaway 2007; Yarris and Castañeda

2015; Zetter 2007). Throughout the book, I likewise use quotation marks around concepts such as "legal" and "illegal" to signal their sociohistorical construction rather than see these concepts as self-evident or natural (Coutin 2005; Dauvergne 2004; De Genova 2002; Heyman 2013). These legal categories, moreover, often "obscure rather than disclose the life-worlds" of those living under these labels (Perdigon 2017, 182), and are also, in practice, fluid and shifting rather than bounded (McGuirk and Pine 2020). Anthropological work on refugees has been important in serving as a corrective to the problematic tendency in academic and policy work to dehistoricize and/or depoliticize refugees, and thus treat "refugees" as a universal construct (Malkki 1995, 1996, Peteet 2005). Likewise, "asylum seekers" cannot be seen as a naturalized or monolithic category. Yet, as an ethnographic investigation of the asylum-seeking process specifically, my project focuses on those who were subjected to a set of common practices, including specific mechanisms of power and techniques of "management," because of their positionality as legal asylum claimants.

The US Asylum Process

Asylum law is relatively new within the United States: it was not until the passage of the Refugee Act of 1980 that the right to seek asylum was formulated and a system for processing asylum claims was established (Cianciarulo 2006). Up until this point, many, if not most, refugees to the United States came from Communist countries, and US refugee policy was adjudicated on an *ad hoc* basis. The Refugee Act of 1980 amended the INA, adopting the INA's definition of "refugee." The Act's main purpose was to establish a uniform system for admitting and resettling refugees domestically, and thereby created the Office of US Coordinator for Refugee Affairs and the Office of Refugee Resettlement. Moreover, the Refugee Act of 1980 also outlined for the first time in US law a category of "asylum," and established a systematic protocol for the Immigration and Naturalization Service (INS) and immigration courts to adjudicate asylum claims (Einolf 2001).

Affirmative asylum claims are currently filed with INS's successor, the Office of Citizenship and Immigration Services (USCIS) within the Department of Homeland Security (DHS), while defensive claims are filed with the Executive Office for Immigration Review (EOIR), part of the Department of Justice (DOJ). A person may file an affirmative claim regardless of legal status if they have not been apprehended by DHS. In an affirmative case, the asylum applicant is interviewed by a trained officer associated with one of the eight asylum offices in the country. Because the asylum office responsible for the jurisdiction of my field site was in another state (located in Chicago, IL), asylum applicants in Minneapolis-St. Paul needed to wait until asylum officers from that office conducted "circuit rides," during which an officer would interview applicants at the local immigration court outside of St. Paul. Circuit rides, on average, happened a couple of times per year.

An asylum officer can grant an applicant asylum, deny asylum (only if the applicant has valid immigration status), or refer the applicant to an immigration judge (IJ), whereby the case is taken up by the EOIR, within the DOJ, and the applicant is put in "removal proceedings." While statistics vary, reliable information suggests that, at the time of my initial fieldwork, asylum officers nationally referred to an IJ 65–70 percent of cases that they heard, granting around 30 percent and denying fewer than 5 percent (Ramji-Nogales, Schoenholtz, and Schrag 2011). Even though my interlocutors had filed affirmative asylum claims, few of them were granted asylum at the level of the USCIS interview. If a case is referred to the DOJ, an immigration hearing is scheduled. Trial attorneys from Immigration and Customs Enforcement (ICE), part of DHS, act on behalf of the government during the hearing. Because an asylum hearing is considered adversarial, trial attorneys conduct cross-examination and attempt to present evidence that asylum is not warranted. In 2010–2011, judges presiding over cases at the immigration court in Minnesota had a significantly higher denial rate than the national average for IJs. The overall denial rate for Minnesota judges was 72.8 percent, compared to the national average denial rate of 53.2 percent (TRAC 2012).

The immigration court also hears defensive asylum claims: cases where an asylum applicant who is without valid immigration status has been apprehended by DHS before they filed an asylum application. Asylum applicants filing a defensive claim do not have the opportunity to have their cases heard by a USCIS asylum officer. Rather, the case is immediately handled by an immigration judge, and follows the same protocol as

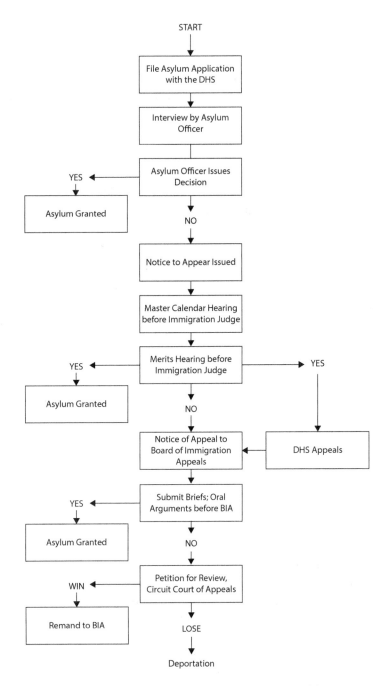

Figure 1. Flow Chart: Affirmative Asylum Process. Adapted from "Asylum Process Flow Chart," National Immigrant Justice Center, Heartland Alliance, 2014.

outlined above. Regardless of how their initial claim was filed (affirmatively or defensively), if an asylum applicant is denied asylum by an immigration judge, the applicant may appeal their case to the Board of Immigration Appeals (BIA), which will then decide whether to uphold the immigration judge's decision. Only 8 percent of immigration court cases were appealed to the BIA and the BIA upheld the IJ's decision 89 percent of the time (U.S. Department of Justice 2012). If not successful upon appeal to the BIA, most cases end at this point, largely due to the cost of further appeal as well as the requirements regarding eligibility for relief in federal court. At this point, "failed asylum seekers" are ordered to leave the country. It is critical to point out here that unlike those within the US criminal court system, asylum claimants are not provided legal representation at any level of their cases. My interlocutors were fortunate to have secured *pro bono* legal representation through CHR, as statistics show that the majority (90 percent) of unrepresented asylum claimants are denied asylum status in immigration court (Ramji-Nogales et al. 2011; Bohmer and Shuman 2018).

In 2010, when I first began my research, the United States received just under 33,000 asylum applications. That number steadily rose over the course of my fieldwork and subsequent follow-up research. In 2019, there were 307,704 asylum applications filed in the United States, and 96,952 of these were affirmative applications (Baugh 2020). Importantly, asylum may be granted to any person meeting the above definition, regardless of how they entered the country. That is, under both international and domestic law, if a person meets the legal criteria of a refugee, the nature of their border crossing is irrelevant. Thus, asylum claimants may have arrived in the United States clandestinely, without "legal" authorization, or they may have entered the United States through identified authorized channels, such as with temporary travel or student visas. So, whether a person files an asylum application in a USCIS office in Bloomington, MN, or after being apprehended at the US-Mexico border, they are acting in accordance with the law.

A significant problem with the asylum system has been the enormous backlog of cases. In 2011, the backlog for all asylum cases in immigration courts (those filed defensively or affirmative claims that were referred to the EOIR) stood at a then all-time high of 320,331 (TRAC 2012). This hefty backlog resulted in delayed court hearings and adjudication of claims. This situation has only become more entrenched. As of September 2021, over 400,000 affirmative asylum claims were pending with USCIS (Dzubow 2021) and the backlog of asylum cases in US immigration courts grew to its highest ever at 667,229 (TRAC 2021). This translates to average wait times for an asylum hearing of over five years, which does not include time spent waiting prior to the filing of the asylum claim or time spent at the USCIS level. As a 2021 Human Rights First report succinctly summarized, "(t)he human consequences of the [US asylum] backlog are devastating."

To explore the lived experiences of the protracted and onerous asylum process, I conducted in-depth ethnographic fieldwork with a multi-ethnic, multi-national group of twenty-six asylum seekers from seven different countries[5] during sixteen months of continuous ethnographic fieldwork in and around Minneapolis-St. Paul, Minnesota from 2009 to 2011. This fieldwork was augmented by shorter follow-up trips in 2012, 2015, and 2019. Data collection with my asylum claimant interlocutors included the collection of life histories; multiple open-ended, ethnographic interviews; ongoing recording of everyday conversations with my research participants; and extensive participant observation (for which I wrote daily fieldnotes). A nongovernmental human rights organization in Minneapolis, which I earlier introduced as the Center for Human Rights (CHR), assisted me in the initial recruitment of study participants by sending out flyers about my study and subsequently referred interested asylum claimants to me.[6] CHR has a well-established legal aid program for assisting asylum seekers on a *pro bono* basis, as they did for Louise.

The Minneapolis-St. Paul area has been a rich site to investigate the lived experiences of asylum seekers. The area has a rich and diverse history of migration and has been identified as a "twenty-first-century gateway" for migration, with a resurgence in immigration to the area in recent decades (Singer, Hardwick, and Brettell 2008). In addition to being home to a large number of refugees from Southeast Asia (Hmong, Vietnamese, Laotian, and more recently Burmese), who have settled in the Twin Cities since the mid-twentieth century, the Twin Cities continue to see the arrival of large numbers of asylum seekers and refugees, not only from Southeast Asia, but also in recent decades from African countries such as Ethiopia,

Liberia, Somalia, Guinea, Ghana, Togo, Cameroon, and Democratic Republic of Congo (MN Department of Health 2012, 2021). An estimated 25–50 percent of immigrants in Minnesota were refugees and asylum seekers, compared to 8 percent nationally, and Minnesota currently has the highest number of refugees and asylum seekers per capita of any state (Immigration Law Center of Minnesota 2018).

Asylum seekers from the northwest region of Cameroon were the largest subset of my sample, thirteen of twenty-six, and were a group of particular ethnographic focus in my research. Having a multi-ethnic/multinational sample along with a more focused sub-sample provided me with invaluable insights. First, working with a nationally and ethnically diverse sample allowed me to track themes that emerged across my sample, including ways of being-in-the-world that my interlocutors themselves attributed to their positionality as "asylum claimant." While I do attend to the variability of participants' experiences—informed by diverse sociocultural, political-economic, historical, and personal factors—there are many salient, shared aspects of asylum claimants' lives that emerge from their engagement with a specific politico-legal system. This book, then, is perhaps best understood not as an ethnography of a particular group of asylum seekers but as an ethnography of asylum *seeking*.

At the same time, I bring into focus aspects of my Cameroonian interlocutors' lives and narratives that were distinct from my other research participants. For example, my Cameroonian interlocutors frequently referenced their past political struggle and asserted their identities as "freedom fighters" to communicate their moral agency as they tried to make sense of their displacement and exile in the United States. This is not to say that other (non-Cameroonian) asylum claimants did not feel the same way or share similar forms of political subjectivity. But this was a marked aspect of my Cameroonian participants' speech. These narratives provide an important window into the collective lived effects of the asylum system. Cameroonians' narratives of their pasts, as they are recalled in the present, reveal subjectivities and identities that are often elided in legal and public arenas, as well as in some academic scholarship on refugees and asylum seekers. I see these narratives of "freedom fighting," moral agency, and familial and community obligation as meaningful counternarratives, or what critical race theorists have framed as "counterstories" (Fan 1997;

Solórzano and Yosso 2002). As reflections of lived experience and subjectivity, these counternarratives expose the profound disconnect between asylum seekers' own perceptions of themselves, their situation, and their deservingness of protection and the institutional labels and techniques of discipline within the asylum system.

In addition, though a sense of social isolation was fairly ubiquitous among my study participants, Cameroonians, as opposed to some of my other interlocutors, often maintained a connection to local communities throughout the asylum process. As I discuss further in later chapters, having a shared (ethnic/national) local community shaped one's experiences of the asylum process. Finally, though wholly unanticipated, my follow-up field visits and data collection in Minnesota in 2019 took place during a resurgence of violence and terror in the Anglophone regions of Cameroon, which began anew in late 2016/early 2017. In important ways, I was able to track how the newly revived violence in my interlocutors' country of origin challenged and reconfigured their sense of belonging and security in the United States, even if they had been granted asylum. Violence in Cameroon intersected with the enduring effects of the violence of the US asylum system in complex, fraught, and ultimately tragic ways (see chapter 5 and the conclusion).

The intensive ethnographic fieldwork with asylum seekers constituted the bulk of my data collection; I spent my days with asylum seekers in their homes, at their jobs and places of worship, and accompanying them on errands and to various bureaucratic appointments and legal proceedings. But I also knew that to fully capture the complexity of the asylum-seeking process, I needed to cast a broader net. To this end, I interviewed dozens of immigration advocates, attorneys, and USCIS asylum officers. I also observed numerous asylum hearings, attended immigration conferences, and sat in on several training sessions for immigration attorneys. Attention to these institutional actors and bodies, and especially being granted the unique opportunity to interview adjudicators, gave me a better understanding of the various, and often, conflicting logics at play in this context. In chapter 4, I engage directly with my data culled from these sources. If asylum claimants have only intermittent and limited contact with asylum adjudicators and other immigration officials, the ideologies reflected in my interviews and observations among these legal actors are indicative of a larger culture of suspicion and conceptions of asylum seekers as problematic subjects that "spills over from the formal space of asylum law" (Cabot 2014, 7). These underlying ideologies and moral evaluations undergird not only the intersubjective milieu of the asylum interview or court hearing, but also inform the everyday practices of governing asylum seekers and, in turn, the subjective and social lives of asylum seekers themselves.

Asylum Seekers as "Problematic Subjects"

The continuum of violence embedded in the asylum system emerges from and is reproduced and justified by the assumption that asylum seekers are a problem to be solved. The *ethos of suspicion* that I identify relates to the state's ambivalence regarding asylum seekers. In the logic of the state, a primary question is whether asylum claimants are "true refugees" who deserve protection or potential threats who warrant, or even necessitate, exclusion. This is what was at the heart of DHS's decision to conduct an overseas investigation of Louise's asylum claim.

The presumptive distinction between the economic migrant and the humanitarian/political refugee lies at the heart of asylum adjudication—a theme I explore more fully in chapter 4. And while the distinction between these two categories of migrants has been shown to be untenable—if not a "dangerous legal fiction" (Hamlin 2021)—it remains a cornerstone of policies and discourses surrounding asylum (Bohmer and Shuman 2010; Crawley and Skleparis 2017; Dauvergne 2004; Yarris and Castañeda 2015). The deployment of ideologies surrounding "proper" (humanitarian/political) versus "improper" (economic) reasons for mobility becomes a way of "morally delineating the deserving refugee from the undeserving migrant" (Holmes and Castañeda 2016, 13). Thus, the asylum process is ultimately much more than a set of political-legal procedures. It is also an inherently sociomoral process. That is, in declaring—and thus producing—an asylum seeker as either an illegitimate/"bogus" asylum seeker or a legitimate/"true refugee," asylum officials confer not only legal categories, but categories of moral personhood. Louise's reaction to being interpreted as potentially suspect ("It's very, very painful") highlights the embodied and social implications of being subjected to these moral categories.

The idea of refugees and asylum seekers as "problems to be solved" has been subjected to critique yet continues to inform both academic and policy work (Espiritu 2014; Malkki 1992, 1995; Ramsay 2020a). Refugees, as Liisa Malkki (1995) has argued, have long been constructed, historically and discursively, as a threat to the "national order of things." State (and non-state) actors have conceptualized and responded to this supposed threat to the national order in a variety of ways. First, while human rights scholars and activists have focused on asylum seekers as rights-bearing individuals within the context of international law (Edwards 2005; Hathaway 1991), this human rights framework has been increasingly eclipsed by the discourse of humanitarianism, whereby asylum seekers' legitimacy relies on appeals to compassion and moral sentiments, including the invocation of trauma (Fassin and Rechtman 2009; Ticktin 2011). Second, refugees and asylum seekers have, in both policy and academic scholarship, been cast as people in need of therapeutic intervention. While not denying the psychological impact that displacement may cause, the tendency to unquestionably equate displacement with pathology or trauma is problematic (Espiritu 2014; Malkki 1992; Summerfield 2012; Watters 2001b). While psychological studies have been helpful in shedding light on the mental health effects of specific vulnerabilities that underlie the asylum seeking process (e.g., lack of or limited access to health care, education, and employment; prolonged family separation; looming threat of deportation) (Carswell, Blackburn, and Barker 2011; Hocking, Kennedy, and Sundram 2015; Li, Liddell, and Nickerson 2016; Silove et al. 2007), anthropologists have cautioned that the translation of refugee experiences into psychological categories may delegitimize alternative understandings of displacement (Jenkins 1991, 1998; Malkki 1995; Salina Gross 2004; Zarowsky 2004). Following this, I argue that the feelings generated via the asylum system, such as anger, sadness, fear, and anxiety, are better understood not necessarily as psychopathology but as sociomoral indictments of an unjust politico-legal process.

Finally, the rise in the criminalization and securitization of asylum and asylum seekers, both in the United States and globally, constructs refugees and asylum seekers as problematic subjects not based on their victimhood, but rather on their supposed threat to the state, from the threat of physical destruction of the "host" country to the destruction of the economic and cultural integrity of it (Anderson 2013; Bigo 2002; Coutin 2011; Gibney 2004; Haas and Shuman 2019; Squire 2009). The institutional and societal framings of asylum seekers as criminals/threats are important to the arguments of this book and to the lived experiences of asylum seekers, as is the problematic frame of victimhood. It is on the bodies of asylum seekers that tensions between security and humanitarianism play out. Asylum seekers occupy an ambiguous positionality whereby they must confront disciplinary techniques that construct them as both humanitarian victims and threats to the state (Fassin 2005).[7] Globally and domestically, the criminalization and securitization of migration has meant the emergence and implementation of restrictive border control measures, ranging from the collection of biometric data to detention, interdiction and deportation (Bigo 2007; Broeders 2007; De Genova and Peutz 2010; Fassin 2011; Huysmans 2006; Mountz 2010). The discourse of national security has been mobilized by states, including the United States, to repress the rights of migrants or to justify the infliction of violence upon them (Fassin 2011).

Importantly, these formulations of asylum seeker as a threat or as a problem to be solved are highly racialized. Critical race theorists have long argued that race and law are inextricably enmeshed (Calavita 2007; Fan 1997; Hirsch 2019). These theorists have been crucial in exposing white privilege and the subordination of people of color within immigration law and enforcement (Sanchez and Romano 2010). Yet the immigration system not only produces racialized Others, but also reflects broader forms of racism and racial hierarchies already in place. Othering based on immigration status allows "animosity for domestic minorities [to be] displaced to a more publicly palatable target for antipathy" (Sanchez and Romano 2010, 781). Key to these forms of racialization via the asylum system is the way in which the racial logic of the state is rendered invisible but remains intrinsic to its very process (Garner 2007; Hirsch 2019; see also de Genova 2018). Critical race scholars have underscored the normalization of the racialized effects of immigration law and enforcement, calling out "racial discrimination masquerading as neutral controls on immigration" (Fan 1997, 1204). Lucy Mayblin (2017, 2020) extends this theorizing, arguing that legacies of colonialism, and not solely racism, have been fundamental to the construction of asylum seekers as undesirable and excludable. Processes of asylum seekers' racialization, Mayblin argues, are grounded in colonial logic regarding differential human worth and access to rights. These logics of differential worth extend not only to extreme situations of physical and political marginalization and/or bodily violence (e.g., the Calais migrant camp or the US-Mexico border) but also the everyday lives of asylum seekers. In this way, "states can also be seen to deploy these same definitions of who matters and who does not *while* fulfilling their legal obligations to those making an application for asylum" (Mayblin, Wake, and Kazemi 2020, 120).

Forms of racialization or "racial ascription" (Hirsch 2019) have both personal and social consequences for asylum seekers. I found it notable that many, though not all, of my research participants spoke of any perceived discrimination in terms of "anti-immigrant" sentiment rather than in racialized terms, even though all my participants were people of color. That is, my interlocutors mostly framed the everyday and bureaucratic violences upon their (black and brown) bodies as motivated not by racism but by xenophobia—though in practice these are, of course, inseparable. I return to these issues in later chapters, but I want to comment briefly on this here. First, as highlighted above, anti-immigrant sentiment is always racialized. In this way, feeling discriminated against because one's foreignness or legal status in many ways indexes racism or racialized forms of Othering. My participants' lack of explicit mention of (and sometimes, when pressed, even the denial of) feeling targeted due to their racialized identity brings into relief just how much the racial logic of the asylum system is hidden even as it exerts enormous force.

Second, my interlocutors' resistance to labeling experiences of the asylum system's violence continuum as informed by race may underscore the disconnect between lived and ascribed identities. That is, racialization processes are not uniformly experienced and thus do not have the same effects on all immigrants (Viruell-Fuentes, Miranda, and Abdulrahim 2012). It may also be the case that identifying forms of locally-patterned racial discrimination (that is, in the United States) is a learned process (Viruell-Fuentes 2007). Finally, in stressing that the stigma and dehumanization they faced was a result of anti-immigrant (and not anti-black or brown) logic, my research participants left room for racism to be evaded in the future, should they be granted asylum and, as most of my participants hoped, become US citizens. Attention to race, along with gender and class, was also critical in understanding my own positionality and how it shaped the research milieu.

ENTERING THE FIELD: ETHICAL AND THEORETICAL STANDPOINTS

I entered my fieldwork with a heightened sense of sensitivity about research with asylum seekers, having worked as a volunteer and advocate for numerous refugee and asylum aid organizations for years. Though many enthusiastically joined my research, I was nonetheless struck by other asylum seekers' trepidation regarding my work, as the following stories illustrate. When I first met Esther, a Cameroonian asylum seeker in her late forties, at an after-church gathering that I attended with Louise, we seemed to hit it off, moving quickly into an easy banter. Over the course of the afternoon, we discussed my research and she took my number, saying she would call me to set up a time to enroll in the study. After not hearing from Esther for over a week, I called her and left a message.

Later that week I met Eric for a meal at an inexpensive all-you-can-eat Chinese lunch buffet. Eric, an asylum claimant who became a close interlocutor and friend during my fieldwork and who will appear throughout this book's chapters, seemed to know everyone in the local Cameroonian community. After we filled our plates and prepared to eat, Eric looked at me, chuckling, "So I hear you tried to get Esther to talk to you." I looked at him quizzically. "Yeah," Eric continued, still laughing, "Esther calls me and says 'there's this lady, a white lady, and she's asking me to talk to her.'" My continued confused look only made Eric laugh harder. "Yeah, she [Esther] was like trying to explain how scared she was about the white woman, the white woman." While Esther conceded to Eric that I seemed nice, Eric's attempts to put her fears at bay were moot. She remained certain that I had a nefarious reason for talking to her about her asylum-seeking experience and that perhaps I would report her whereabouts to the Cameroonian government, from whom she was fleeing.

"Why do you think she has so much fear about me and the study?" I pressed Eric. "Because," Eric said, "there's been so much betrayal. What we

English Cameroonians have been through, what we've experienced at the hands of the French. We learn to trust our own. I tried to explain to Esther [that] it's okay to talk to you but she just said 'tsk, tsk. $25! [the IRB-approved honorarium for interview sessions.] They want to buy your conscience! They want to buy something from you! You know these white people. They don't give you money for nothing.'" Eric speculated that Esther's suspicion of me may have partly been informed by "naïveté" and a lack of understanding about research more generally, but that the fear surrounding how I would use information would likely be a challenge in finding asylum seekers willing to talk to me.[8] "They're afraid. They worry that this white girl is taking information and maybe trying to send it back to their governments [in countries of origin]. We were in life-and-death situations, so, it becomes really threatening." Indeed, I never heard back from Esther.

Weeks after my lunch with Eric, I met with Linda, a Liberian asylum seeker in her early forties who had responded to a study information letter sent out by CHR. We spent an hour chatting and going over the study, after which she signed the informed consent to enroll. But when I arrived at her house the following week for our first interview, she seemed hesitant and uncomfortable. It was only after talking for a bit that she revealed her concerns: her boyfriend, after hearing about Linda's enrollment in the study, had warned that I may have been "a spy for INS or the FBI" and that my motives in talking to her may have been to "catch her in lies" and have her "taken away."[9] I was able to allay her fears only slightly by reiterating my position as a researcher, underscoring that I had no ties to the government, and reassuring her that everything would remain confidential. She listened to this, but then brushed it off by telling me a story of a Liberian acquaintance who had applied for asylum and then was arrested and detained by "someone from immigration or FBI." I again did my best to put her at ease. She nodded but added, rhetorically: "But do you know what happens when Immigration comes to your house!?"

These episodes and interactions served as critical lessons in several ways. First, these interactions helped me quickly apprehend the pervasiveness of asylum seekers' fear and anxiety, and how these feelings stretch from countries of origin to "host" country. Esther's concern was that information she shared with me would get back to the Cameroonian government. Linda's fear was that it would get back to the US government. For each of them, this was an existential threat. Moreover, as these moments illustrate, fear and anxiety were not bound to legal settings, but rather permeated everyday life. Second, these recruitment "challenges" provided insight into the potential ways that my positionality could impact my fieldwork. Esther's mistrust of me as a white woman, who might be trying to "buy [her] conscience," speaks to "the haunting presence of the colonial" (Good et al. 2008, 5) or what Ann Stoler (2013) terms "imperial debris" that continues to structure present-day relationships for many asylum seekers who have fled countries where violence and oppression are rooted in legacies of colonialism. For example, among Anglophone Cameroonians, the struggle over political voice in the postcolonial era has echoed colonial experiences of oppression, violence, and marginalization. France's support of the current regime in Cameroon, the Cameroon People's Democratic Movement (CPDM), and its leader Paul Biya, has led political opposition leaders to decry the current political situation as one of "French neo-colonialism" (Konings and Nyamnjoh 2004, 2019; Chiatoh 2019). As a white woman, a symbol of both the colonial past and the current context of neo-colonial rule in Cameroon, I was confronted with entrenched historical and racial histories that informed the already-existing power differential between me, as the researcher, and Esther, as a (potential) research subject. While the United States was not the colonizer of Cameroon or my other interlocutors' countries of origin, it was not uncommon for my African asylum seeker friends to point to America's silence regarding the suffering in their home countries, as well as the United States's support of such oppressive foreign regimes. This point has been argued by Grosfoguel and Georas (2000), whose research on Latino Caribbean migrants in New York draws on Quijano's (1992, 2000) theory of the "coloniality of power." Grosfoguel and Georas's use of the term "colonial immigrants" explicitly includes groups of migrants that came from countries not colonized directly by the United States but still "dominated by the US" (2000, 89). They argue that these groups "still suffer from forms of racial discrimination and stereotypes that are similar to those suffered by the 'colonial/racial subjects' of empire" (89). Indeed, similar dynamics were at play in my research context.

Yet, if I or my research was initially seen as a threat to some potential participants, for most others I was viewed as an empathic witness, and even a potential source of help with one's asylum case. Many asylum seekers were eager to tell me about their experiences of the asylum process and I was constantly fielding questions about the asylum system, even among those who never joined my study. In her research among migrant farmworkers in the United States, Sarah Horton (2016) frames her position as ethnographer as simultaneously one of advocate, arguing "that ethnographers who work with vulnerable populations must go beyond the imperative of sympathetic representation: they must honor an unspoken ethical contract they establish with their research participants through the very conditions of their entry" (11). As part of my everyday fieldwork, I assisted asylum claimants in completing legal and bureaucratic paperwork, such as work authorization applications; drove them to and from asylum interviews, court hearings, and ICE appointments; and helped them schedule medical and therapy appointments. These activities helped build trust and connection with my interlocutors and provided me with invaluable information about the asylum process. I also think of these quotidian forms of assistance as forms of solidarity. Framing these shared moments as forms of solidarity also underscores knowledge production as coconstituted, emerging from my relationships and interactions with asylum seekers. In this way, my interlocutors were not objects of investigation but social actors whose experiences and stories allowed for important insights into the asylum process—insights that would otherwise remain hidden. At the same time, my positionality gave me access to information and observations which asylum seekers were denied or to which they were not privy, such as the data I collected among institutional actors (adjudicators, attorneys).

Ethnography is an ideal approach for getting at the lived dimensions of the asylum system. Ethnographic methods of in-depth interviewing and extended participant observation offer a way to capture and better understand how sociolegal categories come to be inhabited, negotiated, or resisted by asylum claimants. My follow-up fieldwork afforded me the opportunity to trace the impact of the asylum process on my interlocutors over time, including after the resolution of their claims. Ultimately, an ethnographic approach was vital in revealing the complex subjectivities of asylum seekers and their responses to the asylum process. My interlocutors were well-versed in telling their stories of persecution and flight. Each told their "story" to doctors, therapists, lawyers, asylum officers, immigration judges, and legal advocates. The institutional co-opting and subsequent translation of asylum seekers' stories into legalese or into psychological categories risks alienating asylum seekers from their own experiences. As an ethnographer I was careful to listen differently. Asylum claimants' counterstories challenge dominant public and even scholarly representations of them as either passive victims or potential threats and expose the asylum system as a site of political and social injustice.

Theoretically, this book sits at the intersection of political-legal studies of immigration regimes and analyses of power and subjectivity rooted in psychological anthropology. My focus is on asylum claimants' lived experiences and subjectivities—the "everyday modes of experience, the social and psychological dimensions of individual lives, the psychological qualities of social life, the constitution of the subject, and forms of subjection" as they emerge within the US asylum regime (Good et al. 2008, 1). I see the social and psychological, or political and phenomenological, as inextricably linked. By this approach, I take my cue from scholars of migration who have engaged the framework of critical phenomenology (Lucht 2011; Willen 2007, 2019). In her research with undocumented migrants in Israel, Willen (2007) proposes a "critical phenomenology of 'illegality,'" which rests on a threefold idea of illegality as: a) a juridical status, b) a sociopolitical condition, and c) a mode of being-in-the-world. Describing illegality as "a form of politically and socially abject status," Willen connects legal and transnational anthropology to an anthropology of experience, by highlighting how illegality shapes migrants' sense of time, space, home and embodiment (12). Like Willen, Hans Lucht (2011) draws on critical phenomenology and existential anthropology in his ethnography of Ghanaian migrants in Italy. Lucht's theoretical project is to understand how these migrants subjectively navigate harsh conditions as laborers in Naples, "to explore being not as a contemplative effort, but as a question of action and constraints on action" (16).

Lucht and Willen share an interest in the phenomenology of illegality and their work makes clear how processes of illegalization intimately shape migrants' ways of being-in-the-world and their struggles to realize moral lives. While anthropological attention to the lived experience of illegality (see also Coutin 2005; Castañeda 2010; De Genova 2002; Quesada 2012) informs my analyses, I draw urgent attention to particular spatial-temporal orientations—a space of ambivalent refuge—and associated modes of disciplining that are specific to asylum seekers and to asylum *seeking*. In turn, these context-specific orientations and techniques evoke modes of being-in-the-world that are unique to the status of "asylum claimant." I thus depart from the above body of scholarship by offering a distinct *critical phenomenology of asylum seeking*.

The phenomenological method in general is committed to investigations of the everyday, and the "refusal to accept the taken-for-grantedness of experience" (Weiss, Salamon, and Murphy 2019, 3). A phenomenological approach engages with experience as it is lived, emphasizing intentionality as a key—that "our understanding is always engaged within the world" (Davis 2019). This means that experiences are interconnected and emergent, tied to particular temporal and spatial contexts and to other people. A critical phenomenological lens advances this approach by connecting everyday experiences and ways of seeing and being in the world to broader structural conditions and relations of power. In other words, the critical phenomenological method asks how historical, political-economic, and sociocultural forces get 'under the skin' or, more specifically, "how states put their laws in migrants' 'inner parts'" (Willen 2019, 87). Here, asylum claimants' bodies and lives serve as important sites of critique.

This theoretical framework allows me to tack back and forth between the examination of modes of subjectification and considerations of subjectivity and subjective experience. Judith Butler (1992, 1997), for example, argues against the subject as an a priori fact, arguing that the self is constituted by "matrices of power and discourse" and is dependent on these external powers for her very existence, even if from a position of subjugation (1992, 9). I draw on this line of theorizing in considering the various ways in which asylum seekers are constituted by the forms of surveillance, control, and management to which they are subjected, yet argue that their subjectivity is not reducible to these. By attending to the affective and embodied aspects of asylum seekers' everyday lives I want to push us to see the political meaning of emotions like anxiety, fear, and anger. What do the thoughts, feelings, actions, and desires of asylum claimants in the United States tell us about the asylum system and the broader logic and moral assumptions that inform immigration practices and policies?

A critical approach is essential to the study of refugees and asylum seekers if we are to destabilize notions of the refugee as a naturalized, dehistoricized, and depoliticized category, in particular one that assumes the refugee as a problem to be managed. Espiritu's (2014) elaboration of a field of critical refugee studies "begins with the premise that the refugee, who inhabits a condition of statelessness, radically calls into question the established principles of the nation-state and the idealized goal of inclusion and recognition within it" (14). Indeed, the asylum seeker, emerging as a central figure in debates surrounding humanitarianism and security, challenges "both the norms and the exceptions of the state" (Squire 2009, 3). Because asylum claimants are caught within the very system that will produce them as desirable or excludable, their lived experiences offer a critical lens into the workings of the state, particularly as it relates to the distribution of "deservingness" of inclusion and recognition. Espiritu (2014) suggests, however, that critical refugee studies must move beyond critique, and recuperate the refugee not only "as a critical idea but also as a social actor" (14). Anthropological work has revealed the complex ways in which transnational migrants negotiate political-legal and socioculturally-produced identities (Cabot 2014; Horst 2006; Heyman, Slack and Guerra 2018; Ong 1996, 2003). Whether conceived of as tactics of resistance or strategies of survival, this body of scholarship has highlighted refugees as engaged social actors who creatively refashion subjectivities even within contexts of structural constraint.

Likewise, this book illustrates the creative and agentic capacities of asylum claimants. It is a story of violence but not victimhood. The stories of suffering, like Louise's story that opened this chapter, serve not as representations of passivity but of critique and endurance. That my asylum-seeking friends confront, withstand, and push against the US asylum regime's continuum of violence—that they endure this system and weather its harms—exposes their unwavering commitment to their right to protection and the desire for a life worth living. At the same time, the fact that they must endure these forms of violence is evidence of the injustices, indignities, and, sometimes, absurdities of the US asylum system. In a world increasingly hostile and harmful to asylum seekers, ethnographic attention to the routinized and often hidden consequences of immigration policies is crucial to understanding both the suffering evoked by such systems and the capacity of people to endure.

1 Violence of In/Visibility

On a grey, winter afternoon in early 2010, I sat with Ruth at the office of Behavioral Interventions, Inc., a private company contracted by US Immigration and Customs Enforcement (ICE) to oversee one of their "Alternatives to Detention" (ATD) programs. Ruth had fled Cameroon's Anglophone Northwest region after enduring brutal oppression and political violence and had applied for asylum with the US government in early 2006. Her asylum claim had been denied by an immigration judge, after being referred by an USCIS asylum officer. With assistance from volunteer lawyers with CHR, she had appealed her case to the Board of Immigration Appeals and was awaiting a decision. On this Monday afternoon, like every Monday for months, I had taken Ruth to her mandatory check-in appointment, as part of her participation in ICE's Intensive Supervision and Appearance Program (ISAP), in which she was enrolled while awaiting the appeal of her asylum claim. Ruth and I sat quietly on uncomfortable folding chairs, as Ruth clutched her ISAP identification card—what she had come to refer to as her "prisoner card"—and waited for her assigned caseworker to call her name.

The lobby door suddenly burst open and a young woman, who I later learned was from Ghana and also an asylum claimant, appeared, looking distraught and panicked. Despite the single digit temperature outside, she wore only thin plastic sandals, fleece pajama bottoms, and a short-sleeved soccer jersey. "Be honest with me!" she shouted as she moved toward the desk. "Am I leaving!? I'm leaving, aren't I? Just tell me," she pleaded, tears streaming down her face. The man at the desk, twenty-something with rumpled khakis and a shaggy haircut, curtly asked for her name and told her that she'd have to wait for her caseworker to return from his lunch break. I caught a glimpse of the hard, black plastic monitoring bracelet on her right ankle—the same model as Ruth's. The young woman paced the small lobby, crying and pleading for information from the man at the desk; "Just tell me what's going on," she repeatedly implored. The young man at the desk busied himself with paperwork, averting his gaze and said nothing. Dropping her petite frame into a chair, the woman wailed "I can't do this anymore. I'm gonna have a heart attack. What am I going to do? What's gonna happen?" Ruth looked uneasily at me, then leaned close and whispered bitterly: "You see, we're prisoners. Prisoners in America. As if we're criminals! As if we're garbage!"

This was not the first time that I had heard Ruth use the language of criminality and the carceral to describe her treatment within the US asylum system. In my everyday conversations with her—while mashing cocoyams and cooking ndolé together, driving her to the store or doctors' appointments—Ruth regularly decried the dehumanizing treatment she received.[1] "Asylum seekers here are treated like animals. But we are not animals. We only want to be safe," she had told me on the very first day I met her in the fall of 2009. And while I had been documenting for many months the everyday, often subtle, forms of bureaucratic and discursive violence to which asylum claimants were subjected, this incident at the ISAP office was nonetheless jarring. Now, slumped in her chair, the young woman who had barged into the ISAP office was quiet, save the sounds of stifled crying that would periodically emerge and permeate the otherwise silent waiting room. Ruth kept her eyes on the ground. I shifted uncomfortably in my chair, wrestling with conflicting thoughts and feelings. I felt pained by the young woman's anxiety and fear—emotions that I knew Ruth also embodied. I was outraged both by the dismissive attitude of the front desk employee and the broader institutional ethos of the (putatively humanitarian) asylum system that justified and normalized such indignities. And yet I felt helpless as I contemplated possible actions I could take. If I confronted the front desk employee or an ISAP supervisor, then I feared I would risk putting both the Ghanaian woman and Ruth in jeopardy. Might my hypothetical rebuke of ISAP staff impel them to act even more aggressively towards these two women? I knew that Ruth would not want me to say anything. To be sure, despite her biting critique of her treatment at the ISAP office and the frustration at being made to always wait, sometimes up to an hour past her scheduled appointment, Ruth never communicated this to ISAP or other immigration officials. But I also knew that her silence was not complicity. My ruminating was disrupted by Ruth's name being called loudly by her ISAP case worker, who took Ruth to her office, out of sight of the waiting room. Shortly afterwards, the woman in the soccer jersey and fleece pants was also called to the back offices. By this point, the woman's face revealed less a sense of panic and more a look of resignation.

After another twenty minutes, the young woman in the soccer jersey re-emerged into the waiting room, accompanied by her case worker. The mood was different now, lighter. "I'll see you next week, okay?" the case worker said to the woman. "And don't worry so much," he exhorted lightly as he exited the waiting room to return to the back offices. I felt a sense of relief, as it seemed the woman's fears of immediate deportation would not be realized. Ten minutes later, I left the ISAP office with Ruth. We ran into the young woman near the exit doors of the office complex. She was waiting for her friend to pick her up. "Is everything okay?," I asked her. She proceeded to explain to Ruth and me that she was an asylum seeker from Ghana. Like Ruth, she had been placed on an ankle monitoring bracelet after her asylum denial had been upheld by an immigration judge and she filed an appeal with the BIA. "This thing," she said, shaking her leg to expose the ankle monitor, "is so terrible." In what she would later learn was a technical malfunction, the ankle monitor had communicated a message that she was to report to ISAP immediately. She was convinced she was being deported. "It [the ankle monitor] was telling me that I need to report. I need to report. I told myself, 'This is the end.' Why else would I need to report like this?" Unable to get through to the ISAP office by phone and unable to stop the beeping messages of the monitor, the woman, in a panic, took a bus to the ISAP office. Although her case worker's explanation that this was a malfunction and that there were no imminent plans of deportation put her immediate stress at ease, this did not seem to allay the deeper anxiety that the ankle monitor reproduced and exacerbated.[2] "I just don't know how long I can keep on like this. What kind of a life is this?" she said, rhetorically, as she quickly exited into the cold air and jogged through the snow to the car that had just pulled up.

I looked at Ruth, who was shaking her head. "I just don't understand it, Bridget. Are we supposed to be treated this way? When we have done nothing wrong." Indeed, Ruth and the young Ghanaian asylum seeker had, in fact, done nothing wrong. They were acting in accordance with the law. They had filed legal claims for protection, exercising their right to do so under international and domestic law. Both were following an established legal and administrative protocol for appealing their asylum decisions. And yet their experiences of this process were shaped by the state's framing of them not foremost as rights-bearing subjects but rather as potential criminals and threats.

The experience at the ISAP office that afternoon had a lasting effect on me. The raw emotions, the unfiltered fear and anxiety of the young Ghanaian woman, gave me some insight into what it *felt* like to be an asylum claimant in the United States. Her body—its cries, its collapses, clenched teeth, and wringing hands—both reflected an internalization of the routinized, bureaucratic violence of the asylum system and served as a critique of it, exposing the fiction of the system's humanitarian imperative. And although this incident was not routine in my fieldwork (in fact, only seven of my research participants were enrolled in ISAP) it became evident that the forms of violence on display that afternoon were not exceptional. This episode at the ISAP office highlights what I call a *paradox of visibility*. Like Louise, whose story opened this book, Ruth and the Ghanaian woman, in filing an asylum application, sought to be visible, to be recognized in need of protection by the state. In this way, their (hyper)visibility was a prerequisite to their desired sense of security, conferred by a granting of asylum. And yet the events of that afternoon exposed how much that (hyper)visibility can also serve as a potent form of *in*security. While the paradox of visibility is magnified via the heightened surveillance of programs like ISAP, the violence of in/visibility is evident across the asylum system's practices and institutions, impacting all asylum applicants.

This chapter explores the myriad ways in which both visibility and invisibility emerge as technologies of power and governing in the context of asylum seeking. Perhaps more aptly, this is about the power to *make* (things and people) visible or invisible. As Khosravi (2010), in his poignant auto-ethnography of borders, asserts: "The gaze is not an innocent act of seeing, but an episteme determining who/what is visible and invisible" (87). I uncover various technologies of in/visibility and trace their enactments and their lived effects as asylum seekers sought to make sense of and respond to these forms of power. Beyond highlighting the paradox of visibility that confronts asylum claimants, the ISAP office incident brings to light additional aspects of the violence of in/visibility within the asylum system. First, while the asylum system produces applicants as (hyper)visible, that very system remains largely opaque—*in*visible—to asylum seekers. The cruelty of this was epitomized by the Ghanaian woman's panicked, but unanswered, pleas of "tell me what's happening." Second, while the asylum system works to make asylum claimants visible, it also engages in acts of invisibilizing. Thus, the power to render visible or invisible are two sides of the same coin. Standing in the ISAP office lobby, the Ghanaian woman was simultaneously made (hyper)visible, via a monitoring device, *and* invisible, as the front desk worker avoided her gaze and ignored her physical presence and obvious distress. Third, if the violence of in/visibility entailed the institutional power to control when asylum seekers were visible or invisible, it also involved unevenness surrounding *how* asylum seekers were visible. As both the events in the ISAP office and Ruth's commentary about it underscore, asylum applicants were often made visible to the state in terms of their potential criminality rather than on terms of their own making. Asylum seekers like Ruth felt the injustice and indignity of this not only because they had committed no crime, but also because this imputed subject-position of criminal/threat was so at odds with their own sense of self.

In what follows, I elaborate on these themes to explore how the violence of in/visibility is enacted through various institutional technologies and practices within the asylum process. In doing so, I also importantly illustrate that asylum claimants are not passive in the face of these forms of violence, despite their often-painful effects. I will return to a more robust discussion of Ruth's and others' experiences of ATDs later in the chapter, after exploring the powerful ways in which technologies of in/ visibility pervade asylum seekers' lives outside of electronic monitoring and heightened surveillance programs. First, it is necessary to contextualize the broader landscape of the growing securitization and criminalization of asylum seekers. It is within this larger political-legal context of suspicion that local technologies and practices of in/visibility are embedded and routinized.

IMMIGRATION RESTRICTION AND THE RISE OF A CULTURE OF SUSPICION

The frameworks of criminalization and securitization both produce and justify restrictive immigration policies. How is it that suspicion often comes to supplant humanitarianism in approaches to asylum? A partial answer to these questions lies in the recent history of political asylum and the ideologies that undergird it. Asylum seekers have always been met with some level of suspicion and ambivalence across the globe, though this has greatly increased in recent decades. In the United States, since the inception of the asylum system established by the Refugee Act of 1980, asylum policies and procedures have become increasingly restrictive.

The Illegal Immigration Reform and Immigration Responsibility Act (IIRIRA) of 1996 made the asylum process more difficult and exclusive by creating new restrictions on asylum seeking, in one of the most significant pieces of immigration legislation in US history. These new restrictions included the imposition of a one-year filing deadline, delays in work authorization eligibility, a broadening of the grounds for rejecting asylum claims, new restrictions on asylum appeals, and new policies of expedited removal and detention of asylum seekers (Gibney 2004, 164). The latter policy of "expedited removal" gave low-level immigration officers the power to immediately deport individuals arriving without proper travel documents. And yet, because asylum seekers, by definition, are fleeing persecution, they often do not have adequate time or resources to obtain proper documents (Bohmer and Shuman 2018). In addition, the IIRIRA gave Immigration and Naturalization Services (INS) officials unprecedented power to indefinitely detain asylum seekers and to invoke secret evidence against them. The IIRIRA also eliminated judicial review of detention and deportation decisions.

Immigration policies passed in the wake of September 11, 2001, have continued to be defined by modes of securitization and criminalization, including such measures as the rise of mandatory detention for asylum seekers without proper documentation, increased border security, heightened surveillance measures, and increased detention and deportation (Peutz and De Genova 2010; Schoenholtz 2005; Tazreiter 2004; Welch and Schuster 2008). Massive organizational changes were also implemented following September 11, 2001. The Homeland Security Act of 2003 dissolved the Immigration and Naturalization Service, removing it from the Department of Justice, and divided it into three new structures under the newly created Department of Homeland Security (DHS): US Citizenship and Immigration Services (USCIS), Immigration and Customs Enforcement (ICE), and Customs and Border Protection (CBP).

Operating on an "alarmist agenda," Congress passed the Real ID Act of 2005, touted as an anti-terrorism measure and specifically targeting asylum seekers (Cianciarulo 2006, 2). This act made significant changes to the asylum process, including an expansion of the basis upon which cases could be denied (e.g., immaterial inconsistencies); implementation of new corroboration requirements; and a loosening of criteria for assessing credibility of applicants, for example by allowing applicants' demeanor to be considered grounds for lack of credibility. Also in 2005, the DHS budget increased funds for screening procedures of asylum seekers, detention, removal, and enforcement, with ICE seeing a budget increase of 10 percent (Schoenholtz 2005, 344). This had local effects. The ICE budget in the Minneapolis-St. Paul area was tripled in 2009 and the number of ICE staff increased significantly. Furthermore, St. Paul was included as one of eight cities to test the Intensive Supervision and Appearance Program (ISAP), which was then a new pilot program. As is evident from the opening scene of this chapter, ISAP employs heightened surveillance and policing techniques to monitor non-citizens in the United States, including some asylum seekers.

Throughout the last decade, political asylum has continued to be the target of restrictive measures motivated by mistrust, at best, and outright hostility toward asylum seekers, at worst. Mass deportation steadily grew through President Obama's tenure, bolstered by previous administrations' policies, mostly notably IIRIRA in 1996 (Martínez, Slack, and Martínez-Schuldt 2018). Shortly after entering office in 2017, President Donald Trump issued a series of Executive Orders aimed at severely limiting immigration, including the so-called Muslim Ban, which barred entry to the United States for refugees and immigrants from seven predominantly Muslim countries. Though the initial travel ban was quickly met with widespread protests and legal challenges across the country, the Trump administration ultimately prevailed in enacting another iteration, barring or restricting immigrants from seven countries (five of which are Muslim majority) in December 2017. Moreover, in October 2017 Trump laid out a new immigration strategy that focused specifically on overhauling the US asylum system, including narrowing the standards required to gain asylum and imposing penalties on asylum seekers who file claims deemed to be "fraudulent." Yet, perhaps the Trump administration's most visible assault on asylum emerged through the policies directed at the US-Mexico border. These measures include the Migration Protection Protocols (MPP), aka "Remain in Mexico," begun in January 2019, which forces Central American asylum seekers to return to Mexico while their claims are processed; and a new rule in July 2019 that prevents migrants from applying for asylum if they traveled through another country before reaching the United States and failed to apply for asylum there.

Upon winning the presidency in 2020, Joe Biden and his administration swiftly reversed many of Trump's egregious immigration policies, including attempting to end MPP and overturning former Attorney General Jeff Sessions's 2018 ruling that gang violence and domestic abuse would no longer be an acceptable basis for granting asylum. However, given the Trump administration's numerous and incremental restrictive changes to asylum policies, the asylum system has sustained damage that will take years to unravel, if even possible (Herrera 2021). Moreover, the Biden administration has kept in place some very troubling Trump-era immigration policies, including the expulsion of migrants under Title 42, a provision of US health law that allows the barring of foreigners if they pose a dangerous health risk—a move that many have rightfully criticized as unnecessary, violent, and exclusionary.

Increasing mistrust and hostility towards asylum seekers is not a situation unique to the United States, but rather reflects a global trend. Scholars working in the United Kingdom and Europe have highlighted a similar longstanding wariness of foreign migrants, yet also note an increase in exclusionary border enforcement and asylum policies in more recent years, whereby an asylum regime "predicated upon suspicion" has solidified (De Genova 2020, 163; Anderson 2013; Andersson 2014a; Gill and Good 2019). This has particularly been the case in the wake of public and some academic framing of migrant movements as "crises" (e.g., the so-called European "migrant crisis" of 2015). Critical refugee scholars have importantly cautioned against the deployment of the frame of "crisis" as it obscures the historical trajectory of such mobilities and effaces migrant autonomy, as well as serves to politically justify the use of restrictive and often violent measures in response to migrants' movements (Cabot 2019; De Genova 2018; Goździak and Main 2020; Tazzioli, Garelli, and DeGenova 2018). As Gill and Good (2019) astutely note, "asylum is the rare example of a moral panic that is chronic rather than acute in nature" (2). Likewise, in the US context, the Trump administration policies did not emerge in a vacuum, and it is important to recognize that decades of suspicion and exclusionary measures directed toward asylum seekers—like those facing my asylum-seeking friends in 2010—worked to scaffold these extreme policy changes. And, of course, national policies and discourses surrounding asylum do not exist in isolation either. Individual nations' policies and leadership concerning im/migration influence each other, and in turn reproduce and normalize a global framework of suspicion of asylum.

   This political-legal history helps to appreciate the broader framework that gives rise to an ethos of suspicion that was on display at the ISAP office in early 2010 and that persists. This global and national framework of suspicion and its attendant violences of in/visibility do not just impact those who file claims for asylum with governments. Those classified, for example, as undocumented migrants or as refugees are subjected to the punitive gaze of the state as much as formal asylum applicants, even if their experiences may be very different. Yet there are distinct technologies of in/visibility that are specific to the experiences of asylum applicants. This starts with the filing an I-589, the Application for Asylum and for Withholding of Removal form, whereby one legally becomes an "asylum claimant." The filing of an asylum application is a form of "bureaucratic inscription" (Horton 2020) in which migrants enter into what Anna

Tuckett (2018) has described, in the Italian context, as a close and protracted relationship with a "documentation regime." These forms of relationships and inscription "entail discrete—and sometimes prolonged—moments of visibility to a field of power" (Horton 2020, 3). Applicants show proof of identity (if they have traveled with identity documents), provide photographs of themselves, and must notify USCIS or DHS of any changes in address or other contact information. Applicants are tracked at every step within the asylum process. As an initial part of the asylum process, applicants must be fingerprinted and all biometric and informational data are put into myriad national databases. The USCIS Affirmative Asylum Procedures Manual lists a dozen different databases into which all asylum applicants' information is entered (USCIS 2016). Many of these databases are shared with other branches of DHS, including ICE and Border Patrol, and even the database names call attention to the increasing enforcement focus of immigration policy more broadly: Deportable Alien Control System, Nonimmigrant Information System, National Automated Immigration Lookout System, and the Interagency Border Inspection System. It becomes evident that these databases are aimed not only at managing or tracking individuals who apply for political asylum, but that such management has a larger, ideological and practical aim: to discern and identify fraudulent, suspect, or criminal migrants. These additional forms of bureaucratic inscription produce a visibility for asylum claimants that is at once protective and threatening (see also Cabot 2012, 2014).

BUREAUCRATIC OPACITY AND INVISIBILIZATION

As we saw with Louise, whose story opened this book, not being visible to the US government meant she lacked a sense of security and protection. Because her file had gone missing from the USCIS asylum system, Louise felt her existence was threatened ("If I died, no one would know," she said). Many asylum seekers likewise positioned legal recognition in terms of physical existence in the United States, declaring, for example, that "my case is my life" or "without asylum, I am nothing here." Yet we also saw that Louise's eventual visibility to the state was not a panacea for her sense of insecurity. And certainly, in the case of Ruth and the young Ghanaian woman in the ISAP office, visibility could provoke profound fear. The simultaneous (hyper)visibility of asylum claimants and the opacity of the asylum bureaucracy was an important component of how in/visibility worked as a technique of power. A conversation with my friend Maurice, an asylum claimant from Cameroon, illustrates the painful effects of this.

Maurice, a kind and usually animated man in his late thirties who had been a political activist in Cameroon, appeared rather somber and a bit agitated when I paid him a visit one afternoon. The week before, Maurice had received a notice in the mail from the asylum office informing him that his claim had been denied. While the notice had informed him of his right to appeal the decision, there was no information about the denial's reasoning, leaving him puzzled and unnerved. Maurice, who did not have legal representation, had been trying unsuccessfully all week to get this additional information about his case by calling the USCIS office. "This [asylum] system is inhumane," Maurice declared, as I read the letter myself. When I expressed my own sense of dismay at the brevity and lack of information provided to him, he nodded emphatically, reiterating that immigration officials failed to "recognize the human side" of the asylum process.

MAURICE: It's really hard to know what is going on. . . . (A)t least if you could just speak with somebody who is handling the case over the phone. Just to talk with that person, let the person be accessible. So that you can talk. The person [the asylum claimant] can ask questions. The office should be able to put their document before you, to take a look at it and talk to you about it, you know, to say this is what is going on. . . . But no. I receive instead a letter that only says we denied your case.

BRIDGET: And they [asylum officers] aren't accessible like that, to talk to?

MAURICE: Oh, no! Everything is by mail. And if you do ever get someone on the phone, they are just repeating the same thing that you see online, not 'so do you have any other questions?' You get nothing. It's really terrible. To be honest with you, until you get here and get into the immigration system, you will never believe that there is any department in the United States that works this way. You would never believe it. You cannot. Because it is either exactly the way things are done in Africa, or worse.

Without legal representation and unable to find anyone at USCIS to explain the circumstances of his denial, Maurice was unsure how to proceed.[3] He had been referred to an immigration judge, with the first step to attend a master calendar hearing, where he would be given a date of his asylum hearing. I encouraged him to reach out to CHR, noting that his chances of getting asylum would be greatly enhanced with legal representation. He asked me about the procedures of immigration court. I outlined for him the steps involved and, without thinking about it, referenced the legal term "removal proceedings." Maurice's eyes went big. "What do you mean *"removal* proceedings"? I quickly (and humbly) realized how easily this terminology had rolled off my tongue and that despite my analytic critiques of the concept, I was not forced to experientially reckon with the existential threat that such terminology signified. The idea of "removal"— the sting of the word—hung in the air, despite my attempts to assure Maurice that he was still able to legally stay in the United States while his case continued. "But anything can happen when you go to immigration offices," he replied. As a way of illustrating this to me, he then recounted a story of a friend who had been arbitrarily detained and held in detention without access to any information on his case. I had heard other asylum seekers talk about this and similar cases.

MAURICE: He [Maurice's friend] went to the immigration office to renew his work authorization. And they arrested him! Four years ago. For four years he has been in different jails, from jail to jail.

BRIDGET: What did they—?

MAURICE: —They don't say anything!

BRIDGET: Are they trying to deport him?

MAURICE: We don't know. He has said . . . just allow me to go. But nobody's saying anything. They just—they keep pushing him left and right. Left and right. For four years! Oh, God. I'm telling you, just one morning he left the house to go renew his work authorization. He was trying to do the right thing.

BRIDGET: And at that time, was he still—was his decision pending with the court?

MAURICE: Yes! His decision was still pending. So his heart is really hard. The immigration system is—it's really hard to find out information. To know what is going on. . . . And then one guy from immigration [a deportation officer] last year said, 'We're going to deport him. Come around with clothes. We're going to deport him.' And that was last year. He's still there! Still in jail!

Maurice's narrative illustrates how opacity works as a bureaucratic technology in the asylum system. This starts with Maurice's inability to get additional information about the reasons behind his asylum denial. While asylum officers must produce written justifications of their decisions for their supervisors, this information is not readily imparted to applicants themselves. But bureaucratic opacity characterizes the asylum system on a broader level. Indeed, a salient complaint among my asylum-seeking friends was that they were often unable to get questions answered about their cases and/or their status at myriad points during the asylum process. These questions ranged from what forms they needed to complete ahead of an appointment to the reasons for delays in hearings or questions about removal orders. If calls were answered then they were mostly directed to an automated system, which prompted callers to input their "alien ID number," after which they would receive minimal information about their status (e.g., date of asylum hearing, whether decision was still pending). Thus, while asylum claimants were surveilled and tracked in a way that made them highly visible and legible to the state, this visibility and access were not reciprocated.

For Maurice, being refused information about his asylum denial magnified larger concerns about bureaucratic opacity and its potential consequences. If Maurice could be denied asylum without sufficient explanation or information, then he figured he could certainly be, like his friend, detained and/or deported without explanation or justification. Throughout my fieldwork, asylum seekers expressed continuous fear and confusion surrounding detention and deportation policies and procedures. While I cannot comment on the veracity or the details of the case of Maurice's friend, the recounting and circulation of stories like this speak to the fear evoked by "deportability" (De Genova 2002; Núñez and Heyman 2007; Peutz and De Genova 2010) and "detainability" (Campesi 2018; De Genova 2007) as state- and institutionally produced conditions of vulnerability. It was, however, not just that detention or deportation remained possibilities for asylum seekers with pending claims that was so anxiety-provoking. It was also the "black boxes of bureaucracy" and the seemingly arbitrary nature with which policies were overseen that increased asylum claimants' sense of insecurity and fear (Thomson 2012). Like Louise, who thought she was "doing the right thing" in filing her initial asylum claim, Maurice explained that his friend was "trying to do the right thing" in renewing his work authorization. Such confusion over the "right thing" reveals not just the illegibility of the system but a disconnection between the representation of the asylum system as rational and lawful and asylum seekers' actual experiences of that system (Whyte 2011).

These incidents of unanswered phone calls, lack of access to information, and stories of arbitrary detention were institutionally normalized as aspects of the asylum process. But these bureaucratic practices are performances of state power, engendering states of anxiety for applicants, or what Juan Thomas Ordóñez (2008) has described as the US asylum system's production of a "state of confusion." Regarding deportation, asylum applicants are considered to be "living under the color of the law" and thus cannot be deported while their claims, including appeals, are pending, though many will never be able to permanently stay. Yet the misapprehension and fear surrounding detention and deportation that Maurice expressed are exactly the point here. In other words, the manufacturing of confusion is not a side effect of the asylum system's bureaucratic complexity, but rather is integral to its very operation. "Strategic uncertainty," to borrow from Whyte (2011), is productive in that it works to distance asylum applicants from the asylum determination process, facilitating their exclusion and marginalization. As an increasing number of scholars have argued, this model of disciplining asylum seekers—"governing through uncertainty" (Biehl 2015) or through a "politics of unease" (Bigo 2002)—has emerged as an effective form of governmentality (see also Darling 2011; Fassin, Wilhelm-Solomon, and Segatti 2017).

Put together, Maurice's experience of legal procedures, including imagined ones such as detention and deportation, highlight what Eule et al. (2019) have described as "the illegibility effect" (113). Writing about the legal migration apparatus throughout Europe, Eule et al. draw on Veena Das's (2004) work on the illegibility of the state to capture "the feelings of disorientation and uncertainty about the course of action of legal procedures" within European migration regimes (121). Migrants' lack of knowledge about legal procedures and policies, Eule et al. argue, often reflects a deliberate withholding of information on the part of immigration bureaucracies, whereby "opaqueness is strategically used" as a tool of governing (126). These observations build on previous refugee and migration scholars working primarily in the European context, who have likewise highlighted the complexity and opacity of border enforcement and asylum regimes and their effects on those embedded in these systems (Cabot 2014; Gill 2016; Jubany 2017; Tuckett 2018). Surely Maurice, Ruth, and the young Ghanaian woman at the ISAP office reflected the "disempowering effect of illegibility" as they struggled to make sense of confusing and demoralizing bureaucratic procedures (Eule et al. 2019, 121). Ultimately, while the purpose of the political asylum process is to make legible to the state particular categories of persons, the process itself is rendered opaque—invisible—to those going through it. Asylum claimants are thus visible as *objects* of state power but invisible as *subjects* with claims to full personhood.

To this point, Maurice's narrative underscores the affective consequences of bureaucratic opacity. Just as the Ghanaian woman in the ISAP office was simultaneously (hyper)visible and ignored, Maurice keenly felt the effects of the asylum system's power to invisibilize. His anxiety and confusion were products of both bureaucratic opacity and the system's denial of his humanity. At the same time, in calling out the inhumanity of bureaucratic opacity and acts of invisibilization, Maurice asserted himself to me as a rights-bearing subject, a human being deserving of the dignity of a face-to-face interaction—or, at the very least, a human being on the other end of a phone line. Similarly, Maurice's claim that the USCIS and other immigration offices operate the same, or worse than, government offices in his home country, was both a critique of the US asylum system and an index of the lived consequences of the violence of in/visibility. While asylum claimants experienced an initial sense of relief in making it to the United States, as they became more deeply embedded in the asylum system, it was not uncommon for asylum seekers to tell me that they felt as afraid here as they did in Cameroon or other countries of origin. These comparisons of the US asylum offices with government institutions in Cameroon speak to the perceived inefficiencies of both countries' bureaucracies. Yet, these declarations of America and "Africa" being one and the same are more than descriptive narratives about poor management. Rather, they provide insight into the lived effects of these bureaucratic (non)encounters. For Maurice, the asylum system had rendered him invisible, evoking his experience as a marginalized Other in Cameroon. In this way, Maurice's alienation from the asylum process, like Louise's documentary erasure from the USCIS system recounted in the introduction, were part of "a series of violent erasures of personhood" that had continued from the past into the present (Coutin 2003, 35).

THE DANGERS OF VISIBILITY

If visibility to the state represented the possibility of protection for asylum seekers, it was simultaneously—and paradoxically—experienced as a threat, embodying the potential for their expulsion. As I came to know Roland, an asylum claimant from Liberia, I witnessed the pernicious effects of this paradox of visibility and the challenges of navigating it. Roland was in his early twenties and had come to Minnesota to live with a cousin whose family had resettled in the United States in the 1990s as refugees fleeing Liberia's first civil war. He had recently filed an affirmative asylum application and was awaiting his interview with USCIS.

Roland lived in a suburban area of the Twin Cities that was home to a significant population of Liberians and other African immigrants. Though he had a social network of family and friends, Roland talked to me often about his fear of being in public settings and how cautious he needed to be. Roland complained of being targeted by the mostly white police force in his community, and on multiple occasions he was approached by the police while simply walking to his car outside his apartment building or the local McDonald's. Since he had no US identification documents, police would pepper Roland with questions concerning his asylum claimant-status. "It's just I don't know when they are going to come up to me and start asking lots of question, asking to see papers," Roland said, highlighting the unpredictability of police harassment. "I just get so angry, you know.... It's hard sometimes to continue anymore." His face twisted a bit as he recalled his sense of rage and indignation: "It's almost unbearable." Roland paused contemplatively, and added "I don't know, it's like they are trying to aggravate you so much that you can't take it anymore, you know. Aggravate you to lose your mind, that's what they want to do. And you can't do anything about it." For Roland, this risk of "losing your mind" was directly related to his asylum case. When I asked him what most worried him about his interactions with the police, he was quick to respond: "I worry that I'll become so angry that I may slip up." "Slip up?" I inquired. "Yeah," Roland continued, "like I'll say something, like curse them out, yell back at them. And then they could tarnish my reputation or charge me for doing that and then I'd never win my asylum case."

This fear of "losing [his] mind" speaks to the ways in which surveillance and policing can be productive of a kind of madness. Roland was not being hyperbolic when he suggested the routinized violence of policing was purposefully aggravating people to the brink of insanity. Beyond the material consequences of his potential "slip-ups," he truly worried about his mental health, at times confiding in me that the demoralization and dehumanization evoked by such institutional techniques were compromising his emotional wellbeing: "I'm just not feeling in a good headspace with this happening so much." Roland understood well that these forms of policing were highly racialized. "It happens to my cousins, too. Because of the way we look." I asked Roland how his cousins, who were Liberian-born US citizens, reacted to these forms of policing. "They hate it. They get angry, too. But it's different for them because they have papers [ID cards]. But for me, I have to worry about my [asylum] case." Though he had never been arrested, over the time I knew Roland in Minnesota, he increasingly chose to stay home instead of going out for fear that he would be apprehended by police. He also restructured his days so that he only walked during daylight hours, when police were less likely to stop him. Though this resulted in fewer police interactions, it came at a social and emotional cost to Roland. Over time, he had taken to limiting some of his social interactions and his mood became more somber. He smiled less and lost weight. One afternoon when Roland told me he was debating whether to go to a large outdoor gathering of some Liberian community members that evening, I noted that there would probably be people his age there and it would likely be fun. "Yeah," he conceded, "but I'm scared [of police interactions], you know. I don't want to do anything, say anything wrong. I don't want a problem with my [asylum] case. So, you know, you don't do things when you're scared."

As with other asylum claimants, Roland's fear of police had a historical basis and often reflected a deep mistrust of such authority figures in asylum seekers' countries of origins, where police and government authorities were often the perpetrators of violence and abuse, or at least failed to properly protect them (Daniel and Knudsen 1995; Ní Raghallaigh 2014). In Liberia Roland's family had been a target of government and military violence during and after the country's civil wars. This connection between past and present violence is critical to consider given that police in the United States are increasingly called upon to engage in immigration enforcement (Armenta 2016, 2017; Stuesse and Coleman 2014; Kline 2017). Yet, asylum seekers' fear of police or other authorities in the United States cannot be understood only as an embodied remnant of past experiences. Indeed, the gruesome epidemic of racialized police violence and racial profiling in the United States extends to immigrants of color (Foner 2018). Fear, as Nolan Kline (2017) reminds us, is not just a product of immigrant policing but "instead a mechanism of biopolitical control" (398).

Roland's experience reveals what Frantz Fanon (1967) described as the "psycho-affective" consequences of the racialized gaze of the state. The fear, anxiety, and demoralization that racialized policing provoked sedimented Roland's sense of himself as an object of suspicion in his new environment, "fixed" by state and institutional surveillance (Fanon 1967, 87). Importantly, Roland's status as an asylum claimant—neither fully "legal" nor "illegal"—mediated both his experience of these forms of violence and his perceived ability to act on his situation. Concerns about putting his asylum case in jeopardy heightened the stakes of police interactions, while his sense of powerlessness over the situation ("There's nothing you can do about it") reflected his constrained agency. In this way, his "spatially embodied fear" was an effective disciplinary mechanism that resulted in Roland's increased isolation (Khosravi 2010, 91).

Asylum claimants' fear and mistrust of authorities was not limited to police or immigration officials, however. Often a place that could require or elicit any sort of documentation could be a threat. Asylum seekers who did not have health care coverage largely avoided hospitals and doctors. Even when I informed my asylum claimant friends that they were eligible for a state-funded health insurance program that would provide services, albeit minimal, and offered to help them with the application process, many balked.[4] For example, Rogers, an asylum seeker from Cameroon, told me "I don't like to go there [hospitals or doctors' offices] because it takes so long to explain my [legal] situation to them. I just don't feel like I have security without a [ID] card." When he had gone once to a local hospital for a sprained wrist, he told me "they [hospital staff] treated me like I'm an illegal or something. It made me nervous." Princewill, another Cameroonian asylum claimant, expressed a similar anxiety, telling me: "Even if I'm sick, I don't go to the hospital because I'm not legal." Princewill, like other asylum seekers I met, was either unaware of the fact that he was, as an asylum claimant, lawfully present in the United States despite his lack of an American "ID card," or this fact was unable to allay his fears. Despite Rogers's and Princewill's lawful presence in the United States, they were marked as and felt like suspect Others. Princewill's declaration of himself as "not legal" highlights not just his insecurity, but also the confusion about the meaning of immigration categories, which positions asylum claimants as undeserving of recognition or care. Here, although "'deservingness' is socially produced, politically-determined, and institutionally implemented, the vulnerability that results from being rendered undeserving becomes embodied" (Quesada 2012, 895; Castañeda 2009; Larchanché 2012).

Yet even those asylum claimants who knew their presence was lawful were nonetheless strategic about how they moved about. It is notable that Rogers cited not *being* "illegal" but rather "*treated* like I'm an illegal" as a reason for avoiding hospitals. This, then, is not about Rogers's lack of information. In a subtle but important contrast to Princewill's "I'm illegal" claim, Rogers's frustration at being categorized as occupying an excluded status (that of the socio-politically produced category of "illegal") disrupts the embodiment of undeservingness. That is, Rogers calls out the injustice of being treated as unworthy of care. Though he adapts his movement and presence in public space to evade hostile treatment, his words simultaneously underscore this strategy as a response to bureaucratic violence, not as an identification of himself as undeserving. Asylum seekers' experiences here serve as a critique of a social positionality in which migrants are compelled to constrain their mobility in order to refuse moral indignities.

It was not uncommon for asylum claimants I knew to exercise caution or limit their movement in public spaces. Some asylum claimants told me that they were wary of even taking long walks or drives in case they inadvertently broke a traffic law they didn't know existed. Again, the perceived risk here was not a traffic ticket but rather the fear that such hypothetical wrongdoing might negatively impact their asylum case. Such concerns highlight how anxiety around being "properly visible" resulted in immobility (Whyte 2011, 21). Asylum claimants limited their mobility to mitigate both the feared repercussions to their asylum cases and to allay the anxiety and distress caused by being subjected to policing and surveillance (Coutin 2005; Hasselberg 2016; Talavera, Núñez-Mchiri, and Heyman 2010). Mistrust could become part of asylum seekers' habitus and may have served as a protective strategy. And while this constitutes a form of agency, as an "attempt to make tolerable lives within sets of conditions and constraints," these tactics of restricting mobility could also increase asylum claimants' sense of isolation (Cabot 2012, 23).

As part of the everyday realities of illegality, undocumented persons adopt tactics of invisibility to maneuver through their daily lives, evading being seen, and hence reducing the risk of deportation (Chavez 1998; Coutin 2003, 2005; De Genova and Peutz 2010; Willen 2007). Because asylum applicants were already rendered visible—known and tracked by the government—being invisible to the state was not realizable. Yet during my research I was struck by how many asylum seekers nonetheless displayed similar tactics of avoiding authorities or evading social situations in which they would be asked about their status. This was the case, as Roland, Rogers, and Princewill highlight, even though they were living in the United States with protected status, and could not be deported while their claims were pending. It was clear that their sense of protection was tempered by the mistrustful and othering gaze of the state.

How asylum claimants experience their visibility has much to do with the illegibility and opacity of the asylum system, discussed earlier in the chapter. Though asylum claimants are surveilled, the institutional scrutiny to which my interlocutors were subjected resembled more of what Whyte (2011) has described as a "myopic disciplining," characterized by an "inconsistent and blurred" gaze of authorities. This generated uncertainty for asylum seekers regarding not only *if* they were under surveillance at a given time, but *how* they were being perceived (20). Indeed, for my interlocutors, fear arose not from being rendered visible *per se*, but from the "uneven visibility" of the asylum regime—producing uncertainty regarding how one, as a now-visible subject, would be assessed or, more aptly, produced via the asylum regime—as either legal/deserving or illegal/undeserving (Tazzioli and Walters 2016, 451).

Couched in such illegibility and bureaucratic opacity, asylum claimants' restricted movements make sense. The case studies presented above illustrate how much confusion surrounded the rules and rights afforded to asylum claimants, from conflicting stories and lack of information about arbitrary asylum denials and deportation policies to qualifications for health care to the right to walk down the block to McDonald's without a US-issued license. In a context in which asylum claimants trying to do "the right thing" may wind up erased—deleted from the USCIS system, like Louise, or detained indefinitely, like Maurice's friend—not being seen at all emerged as a technique of self-preservation. In this way, public invisibility was sometimes the best bet for remaining visible on one's own terms. Yet, as noted, understanding this as an agentic strategy should not blind us to the fact that these technologies of surveillance also work as mechanisms of exclusion, keeping particular populations or categories of persons "out of sight" via "processes of erasure [that] are legally facilitated, justified, and normalized" (Price 2010, 153).

While the gaze of suspicion was most keenly experienced in interactions with "public" (state) officials, surveillance and policing occurred in more private settings as well (De Genova 2002; Weber 2013). Both public *and* private spaces, then, became zones of potential criminalization. I will shortly turn to a discussion of ISAP, one of ICE's "Alternative to Detention" programs, in which Ruth was enrolled, and where the dramatic scene that opened this chapter unfolded. By contracting with independent companies like Behavioral Interventions, Inc. (BI), which runs ISAP, the US government is rapidly privatizing its technologies and reach of policing migrants. But here I want to first consider how private citizens are also increasingly involved in the surveillance of asylum claimants. To do so, I return to Ruth.

Ruth was a devoutly religious (Pentecostal) woman and a former preacher. She would often quote from or read me Bible passages or recount stories about her renowned preaching in Cameroon. "People would come from all over to hear me preach," she would beam. Ruth attributed her decision to engage in political activism to her religious faith. "I was seeing all the injustice [in Cameroon] and thinking 'what can I do?' I felt I needed to do something. Then God spoke to me and guided me to join [the SCNC]." In addition to her narratives of political activism as moral action, she also regularly referred to herself as "a woman of God," which she saw as a salient aspect of her identity. Shortly after arriving in Minnesota, Ruth joined a nearby church. While she was aware of other churches that had larger African, including Cameroonian, congregations, Ruth chose instead a church "with almost all white people," where she could "just go and worship and be with God," rather than engage in the social aspects that some enjoyed about church life. The pastor of the church had seemed supportive of Ruth's quest for asylum after she told him about the trauma she endured in Cameroon. Ruth found respite in her church, especially in the contrast it offered to the hostility and stress she experienced as an asylum claimant, separated from her family in Cameroon and mired in a state of uncertainty. However, the sense of belonging she experienced in her church would be painfully disrupted.

When Ruth's asylum claim was denied, she was understandably distraught. She talked to her pastor and asked if he would write a letter in her support that she could submit with her appeal application. Instead, the pastor called ICE several days later to report her whereabouts (even though ICE was aware of her lawful presence). Through information gathered by her *pro bono* CHR attorneys, Ruth learned that the pastor had told ICE, without any evidence, that Ruth might try to avoid deportation should her case be ultimately rejected. "He went behind my back and called immigration on me!" Ruth exclaimed. She felt deeply wounded. When Ruth confronted the pastor, he explained that he was trying to be a good citizen and because she was now "illegal" (an incorrect assumption), he felt compelled to report her. "I never expected to be treated this way by white people here," Ruth told me. "I am really let down. . . . I don't know why I didn't see it before, that he is prejudiced," Ruth lamented, trying to make sense of her pastor's betrayal. "He says he doesn't like Obama because Obama likes immigrants but really he is just saying that he doesn't like black people."

Ruth's incident with her pastor demonstrates how easily asylum seekers "can slip from one side of the moral line to the other, from the role of suspect to the status of victim and vice versa" (Fassin 2015, 2). That is, Ruth's pastor reinterpreted Ruth in light of a juridically and politically imposed label, not according to her identity as a "woman of God" or devoted congregant. Having been denied asylum, in the pastor's eyes, then, Ruth was no longer a "morally legitimate suffering body" (Ticktin 2011, 11), but rather a morally suspect, "removable alien." Moreover, if, as Armenta (2017) has argued, immigrant enforcement is itself a racial project, then Ruth's experience illustrates the stinging force of racialized immigrant policing as it reaches into more intimate realms, even perpetrated by people whom asylum seekers may consider neighbors or friends. Indeed, Ruth identified the slippage between victim and threat as racially patterned, calling out her pastor's anti-immigrant stance as racially motivated. Ruth's narrative draws attention to anti-immigrant sentiment as a more socially palatable frame that serves as a proxy for racialized antipathies. Ultimately, for Ruth, Roland, and so many other asylum seekers of color, their lived experiences in the United States reinforced "a sense of their doubly stigmatized social identity as 'asylum seekers' and 'Black Africans'" (Scott 2018, 381), or what Khosravi (2010) has identified as the "double marginality" of migrants of color (49). This is not to imply that the criminalizing gaze permeated all private spaces or that homes and churches were always sites of marginalization. As I detail in later chapters, asylum claimants found activities and places that were important sites of welcome and emotional refuge. But this example is a reminder that the gaze is not limited to immigration officials and state actors or confined to legal or public spaces. And while there is no way to confirm it, Ruth was convinced that her pastor's call to ICE was what led to her being enrolled in ISAP, where the criminalizing practices ensured a sense of Otherness.

ISAP: "LIKE BEING A PRISONER IN AMERICA"

If Ruth's pastor represented the incorporation of non-state actors into the policing of immigrants, the Intensive Supervision and Appearance Program (ISAP) epitomized the privatization and extension of surveillance into the everyday lives of asylum seekers. ISAP was started in response to ICE's creation of a $3 million Alternatives to Detention (ATD) program that would ensure that immigrants released from detention and/ or those in "removal proceedings" would comply with the requirement to appear in court. In 2004 ISAP began in eight pilot cities, including St. Paul. The administration and oversight of ATDs was outsourced to a private company, Behavioral Interventions, Inc. (BI), a firm that specializes in the electronic monitoring of criminals. In 2009 ICE accelerated and expanded the development of its ATDs and BI was awarded a $372 million five-year contract to operate ISAP (Koulish 2013). By 2010, ICE was operating ISAP in thirty cities across the nation. That same year (2010), BI was acquired for $415 million by Geo Group, a private company that operates numerous immigration detention centers across the nation. Thus, Geo Group, quite problematically, holds "dual roles in both detaining people and managing undetained people" (High 2018).

According to ICE, to be eligible for ISAP, individuals must "not pose a threat to the public or national security," and not be subject to mandatory detention (e.g., have committed a felony, been found to materially support a terrorist organization, or been deemed a risk to national security). All enrolled "participants" of ISAP are subjected to a range of "technologies of suspicion" (Campbell 2004), including wearing tracking devices, observing curfews, regular scheduled and random meetings and check-ins with immigration officials, and having voice recognition software installed on their telephone lines, so that BI caseworkers can confirm the identity of the ISAP participant over the phone. On its website, ICE provides a justification for ISAP, claiming that the program will reduce the number and cost of detained migrants, "ensure [migrants'] compliance" with legal proceedings, and ultimately facilitate "quick removals of individuals from the United States" when necessary. However, the claim that ISAP would reduce the need for detention beds has proved to be patently false. Since 2010, BI has increased the number of individuals enrolled in ISAP, but this increase in ISAP and other ATD enrollment has not resulted in fewer detained migrants—in fact, the number of asylum seekers and other migrants in detention is growing (Bialik 2019). As both detention and ATDs continue to grow, so do profits, and for just the first quarter of fiscal year 2018, Geo Group posted revenues of nearly $565 million (High 2018).

Seven of my interlocutors had been enrolled at some point in ISAP. A few did not allow me to accompany them to any ISAP activities and preferred not to even discuss the program, citing the distress that thinking or talking about it caused—thus underscoring the extent to which purported "humane" ATDs like ISAP in fact traumatized and stigmatized asylum seekers. In the following discussion, I focus on the experiences of two Cameroonian asylum claimants, Albert and Eric, who were enrolled in ISAP at various points during my research, and who, along with Ruth, were the most forthcoming about their experiences of the program. Their experiences help expand our understanding of the everyday effects of these technologies, building on the vignette that opened this chapter. Insights into the lived experiences of ATDs like ISAP are crucial given that despite the proliferation of research on deportation and detention, relatively little is known about the everyday consequences of ATDs (Cervantes, Menjívar, and Staples 2017).

Alternative to Detention or Alternative Form of Detention?

On its website and brochures, BI frames ISAP as a "compassionate alternative to detention," and emphasizes its "voluntary" nature. In one brochure outlining the ISAP II program (renamed after BI's renewal in 2009), there is no mention of any surveillance techniques or even of its classification as an Alternative to Detention (ATD). Rather, ISAP is framed as a program to "help stabilize participants in the community as they move through the immigration court process." Yet, this humane representation of the program is a contrast to ICE's portrayal of the program as one aimed at the surveillance and removal of migrants, and even more at odds with my interlocutors' experiences of the program as an extension of carceral space rather than an alternative to it.

While there are official institutional criteria for being enrolled in ISAP, many immigration lawyers and advocates with whom I talked claimed that who gets enrolled in ISAP seems highly arbitrary. There is a significant lack of transparency regarding the internal workings of the program, with no publicly available information regarding inclusion criteria or metrics used to determine how participants graduate to less intense phases of the program (Fernandes 2017; Reardon 2008). Though all my interlocutors who had been enrolled in ISAP were in "removal proceedings," none of them ever received a clear explanation as to why they were enrolled.

Albert, an ex-SCNC activist and schoolteacher in his early forties, received a vague letter instructing him to report to the Office of Detention and Removal Operations (now called the Enforcement and Removal Office). At this point, he was awaiting his hearing in immigration court, scheduled for the following year. When he received the letter, Albert was certain that he was going to be detained. When he arrived, he was told that he was being enrolled in ISAP and was required to wear an ankle-monitoring bracelet, which officials proceeded to tighten around his leg. When he asked why he was being enrolled, officials told Albert they only carry out the orders of ICE and that if he wished to ask more questions, he could "go next door to ICE" and would likely be detained instead.

Eric had a similar experience. In his mid-thirties and, like Albert, a Cameroonian asylum seeker and ex-SCNC political activist, Eric was the only one of my study participants who did not arrive in the United States alone. He had come with his wife, Victorine, and his toddler son. In Cameroon Eric had been detained and viciously beaten on several occasions but it was when Victorine was sexually assaulted by *gendarmes* in 2004 that the family decided to flee Cameroon and come to Minnesota upon the invitation of an acquaintance. In 2011, Eric was awaiting the BIA's decision, after he had submitted an appeal of the court's asylum denial. By this time, Victorine had given birth to another son, born in Minnesota. During his appeal process, Eric was "enrolled" in ISAP. His description of being inducted into the program was far from the program's benevolent representation:

> They [BI] said it's a new government program and they are working with the government to implement this. So I cannot question it. I don't have a say in any of it. No voice to argue. If you ask a question, it's 'Immigration has ordered us to do this.' So, 'okay, can you talk to immigration, then?' 'Well, do you want to be in jail if I talk to them? Or do you want to listen to us and do what we say?' They [BI] won't explain anything and it's like 'well, if you don't want to do what we say, then we can call immigration and they can take you into custody.' So, they're [BI] just intimidating us.

Albert's and Eric's lived experiences of being enrolled in ISAP contradict the putative "voluntary" nature of the program, given that the "choice" is between "enrolling" in a program about which one is given little or no information and being detained by ICE. ISAP "introduces a scenario in which immigrants who have neither been arrested nor charged with a crime, nor are in custody, are nonetheless forced into a criminal-like process without judicial review" (Koulish 2013, 77). Incorporating asylum seekers into a framework of criminality recasts them as "offenders" who threaten the security of local communities and the nation at large. Legal communities, including the American Bar Association, and advocacy groups across the country have expressed serious concerns about ISAP and have especially questioned its claim as an *alternative* to detention, suggesting it instead constitutes another form *of* detention (Cervantes, Menjívar, and Staples 2017; Rutgers School of Law 2012).

Indeed, once enrolled, ISAP's criminalizing and dehumanizing tactics violated asylum seekers' sense of dignity, provoking a deep sense of humiliation, confusion, and anger. "I think the most frustrating thing about [ISAP] is that they treat us like thieves," Albert told me one afternoon, running his hand over his bulky ankle bracelet. He continued, describing for me the abhorrent treatment he received at the ISAP office:

> It's a mini Hell. It's like [they say] 'We can ask immigration to deport you if we want to. You better listen to us and kiss our ass or else I'm going to call immigration. I'm going to make your life more miserable. I'm going make you come here every day.' [His voice rose]. And hell, no, you don't have any voice. You don't have any power to do anything about it. And they do not listen to anything you have to say. . . . Oh my God, they treat people like they should not exist. They can either kick you out or let you stay. And you have no voice. You just have to comply.

Eric had similar experiences with the ISAP office, telling me, "ISAP is like selling your life, you know. There's no human dignity, there's no privacy." Moreover, like Roland and Ruth, Eric recognized the racialized nature of these criminalizing techniques of policing and surveillance. As he explained:

> But they never ask me why am I here in the first place. Bridget, I wish my country was a nice place. I would *never, never, never* step out of my country to go to *any* country that would treat my nationality like garbage. I'll bet you an American would not be treated like this any place. A European would not be treated like this *anywhere*. Do you know the people I see [at the ISAP

office]? Mostly from Third World countries. Mexicans. Africans. So, I'm treated like a criminal in a land where it's not—I mean, they say America, Land of the Free. It's a lie! Land of the Chosen Free.

For Eric, like my other asylum claimant friends, the question "Why are you here?" was a critical one. That their histories and complex subjectivities were elided or invisibilized by ISAP workers or other institutional actors who policed them was an enactment of violence, a form of "racialized erasure" (Willen 2019, 93). These experiences with ISAP staff reveal the troubling bureaucratic logic of the asylum system and its associated institutions, where asylum claimants, as unclassified/not yet classified persons (Malkki 1995), are often denied moral personhood. Because the asylum system casts the legitimacy of asylum seekers' claims for protection as potentially dubious or meritless, it is as if their rightful claims to dignity are also suspended—to be either restored with a granting of asylum or permanently refused with an asylum denial. While this was true of the asylum system in general, ISAP especially made asylum seekers legible in terms of their putative criminality. It's no wonder Ruth described herself as "under house arrest" or "like a prisoner in America" while enrolled. Though asylum seekers experienced themselves as a multiplicity of identities and subjectivities—a mother or father, a "woman of God," political activists or "freedom fighters"—living under the label of criminal or "failed asylum seeker" had profound bearing on their everyday lives and senses of self. They were, as Willen (2019) asserts, seen as *what* they were rather than *who* they were (101).

Making clear the inextricable link between the criminalizing effects of the asylum system and racism, Eric keenly highlighted how immigration systems both reflect and reproduce existing ideas of ethnoracial hierarchies (Hirsch 2019). His contention that white bodies—those of Americans or Europeans—would not be subjected to the forms of criminalization as persons of color, aptly captures what Moffette and Vadasaria (2016) have described as "racial governmentality":

> The framework of racial governmentality helps to explain the overt and insidious ways that nonwhite populations, and notably their bodies, are read and treated as threatening and violent. Racial governmentality relies upon rationalities of racial difference, which may at times give rise to the exonera-

tion of dehumanizing practices. . . . Because racial governmentality signals to a circular distribution of power . . . it works to mobilize racialization through internalized racial logics and rationalities, self-surveillance and regulation (5).

Immigration systems, and immigration enforcement specifically, serve as agents of racialization, in which migrants are socialized, consciously or not, to marginalized social positions. As a microcosm of this, the exchanges and encounters inside the ISAP office—like Roland's interactions with police or Maurice's (non)encounters with bureaucratic actors—"socialize [asylum seekers] into the 'appropriate' bodily disposition for a 'good migrant': the acceptance of uncivility, lecturing and surveillance" (Codó 2011, 738).

If broader anxieties and tensions surrounding immigration become "laminated upon black bodies" then the ankle bracelet ensured this in a literal sense (Tormey 2007, 86). ISAP participants complained of the monitoring bracelet being heavy, itchy, and cumbersome, causing difficulty with sleeping and other daily activities. Its physical presence on the body served to constantly remind asylum seekers of their deportability while also communicating their Otherness to the social world. Describing the experience of wearing an ankle bracelet, Albert told me: "I mean every second, every minute you feel it, you know? And then you think about your life, how it is here, every second of every minute." Here, "feeling it" had a dual meaning: Albert both physically felt the bracelet as a material object *and* absorbed its symbolic meaning of alterity and criminality.

For ISAP "participants," the materiality of an ankle bracelet or the need to account for every minute of one's schedule meant that they often reconfigured their social and personal lives in significant ways. On a practical level, participation in ISAP restricted daily movement: leaving one's house after curfew was prohibited; during assigned days, one would need to be home the entire day in case of a random home visit from ISAP staff; assigned in-person reporting times to BI needed to be maintained, often several times per week. During every weekly visit to the BI office, ISAP participants were required to fill out and present a schedule for the upcoming week that detailed their whereabouts twenty-four hours per day. Beyond the demoralization and indignity this produced, Albert explained to me the frustration and interference that this caused in terms of everyday social relations:

> They want you to be as comprehensive as possible, like tell them I'm going to go to church. I'm going to go to the store.... If a friend calls me and is, like, 'Hey, can we hang out at the park,' I'm not supposed to do that. So, it's like you lose a chunk of your liberty. And with this [points to ankle monitor] they're monitoring you all the time.

For many asylum claimants, "legal reality is superimposed on daily life" in unexpected and often unwelcome ways (Coutin 2003, 40). The ankle bracelet ensured this. ISAP participants with ankle bracelets went to great lengths to hide them. When in public, my interlocutors carefully avoided sitting or standing in ways that would expose the cumbersome plastic adhered to their bodies, feeling ashamed about what people would think should they see the device. Both Ruth and Eric wore ankle bracelets during the summer and each time I met either of them in a public place (a park, library), despite the hot and humid weather they always wore long pants or, for Ruth, a dress or skirt that skimmed the ground. Eric also went to great lengths to hide his ankle bracelet from his children—a difficult feat given the fact that he wore one for almost a year. "I can't even do crisscross applesauce [sitting cross-legged] with my kids. I can't go swimming with them. When I take a shower, I make sure the door is locked. I mean, look at this," Eric said pointing to the bulky device, "what would my kids think if they saw this. That their daddy is a criminal."

A few weeks later, a conversation between me, Ruth, and Eric—who had met and become friends through a mutual Cameroonian friend in Minnesota—sharply captured how the presence of the device mediated sociality.

RUTH:	It's very aching and so disappointing because you are so stressed and depressed. Every night. This thing talks! It talks, Bridget!! 'Charge me! Charge batteries please!!' [Ruth and Eric both broke into laughter.]
ERIC:	Oh, my God!
RUTH [IN A BOOMING VOICE]:	Battery charge! Charge batteries!
ERIC [IN A LOUD, MECHANICAL VOICE]:	Vreeep! Vreeep!
RUTH:	Yes, yes!

ERIC: And when the battery's running low. It signals. [loudly]
        Tweeeeeet. And then when you charge it. 'Battery charge.'
        [Both were laughing]. If you don't do it, it will start
        vibrating really loud.

RUTH: And you can't take it off!

ERIC: And you can be anywhere and it will start talking.

Any levity in the conversation was short-lived. At this point, Ruth stopped laughing, her eyes instead welling up with tears as she told us about being in the local African grocery—a place she frequented often and that provided her a sense of comfort—when her ankle monitor started making noise. "Oh my God, I was so humiliated." She was forced to abandon her basket of groceries to go home and attend to the device. Wiping her tears, Ruth looked at me and asked with both anger and sadness: "Do we deserve this?" She then answered her own question: "We're immigrants, not criminals."

In their Los Angeles-based research among immigrants wearing electronic monitoring bracelets post-detention, Martinez-Aranda (2022) found that immigrants may be a liability to loved ones and are therefore often stigmatized and avoided by friends and family because of others' fears about immigration enforcement. While I did not find this to be true among my interlocutors, it was the case that this technology of policing—one form of the violence of in/visibility—disrupted social and family relations. The stigma of an imputed criminality, most visible via the monitoring bracelet but communicated through myriad technologies and practices, also meant that asylum claimants reconfigured how they moved in space and among others. Eric's vigilant attempts to hide the monitoring bracelet from his children and the shame that provoked Ruth's quick exit from the grocery show the reach of these technologies of power.

Implicit in Ruth's proclamation "We're immigrants, not criminals" is the presumption that immigrants, like herself and other asylum claimants, do not inhabit the same moral space as criminals. This categorical distinction, however, is not necessarily shared by the state or immigration bureaucracies. As I outlined earlier, the increasing securitization and restriction of asylum domestically and globally reflect the growing tendency of states to conflate immigration, particularly asylum, with criminality. This conflation is not just discursive. In her examination of US border defense and national security policies, Lynn Stephen (2018) argues that these policies "created categories of people . . . who can be systematically excluded by being labeled as dangerous, criminal, undeserving, and less valuable than U.S. citizens" (7). While Stephen is specifically focused on migrants from Mexico and Central America, we can nonetheless see how my interlocutors were constructed similarly as "preemptive suspects" by the asylum regime. Stephen's concept of "preemptive suspects" importantly highlights how technologies of surveillance and policing, informed by "historical racial/ethnic hierarchies and coloniality," not only produce categories of persons but also work to justify the violence inflicted on them (8). Likewise, this chapter has highlighted how technologies of power surrounding in/visibility, which emerge from a broader ethos of suspicion, construct asylum claimants as particular kinds of morally ambivalent subjects, which normalized a range of bureaucratic violence. The embodied effects of this, as I have traced in this chapter, are both intra and interpersonal. Being rendered invisible, as Maurice experienced, or (hyper)visible, as with Roland, Eric, Albert, and Ruth, led to affective responses of demoralization, anger, fear, confusion, and humiliation.

*   *   *

As affirmative asylum claimants, my interlocutors were offered an ambivalent form of refuge, and occupied an ambiguous and precarious positionality. Granted certain "freedoms" as their cases were processed—protection from deportation, ability to legally reside in the country, and possibility for employment—they were seen and interpreted *partially* as potential "true refugees," who could be eventually granted the right to stay in the country. At the same time, they were subjected to a range of techniques that produced and then treated them as potential criminals/threats who could eventually be expelled. Being visible to the state was a necessary step towards desired (but not promised) permanent status and protection, but it also meant being subjected to a racialized and othering gaze of the state. Navigating this landscape was a formidable challenge, made more difficult by the illegibility and opacity of the asylum bureaucracy, where questions about "proper" visibility and rights were unclear and uneven. In response, asylum claimants often restricted their movements, which was an agentive strategy of self-preservation and dignity, but could increase social isolation. This should not be read as asylum claimants' acquiescence to the state, however. Though not in the form of protests or overt resistance, my interlocutors did "talk back" to the state (Stephen 2018). Their narratives of freedom fighting and religiosity, for example, are important counternarratives to the label of criminal/suspect. Moreover, that my interlocutors forged lives within these spaces of criminalization and in/visibility and stayed committed to the pursuit of asylum—what they unequivocally saw as their right to legal protection and inclusion—confirms their refusal to be reduced to the state's interpretation of them.

2 Limbo and the Violence of Waiting

> It's like always limbo. Limbo, limbo, limbo. You don't know
> what to do today, you know. Sometimes it's hard for me to
> sleep. . . . I cannot shut off my brain because of that limbo.
> That uncertainty. You know that is so, so unsettling. . . . I
> try not to worry about the things I don't have control over
> but sometimes I cannot help it . . . . This is my life.
>
> —Eric, Cameroonian asylum seeker

During one of my first weeks in the field, I spent the afternoon in the reception area of the local immigration court surrounded by people awaiting their asylum hearings.[1] At one point, an asylum officer entered and called out a name. A middle-aged man in a mismatched suit that overwhelmed his lanky frame slowly gathered up a handful of papers and walked towards the asylum officer. "Thanks for waiting," the asylum officer mumbled, barely making eye contact, as the man approached. "Ah," the man responded, "but I have no choice." Though this exchange was striking enough that I jotted it down in my field notebook, I did not realize its prescience. As I continued with my fieldwork, I would soon come to understand that waiting—or, more accurately, being made to wait—circumscribed asylum seekers' everyday lives and evoked subjective ways of being-in-the-world. Waiting, as this chapter analyzes, is both a technology of power and a phenomenological event.

Of course, waiting is not unique to the context of asylum seeking and is, in fact, part of the human condition. Yet, I follow Hage (2009) in arguing that ethnographic attention to waiting raises important questions about how temporal categories are shaped and inhabited (see also Jacobsen, Karlsen, and Khosravi 2021). This chapter focuses on what I identify as another iteration of violence on the asylum regime's violence continuum: the violence of waiting. This violence of waiting was likewise a "violence of uncertainty" (Grace, Bais, and Roth 2018). A primary effect of the violence of waiting and uncertainty was the production of a state of limbo for asylum claimants. In what follows, I explore asylum claimants' descriptions and lived consequences of this state of limbo and chart the ways in which they navigated and responded to it. To do this, I draw on multiple voices and narratives with the aim of capturing the scope and depth of this sense of limbo that was shared across my interlocutors.

Before proceeding any further, I want to address my use of "limbo" in this chapter. There has been an abundance of scholarship on migration that has used the frame of limbo (e.g., Cabot 2012; Gonzales 2015; Mountz et al. 2002). Yet, as recent critical migration scholars have importantly argued, academic writing has tended to deploy the concept of "limbo"—as well as similar constructs like "liminality" and even "waiting"—uncritically and hence, problematically (Etzold and Fechter 2022; Jacobsen and Karlsen 2021; Ramsay 2020a). There are a few central concerns, according to this critique. First, when used as an analytic construct, limbo may represent migrants' experiences as static and fixed, with people passively biding time (Jacobsen and Karlsen 2021). Second, concepts such as limbo and liminality presuppose linearity, with the implication being that asylum seekers or other migrants pass from one point to another (or one location to another) and are re-incorporated into an established social order. Finally, and related to this last point, concepts such as liminality and limbo, "by positioning reinsertion into a system of national identification as the solution . . . can inadvertently reify the national configuration of society" (6).

Both Jacobsen and Karlsen (2021) and Ramsay (2020a) caution against a conflation of experiences of limbo or waiting with theoretical conceptualizations of these phenomena. I likewise follow this critique. I explicitly engage with the idea of "limbo" as an experiential, emic category, taking my cue from Eric, whose description of limbo serves as the epigraph to this chapter. For my interlocutors, during the period of asylum-seeking, the object of their waiting was primarily an asylum decision, which they perceived as a resolution to their uncertainty. Though, as later chapters examine, this sense of resolution—and hoped-for end to waiting—was not often realized through an asylum decision, my interlocutors nonetheless experienced or envisioned it as such. Thus, rather than assume a state of limbo or waiting as inherent to asylum seeking, my goal is to trace the lived experiences of limbo as a politically and bureaucratically produced phenomenon.

MANIPULATION OF TIME AS A TECHNOLOGY OF POWER

Lionel had been a successful journalist in his native Liberia, and proudly supported a wife, four children, and an extended family. Lionel built a career on publishing investigative pieces about the Liberian government, beginning with Charles Taylor's regime in the 1990s. As he became more and more established as a journalist and gained greater access to government activities, his writing became bolder and more critical of Taylor and his administration, particularly during and after Liberia's brutal civil wars. He was regularly harassed, followed, and threatened by those inside Taylor's political circle. At several points between the mid-1990s and mid-2000s, Lionel had taken refuge for months at a time with friends in neighboring countries when he felt that the threats he received were growing in frequency or intensity. He would return to Liberia when he thought it safe again after a brief time away. In early 2008, despite Liberia's 2005 election of Ellen Johnson Sirleaf, Lionel was still occasionally publishing critical pieces about Taylor's legacy and was still receiving threats from the same Taylor loyalists.

Lionel's brother, who was living in the United States with a green card in a state bordering Minnesota, suggested Lionel come stay with him for a while until "things over there calmed down." After Lionel had been with his brother for a few weeks in the United States, a group of armed men came to his house in Liberia asking for him. When Lionel was nowhere to be found, the armed group beat his wife and children, vowing to return soon for Lionel. His wife and children fled to another part of Liberia, where they stayed in hiding with relatives. They urged Lionel not to come home the following week as he had planned. Lionel hoped that he could wait out the threats and return to Liberia soon. Yet, as months passed, he routinely received word from other family and friends in Liberia that they, too, had received menacing visits from armed men looking for him. His house and his office in Liberia had also been ransacked. At that point, an acquaintance in Minnesota suggested he might want to apply for asylum and referred him to CHR. At the time I first met Lionel in 2009, it had been six months since he had filed his asylum application and he had been in the United States for almost fifteen months. He had recently submitted the application for a work permit and was hoping that this would be processed quickly. Though he had a modest savings account in Liberia, Lionel refused to access these funds for himself, as they were the primary means by which his large family was surviving without him. "All this waiting is very difficult," Lionel sighed, adding "I just really need to get my papers [legal status] so I can move on with things in my life." He particularly struggled with the fact that he would not be able to quickly access a work permit. "How are people supposed to live if you won't let them work?" he asked me indignantly, genuinely confused about the possible logic behind this policy.

Towards the end of 2009, Lionel had an interview with an asylum officer, who referred his case to an immigration judge. He eagerly counted the months, then days, until his hearing, hoping that he would finally be granted asylum and could begin to make arrangements to bring his family to the United States to join him. In late 2010, I woke to an early winter snowstorm and made my way to the Bloomington, Minnesota, Immigration Court, where I was to meet Lionel for his hearing. He had arrived before me, having driven with his brother the 130-mile trek in blizzard conditions to reach the courthouse. As I entered the lobby area and approached the doors to the courtroom, I saw Lionel, his brother, and Lionel's volunteer lawyer, Dan, staring at a scribbled hand-written note that read "Closed" on the outside of the Immigration Court's door. As I stood there with Lionel wondering what to do next, I observed other asylum claimants with scheduled hearings gathering in the hallways of the government complex that housed the court. They, too, were nervously looking around, clutching laminated folders with documents inside, and peering through the dark, locked glass door of the court's lobby. Dan, also unsure of what to do, had made a phone call to the court, but got only an automated message. Dan stayed with Lionel, his brother, and me near the lobby for close to an hour before concluding the hearing wasn't happening and leaving, promising Lionel he'd be in touch. I stayed another hour with Lionel and the others who still milled about the entryway, hoping in vain that judges and staff would appear, before we parted ways and Lionel and his brother made the three-hour drive back to their home through the persistent snow. The next day, Lionel called to tell me the date of his rescheduled interview: he would have to wait another fourteen months to be back at court.

Over my many years of working with asylum claimants, I became accustomed to abrupt cancellations and rescheduling of asylum interviews and hearings, often without any explanation. The attorneys and other legal representatives I met were, for the most part, unperturbed by this and saw it as part of the bureaucratic humdrum of immigration procedures. Yet the effect these cancellations and delays had on my friends was the opposite. These delays and the additional waiting they produced, along with the opacity of the decision-making process which I outlined in the previous chapter, generated tremendous anxiety and uncertainty. Asylum seekers were made to wait for protracted periods of time at each step in the asylum process. At the USCIS level, this included filing a claim, scheduling and having an interview, and receiving a decision. Most of my interlocutors were then referred to EOIR (immigration court), where they waited again, this time for longer: hearings were often scheduled years out and decisions took months or even years after the hearing. Those who appealed an asylum denial from an IJ waited approximately another twelve to eighteen months to be issued a response from the BIA. Ultimately, my interlocutors waited for the final decision on their asylum claim anywhere from two to six and a half years. If, as I argued in the previous chapter, the opacity and ambiguity of the asylum system generated confusion, uncertainty, and anxiety, the "temporal governance" of the asylum system ensured that this sense of insecurity saturated everyday life for sustained periods (Griffiths 2017).

Lionel's experience drives home the ways in which the control and manipulation of time was used as tool of power (Andersson 2014b; Cwerner 2004; Griffiths 2014; Khosravi 2018; Turnbull 2016). On a broad scale, control over time, what Hill (2012, 247) describes as "the weaponization of temporality," or what Cwerner (2004), more specifically has referred to as the "time politics of asylum," serves as a technology of governing that regulates migration, marginalizing and subjugating persons or populations deemed less desirable (Andersson 2014b). Given the affective dimensions of waiting, and asylum seekers' intense sense of hope, desire, anxiety, and/or fear toward the object of their waiting (an asylum hearing or decision), the institutional control over time was highly productive in alienating asylum seekers from the asylum process. It was an institutional tactic that unequivocally communicated to asylum seekers that they were subordinated subjects. As Lionel's case lays bare, the opacity of the asylum system's time politics only sedimented the sense of institutional power. This was evident in asylum claimants' anxious ruminations on why their hearings were rescheduled and in the collective despondency of the asylum seekers peering into the windows of the shuttered courtroom the morning of the snowstorm.

The Asylum Clock

Though asylum applicants were largely waiting for the resolution of their claims, Lionel's experience reveals the multiple and cumulative forms of waiting embedded in this larger context of "liminal legality" (Menjívar 2006). A particularly challenging period of enforced waiting surrounded the delay in acquiring an employment authorization document (EAD), which grants legal employment eligibility while asylum claims are pending. At the inception of the asylum system in the United States, asylum applicants were immediately eligible for an EAD. However, in 1994, the US government imposed new procedures mandating delays in the issuance of EADs, with the explicit aim of deterring fraudulent or frivolous asylum claims. The stated concern was that migrants were coming to the United States and applying for asylum for the sole purpose of employment. Such concerns over what then-Deputy Immigration Commissioner Chris Sale described as rampant "abuse [of] the system" reflect the ways in which the putative distinction between "economic migrants" and humanitarian/political migrants are core to the adjudication of asylum claims and to the state's assessment of who is determined to be deserving of protection and humanitarian benefit more broadly.

These concerns have found resonance in contexts beyond the United States. For example, in the United Kingdom, migration scholars have critiqued a 2002 change in British law that ended immediate access to employment for asylum seekers in that country, requiring them to wait until twelve months after their initial asylum application (Mayblin 2016a, 2016b; Waite 2017).[2] As Mayblin (2016a) notes, the rationale behind the Home Office's revocation of employment access for asylum seekers was the assumption that economic rights constituted a "pull" factor for migrants, encouraging frivolous asylum claims. This pull-factor imaginary has had significant traction and influence over policy despite compelling research discrediting it (Mayblin 2016b; Waite 2017). Ultimately, in both contexts, the new changes in EAD wait times ostensibly communicated that those who were "true" refugees should—or could—abide the delay, revealing "a perverse valorisation of waiting" (Hage 2009, 105; McNevin and Missbach 2018). From this vantage point, waiting clearly emerges as form of violence, enforced by the state as a punitive measure against asylum claimants, whose presence is viewed with suspicion.

Following the 1994 rule changes, asylum seekers could only file an application for an EAD (I-765 form) with USCIS after their asylum claim had been pending for 150 days. USCIS then had 30 days to process the EAD application, and the EAD could not be issued until the asylum application had been pending for a minimum of 180 days. This waiting period has become known, colloquially, as "the EAD asylum clock" or simply, "the clock." There are several concerns surrounding the asylum clock. First, regarding the *experience* of waiting, it is important to note that "the clock" does not start until the initial application is filed. It took the asylum seekers I knew many months to learn about the asylum application process and, in most cases, to work with CHR to prepare and file the claim. But this time spent without work prior to filing the asylum application does not even figure into the 180-day wait time specified by the EAD clock—even though my interlocutors *experienced* this time as uncertain and precarious, particularly regarding their material and economic circumstances.

Second, though USCIS was, in theory, mandated to process the claims in a 30-day period, a backlog of EAD applications meant that this processing time was longer. During my fieldwork in 2009–2011, the processing time was approximately 90 days and was sometimes much longer. Finally, there are well-documented problems with the EAD clock, particularly concerning the lack of clarity and transparency of the government's management of the clock, as well as the state's misinterpretation of regulation and improper implementation of clock rules (Penn State Law 2010;

Human Rights Watch 2013). Asylum officials and IJs can stop the clock for a litany of reasons, often citing "applicant caused delays" (e.g., failing to show up for a fingerprinting appointment, requesting a change of date for an asylum hearing; asking for additional time to secure necessary documents; and problems in government coding/data entry errors), despite the lack of transparency and dissemination of what constitutes "applicant caused delays" in the first place. Further, the clock is often stopped without the knowledge of an asylum claimant and, if they have legal representation, even the knowledge of their lawyer(s) (Penn State Law 2010, 17). Oftentimes, the clock is stopped indefinitely. This has resulted in significant delays in receiving EADs and, in some documented cases, never obtaining an EAD at all (15). For most of my interlocutors, the total time from arriving in the United States to receiving an EAD was over a year, and many waited closer to a year and a half, with some waiting even longer.

Protracted waiting without access to employment eligibility often poses a real threat to asylum seekers, as they struggle financially to provide for themselves and for others, typically in home countries oceans away. Lionel's shock at learning he was not eligible for immediate employment access was not just demoralizing, as he had taken great pride in his work ethic and professionalism, but it was also a question of material survival. Lionel was not unique in this respect, as many asylum claimants, especially those like my interlocutors who arrived in the United States without significant, if any, financial savings, struggled to understand how they were supposed to put food on the table or buy a winter coat when they were barred from economic opportunities. The next chapter examines how asylum seekers' structural vulnerability and economic marginalization constrained their ability to fulfill social and familial roles as they sought asylum in the United States, as well as how these constraints challenged their own identities and self-conceptions. Here, I have presented the problematic of EAD delays as a particular form of "bureaucratically-induced waiting" (Rotter 2016, 81).

Court backlogs, abrupt cancellations of asylum hearings, and unexplained delays in judicial reviews are often taken for granted or assumed to be an inevitable part of the asylum system. I aim to unsettle this. In framing the institutional control and manipulation of time as a form of violence, my goal is to disrupt the normalization and routinization of such practices. If time could be a "weapon of sorts," then the lived experiences of waiting that asylum seekers are forced to endure gives voice to the injuries that such violence inflicts (Andersson 2014b, 798).

BETWEEN POSSIBILITY AND
FORECLOSURE: METAPHORS OF LIMBO

Much of my field work and time spent with asylum seekers involved waiting with them, be it in the ISAP office or immigration court lobby, or in their homes as they anticipated phone calls from legal representatives or checked their mail to see if USCIS had finally mailed a decision letter. Waiting also suffused our shared space when our conversations turned to my interlocutors' anxiety or fear about their precarious status and uncertain futures. Of course, given my positionality as a researcher, ally, and US citizen, and not an asylum claimant, my experiences of waiting in these situations was profoundly different than those of my interlocutors. For me, waiting did not entail life-and-death stakes, as it did for asylum seekers. Waiting and uncertainty were also states of being that I, unlike my interlocutors, could willingly leave, returning to the comfort of my apartment and family at the end of the day, with a sense of security in the taken-for-granted unfolding of my life. The contrast of these experiences and orientations to temporality—past, present, and future—exposes how time is differentially and inequitably lived and experienced. During my first conversation with Hassan, an asylum claimant from Pakistan, I could see the distinct ways in which asylum seeking—and the positionality of 'asylum claimant'—shaped the experience of time.

Hassan, a kind and animated man in his late twenties, had fled his native Pakistan after suffering years of physical and verbal abuse, including death threats, because of his sexual orientation. By the time I met Hassan, his asylum case had been pending for several years. I was at first struck by how much Hassan seemed to be engaging actively in life despite this period of protracted liminality: he had a romantic partner and a small social network; a steady job as a line cook in a restaurant near his home; and was taking classes at a local community college. Yet, as we talked further, he revealed a simultaneous sense of deep uncertainty, which shaped his life as an asylum claimant:

> You come here for freedom, but then you feel you're locked in here. What's the point of coming when you're given this life and you're going be locked in? You can be gay, you can be yourself, but all they [asylum seekers] can do is live here and that's it. You cannot travel anywhere, you cannot go anywhere, you cannot see your family anymore, and you don't know if you will be here for good or not. They might just send you away any time. So in a way it's even worse. . . . I just came to this country to be an openly gay man. And live a life where I can be free, I can be productive, live a happy life. And I feel it's there, but I cannot touch it. I cannot have it. So, it's like you get a taste of it, but you're not allowed to have it and maybe it's going to be taken away from you forever. It's very painful.

Though uncertainty and waiting were largely productive of distress, Hassan's explication of asylum here also draws attention to the fact that "uncertainty and precariousness . . . can be read by social actors in them and by analysts both as disorienting and as full of potential" (Kleist and Jansen 2016, 388). Hassan framed asylum-seeking as a highly ambivalent temporal, spatial, and juridical space of refuge. He, like other asylum claimants, was able to *partially* inhabit and envision new "possible selves" (Parish 2008) afforded by life in the United States, but always with the caveat—and the lived reality—that these opportunities to live otherwise could be abruptly terminated and might prove illusory. These glimpses, or "tastes," of a good life took different forms for asylum claimants, but it was the precarity of these potentialities that was such an integral part of the asylum regime's power and a source of pain for those embedded in it. The protracted, institutionally produced states of waiting and uncertainty that asylum claimants faced were animated by both possibility and foreclosure.

Hassan's depiction of feeling "locked in" as an asylum claimant underscores a sense of being caught in space and time. My other interlocutors consistently articulated similar descriptions of what it felt like to seek asylum, or to be an asylum seeker in the United States. These descriptions cohere around metaphors that echo Hassan's idea of "locked in," as the additional narratives illustrate:

You are in this dark situation here, and it was a dark situation that led you to be in this country [America] and you can't break out—*you are like in a cubicle*—it's a *dark cubicle* [and] you can't do anything. It's so, so difficult. . . . You are applying for the papers [asylum], you know it's just the grace of God if you get the papers. Now life is, it's like blank. You don't know whether you're going forward or going backwards, to the left or to the right. It's just so dark and you can't see the light. (Sarah, asylum seeker from Zimbabwe)

What worries me is that I can't have this [asylum case] hanging around in the background because I think about it all the time—you know when you're not secure it's something that lays in your mind . . . and it also becomes very tricky because you can't plan your life. It's like you put *your life on hold* for some time. (Rose, asylum seeker from Kenya)

[Y]ou freeze, you know what I mean? If an animal comes to you and you just—you don't know what to do. *You just freeze.* So, just like I'm in that status right now. And I just wait what they [immigration officials] tell me. And I know the end is . . . um, I understand that people were, at the end, detained or deported and . . . and my fate is not different than theirs. So, I'm just waiting. I'm just waiting. I just see where my fate takes me. So, it's just like there's nothing I can do. . . . And it's of course very hard. And every day, I think 'What my destiny will be?' (Mohammed, asylum seeker from Ethiopia)

These narratives capture the "the interplay of temporal and spatial uncertainty" (El-Shaarawi 2015, 38) and its troubling effect on lived experience. Asylum seekers' ubiquitous use of metaphors of feeling "caught," "trapped," "stuck," "lingering," "on hold," "frozen," or imprisoned map on to what Eric and others specifically identified as "limbo." If, as Laurence Kirmayer (1992, 334) posits, metaphoric concepts are grounded in both bodily and social experience, these descriptions then are not mere rhetorical devices, but rather critical indexes of participants' affective and embodied states. Over time I came to understand that the state of enforced waiting that my interlocutors experienced was best understood as an *existential limbo:* a particular subjective orientation or mode of attention in which the asylum process, in its current moment, was seen as the locus of suffering and in which life and meaning making were made challenging. I take my cue here from Hage (2005), who argues that "existential movement"—a sense that life is "going somewhere"—is a necessary component of a viable life (470). Asylum seekers' sense of life moving forward became suspended or stuck as their asylum claims lingered, producing a profound state of uncertainty.

The metaphors used by asylum seekers bring into relief key elements of existential limbo. First, the narratives above emphasize the disorientation, fear, and anxiety that temporal and spatial insecurity provoke. Asylum seekers are often preoccupied with their asylum cases, sometimes consumed by thoughts of it throughout their days. Though some theorizing on waiting has emphasized the derealization of the present due to an orientation toward the future (Crapanzano 1985), for the asylum claimants I knew it was primarily the *present* state of uncertainty that occupied their minds. Asylum seekers' inability to anticipate their futures results in a lived "time without direction" (Brekke 2010, 163), where the present does not recede into the background, but is rather hyperrealized (Bryant 2016; Griffiths 2014; Jeffrey 2010). Their lives are thus characterized by an "enforced orientation to the present" (De Genova 2002, 427). Yet it was the absences of the current moment that so often consumed my interlocutors' thoughts: lack of legal status, security, a home, a job, their families.

A second key element of existential limbo is a concomitant sense of disempowerment. How one experiences waiting is contingent upon one's position within structures of power (Bourdieu 1997; Chua 2011; Kobelinsky 2010; Turnbull 2016). Waiting in this context emerges as a violence, where those who wait are "condemned to live in a time orientated by others, an alienated time" (Bourdieu 1997, 237). Implicit to conceptions of the self as prey to a predator in its path, as Mohammed metaphorically positions himself, or the self as a prisoner in a dark cubicle in Sarah's narrative, is the notion of a more powerful Other—an Other who can place one in a subordinate position. These metaphoric concepts, then, point to participants' lived experiences of limbo *as it relates to* their limited capacity to define the parameters of their positionality. Critically shaping this sense of limbo is the perception that an asylum seeker's fate or destiny is out of their hands, to be decided by immigration officials or, as Sarah suggests, by the "grace of God." In this way, though they are not physically confined, asylum claimants are nonetheless subjected to a sense of "spatio-temporal entrapment" (Jansen 2013) or "social entrapment" (Crapanzano 1985, xiii), limiting how people are able to envision themselves, their social worlds, and their futures (see also Eggerman and Panter-Brick 2010). For asylum claimants, this sense of entrapment often gives way to feelings of futility, of being worn down, or overpowered, evoking what Luhrmann (2006) describes as "social defeat" as a form of subjectivity. Similarly, Welander and De Vries (2016) use the analytic of "exhaustion" to describe the daily reality for migrants caught up in the European migration regime, insisting that this exhaustion also be understood as a particular tool of governance and control of migrant populations.

The existential limbo I am describing here is, like other effects of the asylum regime's power, critically informed by the racialized, colonial assumptions and hierarchies undergirding the asylum system and its ethos of suspicion. We can see asylum claimants' limbo as a suspended state between belonging and unbelonging, or between what Frantz Fanon (1967) labels "zones of being." Those who are denied full humanity—for Fanon, the colonized black man—are locked in a "zone of nonbeing" (Fanon 1967, 82). Asylum claimants occupy "the middle of a spatial and temporal world" in which they are positioned between a zone of nonbeing and a zone of being (83). As I noted in the previous chapter, Fanon's frame of the "psycho-affective" consequences of colonial power helps us develop a deeper appreciation of the ways in which the anti-black/anti-migrant gaze of the state powerfully shapes how asylum claimants experience themselves and their "bodily schema" (1967, 83). The phenomenology of asylum claimants' existential limbo is a further dimension of this. Having outlined the existential limbo produced through the violence of waiting, I now explore how a sense of limbo mediated asylum seekers' subjectivities and social worlds. I anchor this discussion in a poignant conversation between me, Eric, and Louise.

LIVED CONSEQUENCES OF EXISTENTIAL LIMBO

One late autumn afternoon, I had settled myself in Eric's living room with Louise, whom I had just picked up from work. The two had known each other previously in Cameroon and, by coincidence, met again in the United States through a mutual friend, a Cameroonian asylee. As we sipped on bottles of Fanta that Eric had set out, Louise told us about an offer that she had received from her employer. She had left work as a private caregiver and was working as an entry-level nursing assistant in a group home for the elderly. The group home's director told Louise the company would pay for her to attend classes to get her certification in nursing assistance (CNA). A CNA certificate would have provided Louise with opportunities for better paid employment positions, not just with her then-current company but outside of it as well. This seemed to me like a promising opportunity, especially since I knew Louise was barely making enough money to support herself now that she was living in her own studio apartment. But before I could offer my opinion, she declared this a "waste of time." She explained: "Why would I do that? Why should I spend my time doing that? If they send me back to Cameroon, CNA will be useless. It won't mean anything. It won't help me." Shaking her head, Louise continued, "I mean, look at everything that is going on with my [asylum] case right now, with this investigation." Louise was referring to the overseas investigation that DHS had started, putting her asylum case indefinitely on hold (see introduction). "Immigration is the cause of my suffering," she declared, as Eric nodded emphatically, leaning forward in his chair. Louise continued to describe how she was feeling.

> LOUISE: I don't understand why they are making me to suffer so much. There is so much uncertainty. *So much* uncertainty. That is the hardest thing. When people are running from trouble, like political problems, they are going through a lot. So it's very important that they have some sort of shield, some sort of protection. Because I feel as if I'm homeless. I don't have anywhere to go, nothing. And that feeling is like, it's like you're still fighting a war psychologically. You're still in danger, you know?

> ERIC: I feel that same way, too. I feel that same way. And I have a kid here! And if they tell me to go, then what will I do? So, I'm not safe here, but I'm not safe in Cameroon. So, it's like, I'm not safe anywhere.

> LOUISE: Yes, you are in the middle of war. Even here. [long pause] Since I've come here, I don't sleep. They gave me medicine for depression, it does nothing. Sometimes I forget things. Sometimes I leave things and then look for them in a different place.

ERIC: Yes, yes. Psychologically, it's very tormenting. This process is very tormenting.

LOUISE: It's been too long. Too long. I don't know where I belong. It's something I think about every day. *Every* day. *Every* night.

ERIC [TURNING
 TOWARD ME]:   See, Bridget, this is the psychological effect of this [asylum] process! The mind is never at ease. Like she said, she takes medication for depression. It doesn't help. She takes medication just to sleep. But she doesn't sleep.

By this point, we had stopped sipping our sodas and fallen into a somber silence. Eric's and Louise's words had painfully exposed how the asylum system's continuum of violence became embodied, shaping intimate thoughts and feelings. Their words were also an unequivocal and direct indictment of the asylum system as productive of this uncertainty and suffering. Within this conversation, we can identify key elements of the lived consequences of limbo produced through the violence of waiting and uncertainty. Eric's and Louise's vivid depictions reveal limbo as a disruption of life trajectories and limbo as a form of trauma.

Limbo as Disruption

The disruption that a sense of limbo caused was evident in the metaphors and descriptions that asylum claimants used. For example, we have seen that my interlocutors framed asylum seeking as a period without direction ("you don't know if you're going forwards or going backwards" or "you can't plan your life"). This perceived inability to plan one's life or move forward has not just material consequences, but emotional and psychic ones as well. Louise's rejection of pursuing a CNA can be seen as a meaningful and reasonable response when we consider the violence of temporality embedded in the asylum regime. In his examination of Burundian refugees in Nairobi, Stuart Turner (2016) argues that because these refugees do not envision or desire a future in Nairobi or the camp, they resist becoming embedded in the present to allow for future emplacement elsewhere. Though they engage in everyday livelihoods and activities, they nonetheless "avoid becoming too involved, as they prefer to prepare for the future by remaining liminal in the present" (38). Louise similarly resisted a sense of emplacement. A key difference, however, is that unlike the refugees Turner describes, Louise, like all my interlocutors, was in fact hoping to stay in the United States. In other words, my interlocutors hoped to be able to emplace themselves where they were. Thus, Louise's refusal to become more embedded did not reflect her lack of desire to stay, but rather a strategy of emotional self-perseverance and an economizing of her time and energy. That is, emplacing herself in the United States was emotionally risky given that this could all be abruptly ended with a denial of asylum.

It was also the case, however, that time spent devoid of future-orientated activities or acts of placemaking could likewise seem meaningless and emotionally detrimental. Many of my interlocutors drew on the trope of "waste" when discussing the challenge of finding a coherent life trajectory as an asylum seeker. They described periods of protracted waiting without a resolution as "a waste of time," or "time wasting away." One of my Cameroonian asylum-seeking friends, for example, lamented the disruption caused by such a bureaucratically induced limbo. "I was a civil servant for thirty-five years [in Cameroon]. I was supposed to retire, to get my retirement. I was instrumental, a great asset to the younger generation," he said proudly. "But see where I am now? I am wasting." The use of "waste" here emphasizes just how much a sense of limbo could disrupt "imagined life trajectory[ies]" (El-Shaarawi 2016, 82). Given that asylum seekers' temporal experiences were powerfully shaped by the asylum regime's ability to control their time, the wasted time that my friends experienced may best be understood as what Khosravi (2018) labels "stolen time."

It was not just the disruption of time that is evident in Louise's and Eric's conversation. Indeed, Louise's rejection of pursuing the CNA, as I noted, relates both to the challenge asylum claimants experience in "emplotting" their lives—providing temporal coherence—as well as emplacing themselves in the physical spaces they occupy (Garro and Mattingly 2000). This is most striking in Louise's description of limbo as a state of being "homeless." This was not the first time, nor would it be the last, that I would hear this over the course of my fieldwork from many asylum seekers. Returning to the overarching feeling captured by the metaphors of limbo of life being "trapped" or "suspended," this sense of homelessness lays bare asylum claimants' state of "stuckedness" as an effect of bureaucratic violence (Hage 2009). They cannot go back to the countries from which they have fled out of fear for their lives, and yet are constantly aware—and reminded—of the fact that they might not be able to stay in the United States. Louise's suffering, it is clear, was not necessarily, or at least not primarily, caused by the event of displacement but by the protracted state of bureaucratically produced limbo that disallowed *anywhere* to be called home. It is a cruel irony that asylum seekers who are defined by their mobility (as forced migrants) become spatially and temporally stuck in a protracted state of waiting once in the United States. This sense of being stuck is legally codified, as asylum applicants are not allowed to leave the United States while their claims are pending. If they do, they are rendered ineligible for asylum. Thus, limbo-as-homelessness in this context indexes a disruption of both time and space, calling into question both *when* and *where* asylum claimants may claim to belong.

Limbo as Trauma

The language that both Eric and Louise used to describe their existential limbo makes the effects of the violence of enforced waiting and uncertainty undeniable. They described the enforced waiting of the asylum process itself as "tormenting," akin to "fighting a war." In my interviews and conversations with asylum claimants, I documented a range of perceived psychological and emotional effects of limbo, from "worry" and "discomfort" to "trauma" and "madness." While asylum seekers expressed varied levels of distress, all my interlocutors, without exception, viewed the asylum process as productive of some level of suffering, often labeling the asylum system itself as "a kind of trauma," "a form of torture," or a "psychological game." The asylum process, and the limbo that my interlocutors were forced to inhabit, both prolongs past suffering and produces new forms of suffering. Hence, Louise's experience of "*still* fighting a war."

The "torment" caused by the limbo of asylum seeking altered Louise's experience of herself and her social world. She had become someone who misplaced things, who could not sleep, who was never at peace. Hers was a suffering that was impervious to medication, interrupted her rest, and preoccupied her mind. Limbo was understood as traumatic because of the life-and-death stakes it represented, a constant reminder of the precarity of asylum seekers' positionality and the ever-present possibility of a return to life-threatening danger if deported.

While I have noted how asylum seekers vacillated between a sense of possibility and a sense of foreclosure, there were times that the pain of the present moment threatened to overwhelm my interlocutors. For example, Hassan told me that being an asylum seeker was "so scary sometimes it just makes you so numb, some days it's so overwhelming." Sarah described her emotional pain at times as "too big . . . you can't swallow it." If asylum seekers' distress at times threatened to overpower them, it also could, at times, defy apprehension or articulation, as my friends would sometimes fail to find words to express their thoughts and feelings or simply tell me that they felt detached from their own bodies. As Janis Jenkins (2015) observes, "(t)he phenomenological sense of being in the world that deep bodily and psychic trauma can wield can be summarized as *unfathomability* as an enduring lived reality" (12). This was perhaps most observable among my asylum claimants whose experiences of the trauma of limbo were expressed through their bodies. Many of my interlocutors complained of physical symptoms, such as headaches, intense bodily heat, weakness, and insomnia. They insisted that these symptoms or illnesses were produced not by past experiences of violence or torture, but by the limbo produced by the asylum process (see Haas 2021). Physical symptoms such as these may be easily glossed as somatic manifestations of stress. However, such a reductive interpretation obscures the forms of violence that generate these bodily ways of being-in-the-world and are thus inextricable from their expression. Instead, asylum seekers' physical symptoms are best understood as "embodied metaphors" (Low 1994, 139) or the "corporeal effects" (Vogt 2018, 108) of the asylum regime's continuum of violence. If the effects of limbo can reside within people's bodies, it is also the case that these effects ripple outward.

WAITING AS TRANSNATIONALLY EMBODIED

The enforced waiting and uncertainty of asylum seeking are forms of bureaucratic violence perpetrated against not only asylum claimants themselves but also upon loved ones across the globe who wait *with* and *for* them. Waiting, then, is transnationally embodied. Bureaucratically produced states of existential limbo mean that family separation is protracted, often for many years. It is hard to overstate the emotional and psychological toll that such prolonged family separation has on asylum claimants. Sarah, an asylum claimant from Zimbabwe, who had described the asylum process as being stuck in a dark cubicle, was consumed with the pain of being separated from her children. She had fled Zimbabwe after a group of heavily armed men, whom she believed to be members of the country's military, forcibly entered her home. She was raped and her husband—who was involved in a political party opposing then-president Robert Mugabe—was abducted and, she presumed, killed. She left her children in the hands of a neighbor, promising to send for them as soon as she reached the United States. She had expected this to take no more than a month or two. Though Sarah had filed her asylum claim quickly, after one year she was still waiting to have her initial asylum interview.

"This [asylum] process is taking too long," she said mournfully when I visited her one evening. "I can keep waiting, that I know. But without my kids . . . ." Her voice trailed off, before continuing. "I think if Immigration would let me bring my family at least I'd have peace of mind. You know, I would just feel like a human again." This utterance—"feel like a human again"—has stayed with me, and I have recalled this exchange again and again over the years. What was immediately and exquisitely striking about Sarah's words was the equation of her very humanity with the presence of her children. Sarah's sentiment was not unique. Asylum claimants often express their excruciating longing for family they left in their countries of origin, drawing a deep connection between a life worth living and the presence of family. Asylum seekers' yearning for their children is especially acute.

Psychological literature has argued that family separation has a significant impact on refugee and asylum seeker mental health, and is correlated with higher rates of depression, anxiety, PTSD, and grief (Löbel 2020; Miller et al. 2018; Li, Liddell, and Nickerson 2016; De Haene and Rousseau 2020). While I am not focused on psychiatric nosology, I certainly saw the psychic and emotional effects of family separation. But the psychological literature largely assumes family separation to be a feature of displacement or forced migration. My argument troubles this assumption. Rather, Sarah's story reveals the forms of trauma that are an effect of the asylum system's violence continuum. We see in her story intersecting and overlapping forms of violence. This starts, of course, with the horrific acts of violence that catalyzed her flight from Zimbabwe. Once in the United States, both the violence of enforced waiting and the opacity and illegibility of the asylum system—a violence of in/visibility—shaped Sarah's experience of family separation. In suggesting that reunification with her children would restore her humanity, Sarah subtly but critically indicted the US immigration system for the separation. Though she acknowledged that she bore responsibility for leaving her children—a sacrifice she made so that she could save her life, and in doing so, save her children from losing a mother—Sarah rightfully located the *protraction* of separation as an effect of the asylum system. It is not just the fact of family separation that is so difficult for asylum claimants, but also the uncertainty and opacity surrounding its timeline. Drawing on Pauline Boss's (2010) construct of "ambiguous loss," a relational disorder in which a loved one is either physically present but psychologically absent, or psychologically present but physically absent, Utržan and Northwood (2017) argue this point. Because asylum seekers are uncertain of the duration of their separation from family, they suffer a loss that is ambiguous—a loss that they cannot fully, or concretely, mourn, nor one whose reversal (i.e., reunification) they can hopefully anticipate (see also Miller et al. 2018). As Lee (2019) has argued, protracted family separation, as an effect of enforced waiting and bureaucratic illegibility, can constitute a form of "slow death."

Additionally, my interlocutors' grief and worry about their separated families were compounded by persistent feelings of guilt, despite their understandings of asylum seeking as a form of family sacrifice and something they were forced to do, given the existential threats they faced. If waiting is, as I am arguing, transnationally embodied, then family members across the globe also feel the painful effects of this as much as those seeking asylum in the United States. The illegibility of the US asylum system also shapes experiences of loved ones in Cameroon, Zimbabwe, Pakistan or other home countries. It was not uncommon for asylum claimants to tell me that family members in home countries were confused and frustrated about how long the asylum process was taking. My interlocutors recounted painful phone conversations with crying children asking when they would see their mother or father again. While most asylum claimants found their families supportive, interactions with family members could be emotionally fraught. For example, Hassan not only felt grief about being separated from his family, but also labored to find ways to explain his predicament, particularly as his claim remained pending for so long. "They always grill me when I talk to them. They always ask me 'when are we going to see you? What's going on?,'" he said, dejected. "I have to keep telling them to wait for me, but I've been telling them that since 2005. They don't understand. I mean they don't know the whole [asylum] procedure. And then I cry thinking, when *will* I see them again?"

The weaponization of temporality had additional transnational effects. Some of the most difficult moments I witnessed in my fieldwork were the times my interlocutors received news that loved ones, including children, in their home countries were being harassed, threatened, or harmed. Lionel's wife and children, for example, were terrorized by men looking for Lionel after he had already left the country. Likewise, I vividly recall Ruth's panic and sorrow when she learned that her fifteen-year-old son had been physically assaulted on his way to school when military police intercepted his walk, demanding to know Ruth's whereabouts. "What am I to do?" Ruth implored anxiously. "My whole family is in danger. And I am here, not knowing if I am staying or going. I know I cannot go back to Cameroon. I want to bring my children here so that they can be safe. I am doing this for them. But all I am doing is waiting." Ruth, and other asylum claimants like her, had expected that their absence would make their families safer, only to find that their absence could—and sometimes did— threaten to imperil their families. The bureaucratically produced waiting that asylum claimants were forced to endure in the United States only exacerbated this situation. But even family members in home countries who were not harassed or endangered by my interlocutors' departure were not immune to the shared effects of the asylum regime's "time politics" (Cwerner 2004). Many asylum claimants, especially those who fled situations of ongoing political conflict, had family who remained in environments of continuing instability and oppression. Asylum claimants—and their loved ones who remained—thus felt a sense of urgency in resolving their claims in hopes that they could also bring their families to a safer place. Yet, as we've seen, this sense of urgency was not shared by asylum bureaucracies. Ultimately, the slow violence of the asylum regime's temporal governance could have far-reaching and dangerous transnational effects. I focus the remainder of this chapter on the critical question of how asylum claimants endured this painful waiting.

ENDURING LIMBO

I have thus far shown the pernicious lived effects of the asylum system's violence of waiting and uncertainty, including effects that extend far beyond the United States and its asylum institutions. In discussing limbo as a form of trauma, I noted the sometimes-overwhelming sense of desolation that my interlocutors expressed. Consider, as another example, the depth of pain that prompted one of my asylum-seeking friends to tell me: "I'm not sure how I can keep up this waiting. It's been so long and I don't see an end, I see only darkness. Maybe I should find a way to end it all—my life, I mean." Here, in no uncertain terms, my friend identified the violence of waiting as generative of his despair. This friend was not alone in considering death as an end to their experience of ongoing violence, in its myriad forms. On multiple occasions asylum claimants revealed to me that they had thought about suicide.[3] Though I am not aware of any suicide attempts, these were deeply troubling moments in my fieldwork. It would have been easy for me to declare the asylum process as totalizing in its ability to subjugate claimants. I could see the effectiveness of the asylum system's violence continuum in producing asylum claimants as docile, alienated, and dehumanized subjects. And yet, this is not the story my interlocutors told. Asylum seekers were deeply affected, and often emotionally and socially wounded, by the asylum system's technologies of governing, but they were not fully determined by them.

My interlocutors were agentic social actors who were "deeply engaged in finding a way to live" through the asylum process (Garcia 2008, 723). But what does agency look like in this context? In asking this, I speak to a broader dilemma—ethnographic and ethical—that I have wrestled with in representing the stories and experiences of the asylum claimants who have shared their lives with me. How can we recognize and honor asylum claimants' distress and sometimes crushing sense of despair and defeat while also affirming and illustrating their agentic capacities? Where do we locate a sense of agency in the desire to end one's life to escape an institutionally produced state of limbo? I believe that reconciling this dilemma is possible. Feeling a sense of powerlessness and overwhelm, on the one hand, and an orientation towards forging ahead, on the other, are not incommensurate ways of being-in-the-world. Yet the context of asylum seeking does urge us to rethink what constitutes agency. To this end, I have been inspired by theorizations of agency that attend to the constraints that shape movement within a certain context (Biehl and Locke 2010; Coutin 2003; Holland et al. 1998; Ortner 2006). Cabot (2012), for example, defines agency as "the maneuverings through which individuals attempt to make tolerable lives within sets of conditions and constraints" (23).

The affective and embodied dimensions of limbo that I have discussed expose "the multiple and ambivalent forms that agency takes in relation to waiting" (Hage 2009, 2). Depending on one's position within a field of power, waiting could be experienced as productive or generative (Chua 2011; Jeffrey 2010). In her work with asylum seekers in the United Kingdom, Rebecca Rotter (2016) notes her participants' narratives of stagnation, in which waiting is framed as a passive event—a sentiment certainly echoed by my interlocutors. However, rather than take these narratives at face value, Rotter looks to her ethnographic data that highlight more complex lived experiences, concluding that waiting "is not an empty interlude" and can, in fact, be generative of agentive action (see also Conlon 2011; Parla 2019; Rainbird 2014). Similar understandings of agency within migration contexts marked by protracted waiting have been offered, to include "delayed agency and agency from marginal positions" (Ghorashi, de Boer, and ten Holder 2017), "agency-in-waiting" (Brun 2015), and hidden "sparks of agency" (Robleda 2020).

Taken together, these approaches move away from equating agency with resistance, and instead position people's attempts to maintain the status quo and/or ensure their everyday survival as forms of agency (Asad 2000; Zigon 2009). As Parish (2008) reminds us, people are "not passive in relation to the process of suffering" (127). It is this stance, in fact, that enables a view of suicide as "an act of agency [that] allows a person to have some control over his or her fate" (Parish 2008, 169; see also Broz and Münster 2016; Staples and Widger 2012). And yet, none of my inter-locutors ended their lives. They actively weathered the limbo of asylum. How, then, did they do this?

Seen from the vantage point of agency within constraint, many of the quotidian activities and moments I shared with my interlocutors take on new meaning. If, as Mayblin (2020) has suggested, the everyday is a site of slow violence for asylum seekers, then I have come to understand that the everyday is simultaneously a site of endurance. Asylum claimants' seemingly mundane acts emerged as agentic responses to the enforced waiting imposed upon them. My interlocutors often stressed a desire to "keep busy." Free time spent window shopping at thrift stores, hours-long walks throughout the day, weekends spent in the kitchen cooking pots of Cameroonian stews and fish rolls—these were meaningful activities that offered a distraction from the pain of waiting.

Beyond these more mundane and smaller strategies of endurance, sometimes asylum claimants' time was spent on pursuits aimed at not just sustaining life but trying to flourish within it (Willen 2019). For example, Emmanuel, a Cameroonian asylum claimant who we'll meet again in sub-sequent chapters, took advantage of the health care coverage offered to asylum claimants in Minnesota at the time. With my help, he pursued medical care for his faltering eyesight and hearing. "I need to take care of my health," he told me, "so that I can be strong again, and be there for my family in the future." Emmanuel also went to counseling sessions at a local mental health clinic and found this helped him endure the protracted waiting and pain of being separated from his wife and four small children. This was true of others, as well. As I've written elsewhere, some asylum seekers found psychotherapy and therapeutic relationships meaningful, in part because within these encounters the full complexities of their lives and their moral dignity were recognized and honored—something often denied to them within the legal arena and their everyday lives in the US (Haas 2021).

Asylum claimants found meaning in additional spaces and activities, not only because these spaces provide a reprieve from their ongoing sense of limbo, but also because of the social connections they engendered. For many, religious institutions were important sites where interpersonal relationships were forged and sustained. Among my Cameroonian inter-locutors, many attended the same churches, one Protestant, the other Catholic, both lively places, replete with dancing and rousing songs. Services were often followed by gatherings at someone's house, where food was always served and dancing and singing often continued. Religious institutions such as churches and mosques were spaces of welcome, hope, and solidarity for asylum claimants, providing them with a sense of emotional respite.

Within these spaces, though the reality of existential limbo was never far from my interlocutors' minds and bodies, always looming on the horizon, their fears and distress could temporarily recede, even if just a bit. In these moments, the passage of time could unfold less painfully, allowing for different emotional registers, including comfort, contentment, and even joy. Engagement in the activities I've outlined above highlights the agentic capacities of asylum seekers, who creatively navigate an oppressive and sometimes-overwhelming bureaucratic landscape, carving out moments and places where they can "reconstruct forms of sociality within spaces of exclusion" (Reiter and Coutin 2017, 589).

But what about transnational social connections? While I previously underscored the pain of family separation, for many of my interlocutors, the ability to stay connected to and communicate with friends and fami-lies across the world was often vital to the endurance of the protracted asylum process. As research has shown, family separation does not neces-sarily lead to reduced social connection and family members living apart can provide both tangible (economic) and intangible (emotional) support (Baldassar 2007; Dahinden 2005; Grace 2019), in ways that may even protect against mental distress (Löbel 2020). Yet, we also saw how some of my interlocutors wrestled with difficult feelings surrounding their pro-tracted absence in the lives of their families in home countries. Thus, phone and video calls with loved ones in home countries often emerged as a double-edged sword.[4] On the one hand, asylum claimants were able to maintain an important connection to family members. Phone calls were also a medium in which asylum claimants could parent from afar and per-form meaningful care work (Mahler 2001; Baldassar 2007, 2016; Grace 2019; Bryceson 2019). On the other hand, talking to family members could generate painful feelings of longing, guilt, and anxiety, as well as expose interfamilial tensions evoked by the protracted and bewildering asylum process.

It was not surprising to me, then, when Hassan—who felt "grilled" by his family when he talked to them—confessed to me that he sometimes avoided phone calls with his family altogether. "I don't know what to do," he told me. "I feel bad when I talk to them, and I feel bad when I don't call them." The occasional, or even regular, avoidance of family communication as a way of evading difficult feelings was not uncommon. In a broader sense, this tactic of avoiding familial communication is related to the perceived danger of "thinking too much" that has been documented among refugees and asylum seekers (Kaiser et al. 2015; Yarris 2011). That is, even among asylum claimants who didn't feel their relationships with family were strained, talking to family would often cause them to be flooded with sadness and worry. Not talking to them at all could effectively help to bracket those thoughts and feelings of distress, even if only intermittently. Ultimately, then, both the active pursuit of communication and connection with family in one's country of origin *and* the avoidance of such connection/communication emerged as agentic strategies of enduring limbo.

It was not just observable activities that became meaningful ways of enduring limbo, however. For some asylum seekers, a mental bracketing of a sense of limbo was a way of mitigating the pain of existential insecurity and uncertainty in the current moment. For example, Mohammed, who described feeling like a prey animal in one of the brief narratives I presented earlier, was in removal proceedings and was awaiting an appeal decision from the BIA. His case had been pending for almost four years. He found that imagining and mentally inhabiting another way of living became a way of enduring:

> I don't know. It's gloomy. It's very dark. It's not clear for me. But what I know is that I just don't know. It's too much, I mean, in my head. You know, I just make—live just a fake life, you know what I mean? Just like the others. Just like, just live like nothing is happening, you know what I mean?

I heard similar things from other asylum claimants, including the tactic of trying to ignore or resist thinking about their asylum cases. As one asylum claimant described, "Sometimes I just sit and I ignore the reality, the problem that I have." Though Mohammed was often unsuccessful at fully putting these thoughts at bay, there is something important in these attempts at living a "fake life" or "ignoring reality." While it would be easy to interpret this as a form of denial, can we not instead see it as an agentive move that allows asylum seekers to imagine their present situations otherwise, even if fleetingly? Or, at the very least, an act of emotional or psychic self-preservation?

If we see here "the capacity to act in the present" amidst constrained circumstances, asylum claimants' orientation toward the future was more fraught (Brun 2015, 24). Imagining a particular kind of future was often complicated for asylum seekers. Indeed, as Hassan noted at the outset of this chapter, glimpses or "tastes," as he put it, of life as a potential citizen could exacerbate suffering or introduce new forms of distress since this vision of the future was tenuous and partial—never guaranteed. In this way, envisioning a certain future in the form of being granted asylum could be emotionally dangerous. This is not to say that asylum seekers lacked displays of hope. Indeed, for them, hope was critical to the endurance of limbo. In chapter 5, I return to a more critical examination of hope, as some asylum seekers re-evaluated the role of hope in their lives after the resolution of their claims. Here, I close this chapter with a brief examination of how asylum seekers understood and practiced hope during the asylum-seeking process. I frame these practices of hope as enactments of endurance.

CULTIVATING HOPE

"It is difficult to imagine anything," Ahmed, an Ethiopian asylum seeker in his early thirties, told me during one visit. He had just left a voicemail message with his volunteer attorney inquiring about any updates in his case. Likely a futile effort, he thought, but worth a try, as his worry about the uncertainty of his asylum case had begun to consume his mind. "Asylum is the only thing in my mind now. I cannot imagine a free world. I cannot dream freely. I cannot think about the future. I am not finding any hope." Ahmed added, "I've become religious because I don't understand my life anymore. In my country, I never prayed, but now I don't understand my life anymore, so I pray. I need hope."

Ahmed framed hope as both necessary and elusive. Indeed, asylum seekers often identified hope as essential for enduring the protracted situation of asylum-seeking. As Zigon (2009) has argued, hope can be "an existential stance of being-in-the-world . . . that allows one to keep going or to persevere through one's life" (258). The necessity of hope is consistently reiterated by asylum seekers. Its flipside—hopelessness—is likewise seen as an existential danger. Hassan put this eloquently one morning when he was describing the sense of exhaustion generated by the numerous delays and lack of information about his case: "With the conditions now, my asylum situation . . . my motivation has gone out the window. But I haven't lost my hope. If I start losing my hope, then I probably won't be sitting here with you right now. I wouldn't be here at all." Implicit in Hassan's narrative is his understanding of hope as a resource, something on which he could draw during this difficult time. In contrast, Ahmed was struggling to find it. Yet, both recognized how crucial it was to endurance.

If hope is a resource, it is not evenly apportioned. Recent scholarship on hope has focused on the political economy of hope, which draws attention to how particular sociohistorical and structural conditions shape the production and negotiation of hope in specific contexts so that some individuals and groups have access to certain visions of the future while others are denied this (Hage 2009; Jansen 2015; Kleist and Jansen 2016). Certainly, among my asylum-seeking friends, hope was not always readily available or easily found, given the bureaucratic violences and constraints of the asylum system. Bourdieu's (1997) analysis of time suggests hopes and aspirations will be calibrated to meet the objective probability of those hopes being realized. Following this argument, if the asylum regime generated feelings of my interlocutors' lives being suspended or stuck, often so too were their hopes.

However, hope was not just an abstract resource, or an existential orientation. It was also cultivated within daily life. Cheryl Mattingly's (2010) rich analysis of hope is instructive here. She posits hope as a practice that entails "creating, or trying to create, lives worth living even in the midst of suffering" (7), much the same way as some have approached "agency." From this perspective, we can see how asylum claimants' everyday tactics to endure are also cultivations of hope in the way that Mattingly frames it. But this is not always the case, as Ahmed's struggle to hope reminds us. As

Feldman (2016) notes, in some circumstances, even if people can envision a positive future, they may not have the ability to realize that vision. In these cases, hopelessness "is a meaningful response to present conditions" (412). Feldman adds, however, "[b]ut no moment has a single affective register." Indeed, hope is not a uniform concept or activity. Rather, one can experience "ambivalent" or "competing kinds of hopes" (Parla 2019). Hope, likewise, can be experienced as passive or active (Zigon 2009, 2018). Though asylum seekers hope for a positive outcome of their asylum claims, my interlocutors primarily framed hope, orientated toward the future, in more open-ended terms. The bureaucratically produced sense of limbo prompted an active search for meaning and sense of certainty. Hope, or hoping, was critical to withstanding a painful state of limbo or stuckness not because it determined specific future outcomes—what Parla (2019) describes as "goal-oriented hopes"—but rather because "it suggests that something can still be done" (Zigon 2018, 65).

I have already discussed the role that religious institutions play in providing asylum seekers with a sense of emotional relief and social connection amidst the institutional violence of waiting and uncertainty. There is another important aspect to religious practice: asylum claimants' religious faith is a powerful resource for cultivating and maintaining hope, and for "bearing the indignities of their sociopolitical abjection" (Willen 2019, 189). Yet, more than this, religious faith and practices, such as praying or worshipping, provide asylum seekers with a sense of open-ended certainty—exactly what their lives in limbo lacked. Ruth, who we met in the previous chapter—and who had been subjected to years of protracted waiting and heightened surveillance (recall her participation in the Alternative to Detention program)—drew increasingly on her belief in God as her case neared its end. By early 2011, Ruth had received word that, unsurprisingly, the BIA had upheld the immigration judge's decision to deny her asylum. She, along with legal advocates at CHR, had decided to take a rare step and appeal her case again, this time to the appellate court (see figure 1). One day, I asked her if she was worried about the outcome of her case. Though I didn't say this to Ruth, I knew that it was highly unlikely that the decision would be overturned, in which case she would be issued a final deportation order. "If I think about that," Ruth said, "I get even more depressed and stressed. And I have been too stressed for too long. But God parted the Red Sea, and he will make a path for me, too. Yes, God will take control of my situation. God will take control of my case. He knows how much I am suffering so he'll help me. God will help me because I seek the truth."

Though others had not used such striking imagery as the parting of the Red Sea, I had become familiar with my interlocutors' references to the certainty of God's intervention in their lives. For example, some asylum claimants spoke of God's ability to "to make a path for me," "usher me into a better place," or "help me find peace." Importantly, these narratives of hope and potentiality did not refer directly to the possibility of asylum but rather to a more abstract sense of peace. That is, God and religion were not invoked or experienced as a way of envisioning a positive legal outcome. Rather, asylum seekers drew on the certainty of their religious faith to imagine a place free from suffering—a "better place"—that was itself ambiguous. Hope was generative as a way of "making uncertainty meaningful" (Brun 2015, 24). These everyday strategies of navigating a state of existential limbo thus do not serve to mitigate the protracted waiting and uncertainty of asylum seeking. Rather, they provide asylum seekers with an alternate imagined space to occupy, imbued with some semblance of certainty.

* * *

In this chapter, I have analyzed the violence of waiting as an additional form of harm within the asylum system's continuum of violence. Waiting—and the uncertainty it engenders—is both a technology of power and a lived phenomenon. The bureaucratic manipulation and weaponization of time evoked a state of existential limbo in which life is experienced as stalled or stuck during the protracted asylum process. The politically-produced state of limbo, in turn, mediates asylum seekers' intra- and inter-personal lives, with effects that are transnationally embodied. Though asylum seekers can at times be overwhelmed by the pain of waiting, they draw on a multitude of resources to make life not just tolerable but meaningful, actively enduring limbo.

3 Socioeconomic Violence and Its Ripple Effects

Sharon was unusually quiet as I drove her home from her weekly counseling appointment. Though she was mild-mannered and introspective, our time together was normally filled with conversation, as she shared stories about her past human rights activism in Kenya and freely reflected on her perspectives about life in Minnesota and the asylum process. A self-taught scholar of Buddhism, she enjoyed imparting her wisdom on the dharma and she sometimes accompanied me to group meditation at a local mindfulness center. As I solicited her help with finding the correct street—she had recently moved for the second time in less than three months—Sharon finally punctuated the silence: "You know, it's very humiliating to lose your independence." She told me wearily, "I am so uncomfortable being at the mercy of someone else." As she said this, Sharon cupped her hands, stretching them forward to mimic someone begging. She sighed. "You know, no one wants to keep a person in their house whom they don't know, who doesn't contribute. . . . I look into their eyes and can see they are burdened by me."

For Sharon, a native of Kenya in her early fifties, housing instability was not new. Sharon had originally come to the United States by herself in the fall of 2009 by way of New York City. She had been contacted by a NYC-based nonprofit organization that was sponsoring a human rights conference. The organization arranged a plane ticket and travel visa for Sharon to attend, as part of the conference's outreach to smaller, local grassroots movements across the globe. While in New York, Sharon's daughter, who was thirteen at the time, emailed Sharon to say that she had been approached by representatives of the Kenyan government, brandishing what they said was an arrest warrant for Sharon. Sharon was terrified. For years, she had withstood verbal and physical harassment from government officials and local leaders, and she had received anonymous written death threats because of her political activism and opposition to the government.

Sharon's human rights activism began in the aftermath of the trauma she suffered in the summer of 1998, during the bombing of the US embassy in Nairobi, where she worked as a secretary. The psychological trauma caused by the bombing became debilitating for Sharon. She found herself unable to care physically, emotionally, and materially for her family, resulting in a bitter divorce from her husband, who had become physically and verbally abusive. Sharon's family had her admitted to a state-run psychiatric hospital, where she stayed for several months, while her children—two sons and two daughters—went to live with extended family. Upon her discharge, Sharon returned to the state-subsidized apartment she was renting in Nairobi to find the locks changed and her belongings—what remained of them—shoved in boxes and bags outside the door. Alone and destitute, she moved into the slum area surrounding Nairobi. It was there that Sharon's activism took hold. She began to speak publicly about what she saw as the Kenyan government's lack of accountability to the embassy bombing and terrorism victims. For a decade she continued this work, despite constant threats and harassment by the Kenyan government. As her voice grew louder, so did the frequency of late night and early morning visits to her home by government officials, who warned of punishment and even death should she continue her anti-government campaign. Sometimes they also beat her. During these years, Sharon reconnected somewhat with her children, talking to them and seeing them occasionally. However, they continued to live apart and Sharon never received any financial or material support from them or her extended family.

When she received the message from her daughter while attending the conference in New York, Sharon was convinced that returning to Kenya and being arrested would be a death sentence. Someone at the conference suggested she remain in the United States and apply for asylum—a process about which Sharon knew next to nothing. Instead of taking a flight back to Nairobi, Sharon contacted her brother David in St. Paul, who reluctantly agreed to have her stay with him. Within days, the tension between them was palpable. Their relationship was stilted, as they had not seen nor even talked to each other in years. David, who initially came to the United States on a student visa and then obtained an employment-based green card, did little to hide his resentment at having to support Sharon as she sought asylum.

The tension in the house was very distressing to Sharon. She had been working with CHR on her asylum application, which was filed about six months after she arrived in Minnesota. With no financial resources and no work permit, Sharon spent her days in the house, reading, meditating, and listening to classical music, trying to allay her deep anxiety about her situation. She longed to have her own space and to regain a sense of independence. Sharon saw her lack of economic rights as both a material and emotional issue. "Asylum seekers aren't given a work permit; we're not allowed to work. So, there is so much anxiety about all the fear of where you are going, what is awaiting us. And then we don't have an income, which could help ease the mind. You know, people are very anxious when they don't have money. They are lacking this, lacking that."

After nearly a year of living together, David kicked Sharon out of his apartment, telling her she had a week to find a new place to live, as he was tired of supporting her. He did begrudgingly agree to provide Sharon with very minimal financial support until her asylum claim was decided or until she obtained a work permit and secured a job. The money was not near enough for rent, but enough to buy a limited supply of groceries and necessary hygiene items. Distraught at her brother's ultimatum, Sharon called me and together we tried to think of options. I called the director of CHR, and she confirmed what I already knew: because of Sharon's lack of permanent legal status, she would not qualify for any housing assistance, including from nonprofit groups that receive any sort of federal or state funding. The best option, the director told me, was to refer Sharon to a homeless shelter. Sharon, though, was adamant in her refusal of this option. It was not only the homeless shelter itself that was so threatening, but its symbolic and embodied meaning. "It's the same thing all over," she said through tears. "The same abandonment and neglect." Sharon compared being kicked out by her brother in the United States to being abandoned by her family in Kenya after her discharge from the psychiatric hospital. "It's very painful. It really breaks me. I feel even more abandoned. My brother has put me in a position that really confuses me. The homelessness now, it leaves me with so much stress."

After calling a social worker acquaintance of mine and reaching out to local churches, we finally found someone, an international graduate student, who agreed to have Sharon stay with her. Sharon stayed there several months until that woman moved (and did not offer to bring Sharon) and we subsequently found another family with whom Sharon could stay, provided it was only temporary. This was the house where Sharon was staying when I dropped her off that afternoon. While I ultimately knew Sharon was grateful that she did not have to move to a homeless shelter, it was obvious that itinerant living was taking a toll on her. She continued to anxiously wait for her asylum interview to be scheduled and for her employment authorization application to be processed.

In addressing different forms of violence associated with the governing of asylum seekers, the previous chapters have discussed technologies of surveillance, policing, and bureaucratic opacity—what I term the violences of in/visibility, as well as the bureaucratic control and manipulation of time, which generates a subjective state of limbo, or stuckness. These forms of violence have particular affective, embodied, and social consequences, but also intersect, having cumulative effects. For example, a sense of being stuck or suspended in a state of limbo is exacerbated by the bureaucratic opacity that constrains asylum seekers' ability to access information about their cases. Being subjected to routine racialized policing and heightened surveillance measures adds to the pain of waiting. Undergirding these violences is a broader mistrust of asylum seekers, manifested in an institutional ethos of suspicion that casts asylum seekers and other migrants as economic or security threats or as criminals—as "preemptive suspects" (Stephen 2018).

This chapter adds to the discussion of the continuum of violence facing asylum seekers—emergent from this overarching racialized ethos of suspicion—by looking at structural constraints that impinged upon my interlocutors' lives in the United States. More specifically, I focus on economic exclusion and marginalization as particular forms of structural violence inflicted upon asylum seekers. I concentrate primarily on economic exclusion/marginalization for two primary reasons. First, economic exclusion/marginalization was a salient factor shaping my interlocutors' experiences of asylum seeking and their lives in the United States more broadly. In my interviews and everyday conversations with asylum seekers, they talked frequently of their lack of access to employment opportunities. Asylum seekers without a work permit, or an employment authorization document (EAD), awaited the processing of an EAD application as anxiously as they did their actual asylum claim. As this chapter explores, economic precarity is a critical concern for asylum seekers not only because of its significant material consequences but its relational and emotional ripple effects.

Second, I focus on economic and labor exclusion/marginalization because other structural forces, or violences, are critically tied to asylum claimants' socioeconomic position in the United States. For example, as Sharon's story reflects, struggles with housing or cohabiting are often centered on participants' inability to financially contribute to rent or household expenses; and asylum seekers understand their potential need for social services (particularly food and material assistance) as a consequence of being rendered ineligible to work. Thus, in banning and constraining asylum seekers' employment opportunities, the state indirectly "expos[es] them to all of the harms poverty inflicts" (Mayblin 2020, 2).

The socioeconomic exclusion of asylum seekers—the explicit prohibition on their authorized labor—is an effect of US policy that requires a delay in the issuance of work permits to asylum applicants. Though this outright exclusion is often (but not always) temporary, if protracted, the lived consequences of this are significant. In the previous chapter, I discussed the enforced wait time for an employment authorization document (EAD), noting that an asylum application had to be filed and pending for 150 days before asylum claimants could even apply for an EAD. Because of the confusing, opaque, and often seemingly arbitrary rules surrounding the "asylum clock," asylum seekers found themselves without the opportunity for authorized employment for further extended periods, sometimes years. In that chapter, I highlighted this as particular example of the institutional weaponization of time. Here, I consider how delayed access to work authorization, as well as limited employment opportunities post-EAD, produce a state of socioeconomic precarity for asylum claimants. The institutional wait period for EADs is further compounded by other governmental policies that bar asylum claimants from federal or state financial and material support, sedimenting their social-structural vulnerability. It is noteworthy that the United States is the only developed country to simultaneously bar asylum claimants from immediate access to work *and* governmental support, effectively denying asylum claimants their "fundamental right to livelihood and the many other economic and social rights that depend upon it" (Human Rights Watch 2013).

It is also notable that once (and if) granted asylum, an asylum claimant becomes, in legal terminology, an "asylee," and they then have immediate access to state and federal financial, housing, and social service assistance. Yet, in the transitory space of asylum seeking, as "unclassified/not yet classified" subjects (Malkki 1995), asylum applicants are deemed unworthy/not yet worthy of such assistance. As I have argued regarding the range of technologies within the asylum system's violence continuum, the cruel effects of these technologies are integral to its power. In other words, asylum claimants' state-produced economic precarity is not a side effect of asylum policy but part of its design, what Lucy Mayblin (2020) has described as "purposeful impoverishment." Moreover, we see again the way that these institutional violences are both distinct mechanisms and interlocking in their effects. Sharon pointed directly to this by suggesting that the anxiety of a bureaucratically produced state of limbo—fear about, as she put it, "where you are going, what is awaiting us"—was compounded by the economic exclusion that she experienced.

While Sharon's brother provided her with some financial support, she was far from economically stable. And while Sharon was able to avoid homelessness, other asylum applicants are not so fortunate. In the previous chapter, we saw how the metaphor of homelessness had symbolic meaning within a state of limbo—a lived sense of being neither here nor there in both space and time. In some circumstances, homelessness was also literal—a material fact. Indeed, I knew several asylum seekers who were living in homeless shelters, some for a few months until they found someone to put them up or accrued enough rent money through informal jobs (though most asylum seekers were reluctant to engage in the informal economy). Others stayed in shelters for longer periods of time, a year or more, as they waited for both their work permits and the adjudication of their asylum claims. Some asylum seekers I knew at times went without food. Many were referred by CHR to food pantries or nonprofit organizations that supplied donated material items, such as bus passes, winter clothing, and furniture. These organizations filled an important gap left by the state.

But Sharon's story reveals more. Beyond the material effects, economic exclusion and marginalization often challenge asylum claimants' identities. This is clear in Sharon's humiliation about "being at the mercy of someone else," lamenting her lack of a sense of independence. Moreover, Sharon's tense living environment with her brother, a source of great distress for her, highlights how her socioeconomic exclusion had intersubjective consequences. Indeed, asylum claimants' economic exclusion/marginalization can strain and reconfigure familial and social relationships, both near and far.

RELATIONAL EFFECTS OF ECONOMIC EXCLUSION

Emmanuel came to the United States in 2008, after years of political activism with the SCNC in Cameroon. A soft-spoken and erudite man in his late thirties, Emmanuel was a chemist who had become involved with politics during his time at university. After getting married and having three children, Emmanuel continued to support the SCNC. In 2007, he was abducted from his home and taken to a military prison where he was tortured over several weeks. He sustained facial trauma that left him with hearing loss, blindness in one eye, and blurred vision in the other. Fearing additional reprisals from the Cameroonian government and terrified for his family's safety, Emmanuel fled to the United States. A cousin who had recently been deported gave Emmanuel the contact information of a man named Paul, a middle-aged Cameroonian who had immigrated decades before and was now an American citizen living outside of St. Paul, Minnesota.

When I met Emmanuel he was awaiting his asylum interview. It had been close to a year since he filed an EAD application, which was delayed for reasons both he and his *pro bono* legal counsel could not fully ascertain. Such bureaucratic opacity, as we've seen, stokes the already-present feelings of uncertainty and anxiety for asylum seekers. Emmanuel had been staying in Paul's basement, along with several other men who were relatives of Paul's. Upstairs, Paul lived with his wife, two children, and his wife's mother. When I began visiting Emmanuel, our visits often included interactions with Paul and his family. We would share meals or congregate all together in the living room, engaging in lively conversation. Paul's wife would routinely call down to the basement that she had made food to share or would leave a foil-wrapped plate in the refrigerator for Emmanuel. But as the months went by, I saw less and less of Paul and his family during those visits. Sitting on a stained and tattered sofa in the musty basement one afternoon, I noted this to Emmanuel. "Yes," he replied, "it is now as if they do not even look at me anymore. They no longer greet me even." When I asked why he thought that was the case, he was quick to tell me it was because of his inability to contribute to the household expenses. "You know, sometimes when you live with people and you have nothing to give and then you keep having nothing to give, these people eventually start to ignore. They ignore me. I have nothing. I am here like a burden." Emmanuel was very affected by this gradual souring of his relations with Paul and his family, at times telling me he felt "tormented" and "so low." Emmanuel felt that if he could get his EAD and secure a job, he could repair the embittered relationship with Paul, or better yet, move out on his own. One morning, after I had sat with him while we called USCIS and CHR to check on the status of his work permit and then confirmed that it was still pending, he became uncharacteristically flustered. Acknowledging how frustrating this must be for him, I asked if his main concern was wanting to move out of Paul's house. "Yes, that is true. But it's not just that. You see, I'm not a lazy man, Bridget. I'm not a lazy man!"

But the facts behind Emmanuel's inability to contribute to the household were invisible to Paul. Paul saw Emmanuel as someone who did not work, not someone who *was not allowed* to work. As I walked to my car after visiting Emmanuel one day, I exchanged greetings with Paul, who was taking out the trash. After hesitating for a moment, he asked if I knew what was happening with Emmanuel's "immigration case." Not wanting to violate confidentiality, I said I didn't know. "I don't understand why he's always in the house," Paul mused. "When I came here, I worked. Three jobs. I worked hard." I tried explaining to Paul that immigration law is different now than when he first came to the United States and asylum seekers must wait for work authorization. And, I added, coming as a student, as he did, entailed a different procedure altogether. It was kind, I told Paul, for him and his family to support Emmanuel as they've done. Paul nodded, though I'm not sure how much of this information he took in. At least, it didn't seem to have any effect on Paul's treatment of Emmanuel and a couple of months later, Paul told Emmanuel he'd have to find a new place to live as he could no longer support Emmanuel if he could not contribute financially to the household. Emmanuel was lucky that a woman in his church with whom he had become friendly offered him a room in her house.

Whereas Sharon's living arrangement with her brother had been tense from the beginning, Emmanuel's relationship with Paul and his family deteriorated over time, shaped by his protracted exclusion from the labor market and ongoing legal limbo. Paul either didn't understand or didn't care that Emmanuel was barred from authorized employment, instead seeing him, pejoratively, as someone who "stays in the house all day." Paul was also likely not aware of the fact that if asylum applicants are found to engage in unauthorized work, their asylum claims can be rendered ineligible. Thus, it was not only that asylum claimants without EADs were prohibited from working, but also that any participation in the labor market during this time was punishable. Though I discuss exceptions below, this was the primary reason that very few of my interlocutors risked working under-the-table jobs. Putting an asylum claim in jeopardy was not a risk my interlocutors wanted to take, given the life-and-death stakes of an asylum decision. Yet, this often meant they struggled to get by.

Importantly, while the strained relationship with Paul and his family felt demoralizing and distressing for Emmanuel, not all his social relations were made tenuous by his economic exclusion. It was a woman he knew from his church who offered to host Emmanuel until he was able to work and afford to rent a room on his own—which he did within six months of living with this woman. In the previous chapter I described how spaces such as friends' houses, places of worship, or libraries serve as important sites of social and emotional connection, and of cultivating hope. These sites and the social relations they engender are resources for asylum seekers' emotional and psychic endurance of limbo. These sites also can be places of material or economic support. Churches and associated gatherings connect asylum seekers to other people, but they also connect asylum seekers to material items they might need—food, clothing, shelter. For Emmanuel, though his inability to work ultimately damaged his relationship with Paul, it was his relationship to fellow church congregants that helped remedy the social and material fallout of this. There was, however, another critical aspect to Emmanuel's lived experience of economic exclusion. When Emmanuel insisted to me "I'm not a lazy man," he revealed that beyond the interpersonal ruptures, economic exclusion also takes a psychic and emotional toll.

INTERNAL EFFECTS OF ECONOMIC EXCLUSION

Emmanuel experienced his bureaucratically-produced socioeconomic exclusion as a "dignity assault" (Willen 2019). His material dependence on Paul challenged Emmanuel's sense of identity. It was not lost on Emmanuel that Paul interpreted him as lazy. What was so vexing and cruel about this situation was that what Paul perceived as laziness in Emmanuel was a direct effect of a normalized bureaucratic policy (the EAD waiting period)—a hidden violence. Yet, this effect was "misrecognized" by Paul as a character defect in Emmanuel (Bourdieu 1977). This was painful for Emmanuel since he had taken such pride in his active career and identity as a scientist in Cameroon. Emmanuel's "torment," as he described, from being economically excluded had as much to do with the internal conflict this catalyzed as it did with the tensions it created with Paul.

Yet, even within amicable or welcoming living situations, asylum claimants are not immune to feeling the emotional impact of being reliant on others when they are excluded from authorized work opportunities. Let's return to Lionel, the Liberian asylum claimant we met in the previous chapter, who journeyed in a blizzard to immigration court only to find its doors shuttered. As noted, Lionel was living with his brother in a neighboring state awaiting his asylum hearing and, importantly, his EAD. Though Lionel was mournful about being separated from his family in Liberia, the interactions between him, his brother, and his brother's family were strikingly different from the tension I witnessed at Sharon's or Emmanuel's. The time I spent at Lionel's brother's house—a mobile home in a semi-rural area—was always pleasant, filled with playful banter and laughter. Lionel recognized that his brother and his wife were supportive and understanding of his situation. Yet, Lionel felt anxious and distressed by his own inability to contribute financially to the household. "You know my little brother is doing okay [financially]. But he has a very small place. He lives in a very meager income community. He has his kids. A wife. And with all that he is still sharing a little with me. So, I am benefiting from that, but you also know that . . . I'm not supposed to be here [his brother's house] anymore. I've got to earn on my own, have my own place. But I can't. And that preys on my mind a lot. So that has been a big problem for me." As time went on, and his work permit application had been pending for six months, Lionel's distress deepened. When I brought up the fact that his brother didn't seem to mind supporting him while he was unable to access employment opportunities, Lionel agreed, but this did not assuage his stress: "Still, my inability to work, to earn and dispense money by myself, it's a problem. It keeps me down. Downhearted. It's, it's a trauma for me. You keep thinking about it, about not being able to work and earn money and then it becomes a psychological problem."

By declaring his denial of employment access as a form of trauma, Lionel made clear how the government's EAD policy inflicts psychological harm (Human Rights Watch 2013). As Coutin (2003) has argued about undocumented migrants, because wage labor is a "key marker of presence, personhood, and citizenship," lack of work authorization serves to deny migrants' existence in the broader world (31). Lionel's sense of "trauma" at not being able to work illustrates the connection between structural vulnerability and self-identity. His distress at being reliant on his brother did not emerge from any interpersonal tensions, but rather from his own internal conflict. This internal conflict and the sense of trauma it evoked for Lionel was shaped by deeply held cultural and gendered notions of his identity and sense of self. That is, Lionel's dependence on his younger brother for housing and money, albeit a temporary situation, ran counter to his identity as a successful journalist and an older brother.

The assaults on their dignity and sense of identity that both Emmanuel and Lionel experienced as a result of systematic labor exclusion was shared by many of my interlocutors. Such threats to identity have two critical dimensions. First, asylum seekers' sense of themselves as independent and fully agentic is destabilized by being rendered unable to work or to re-engage with previous and, often, longstanding livelihoods (such as political activists, journalists, civil servants, small business owners, farmers). Self-sufficiency provides more than economic stability. Work is essential to asylum seekers' overall health and well-being, providing them socialization, community participation, and role fulfillment (Fleay and Hartley 2016; Hess et al. 2019; McColl, McKenzie, and Bhui 2008).

As a counter to these feelings of constrained or interrupted productivity, asylum claimants would often share with me stories about their employment, professions, or roles as providers in their countries of origin. My interlocutors were most likely to tell such stories of past work experience and professional endeavors when our conversations turned to the topic of their lack of work authorization or their difficulties in finding a job in the United States. While these stories of past livelihoods could be considered normative topics of conversation, I came to recognize and appreciate the more important work that these stories did for asylum claimants and the relationships I was building with them. These stories and demonstrations—presenting me with their published news stories, giving me lessons on the chemistry experiments performed in their labs, outlining the ranks of civil service positions they had climbed, recounting stories of selling their wares at the market or of campaigning for human rights—were ways of asserting aspects of their identities and maintaining a sense of productive personhood that had been stifled or silenced in their new environment. Like the narratives of "freedom fighting" or religiosity that I have previously discussed, these stories of past activities or professional lives were meaningful counterstories that pushed against dominant perceptions of asylum claimants as passive or "lazy," as Emmanuel noted. This was particularly important in the context of displacement, as my interlocutors found numerous aspects of their sociocultural, religious, professional, and familial roles and identities "suddenly missing or unrecognizable to them" (Utržan and Northwood 2017, 11). Along with the support and relationships that asylum claimants forged with other people and organizations as they sought asylum status, these counternarratives become "resources for a bearable life" in this context (Willen 2019, 196). They were discursive acts of restoring a sense of dignity and moral worth.

Beyond discussions of past employment or professional roles, asylum seekers who had been political activists often brought up former political activities as a way of highlighting themselves as productive, active persons. Though most Cameroonian asylum claimants stopped any overt political activism (e.g., publicly speaking out against the Cameroonian government, engaging in local protests) when they fled to the United States, this remained a salient part of their identities. Some of these conversations—with me and among Cameroonians—became quite impassioned. Such "affective intensification" serves to actively connect asylum claimants to the place that they left (Wise and Velayutham 2017). But there is an important material component to this as well. Asylum claimants place great value on their financial support of political movements in their home countries, such as to the SCNC among Cameroonians. Yet, this is often difficult given asylum claimants' systematic economic marginalization in the United States. Eric, who we've already met, echoed other Cameroonian asylum seekers when he told me: "Even if it's only $10, $20 that I can send to them [SCNC], I want it on record that I contributed to the cause. So if I can ever go back home, then I can say yes, I wasn't here but I contributed. I was always with you. With my money, with my heart, my ideas." Likewise, one of the very first things Emmanuel did when he was able to work and earn a meager income was to set aside a small amount of money as a SCNC contribution. "Even though I am here," he told me, "I know we are still supposed to support the movement to change the conditions [in Cameroon]. I am still a fighter. It is not as if I have run away from the situation completely."

Amanda Wise (2006), drawing on Hage's (2002) notion of "migration guilt," has suggested that refugees' transnational engagement with political activities emerges as a way to "share in and produce the moral economy" of their homeland communities, and to simultaneously "appease feelings of guilt arising from the sense that they had fled their war-ravaged homeland to save themselves and their own families" (154). Thus, by offering even scant financial support to the SCNC or through affectively charged conversations with fellow Anglophone Cameroonians, some of my interlocutors were able to maintain a sense of moral engagement with the political movement. In turn, this helped mitigate feelings of guilt for not being physically present to engage in political activism. Furthermore, my interlocutors reflected a sense of productivity through their financial and ideological support of the SCNC. Hence, Emmanuel's emphasis that he was "*still* a fighter" and Eric's insistence that he "was *always with*" the SCNC. This ability to claim, or maintain, some aspect of political identity, particularly via financially supporting the cause, was an important strategy of their "self work" (Parish 2008).

It is not just through stories of the past or via continuity of political ties that asylum claimants seek to reclaim their sense of agency and productive personhood within a context of socioeconomic exclusion/marginalization. In the previous chapter I discussed how everyday activities, such as walking, cooking, or window shopping, served as important tactics of surviving the sometimes-overwhelming sense of uncertainty and anxiety that asylum claimants describe as the lived state of limbo. Similarly, asylum claimants engage in activities that attenuate the emotional and psychic pain and demoralization associated with the systematic prohibition or limitation on employment. Some asylum applicants, like Emmanuel, find meaning in volunteer work while they wait for a work permit. At his church, Emmanuel took pride in cleaning the pews, arranging prayer books, and ushering parishioners to their seats. Likewise, Sharon began doing volunteer work for a local human rights organization, handing out their informational pamphlets at farmers' markets and guest-speaking about her past advocacy at library luncheons that the organization sponsored. Such activities are not only a way to bide time and, as Emmanuel put it, "keep me from thinking too much about my problems." These activities also promote a sense of active engagement with the social world, despite institutional forces that work to marginalize them. Though unpaid, the work of volunteerism is an assertion of productivity, a way for asylum seekers to "regain one's position as an active participant and actor" in society (Fiddian-Qasmiyeh and Qasmiyeh 2010, 308).

A second way that the socioeconomic violence of being unauthorized to work threatens asylum seekers' identities and sense of self is that dominant images, representations, and discourses in the United States equate moral worth with economic productivity. As I noted in the previous chapter, the bureaucratic logic surrounding the delay of an EAD relies on the presumed distinction between economic and political/humanitarian migrants. According to this logic, granting economic opportunities or access to asylum claimants would serve as an unwanted "pull" factor, attracting foreign Others who would file meritless asylum claims merely as a vehicle for taking advantage of labor opportunities. Undergirding the policy changes to delay the issuance of an EAD was the assumption that truly deserving asylum claimants—those who are not deemed "economic migrants"—can and will patiently wait out this time. Thus, waiting for an EAD becomes a kind of test of legitimacy.

The confluence of these state policies creates a painful double bind for asylum claimants. Within the political-legal framework of asylum, too much eagerness to work threatens to disrupt this performance of deservingness, in that asylum claimants are wary of being seen by bureaucratic officials as "economic migrants" and thus not eligible for asylum status. This reflects the larger bureaucratic logic that positions asylum claimants as lacking agency and finds suspect their assertions of autonomy. As Tazzioli, Garelli, and De Genova (2018) argue, "To seek protection is fashioned as a voluntary submission to a regime that authorizes itself to decide for and dispose of 'refugees' as its docile supplicants" (241). Yet, asylum claimants are not immune to the public sentiment and moral evaluations that simultaneously cast immigrants as lazy and unproductive (Griffiths 2015). In this way, being rendered ineligible to work puts asylum claimants in a position where they may be seen and judged as unproductive persons, as Paul did with Emmanuel. And as my exchange with Paul illustrates, the policies that produce such vulnerabilities are invisible to most. Anwen Tormey (2007) makes such a point in her work on African asylum seekers in Ireland, noting that because they are not eligible for work, asylum seekers "are not perceived by Irish citizens as visibly contributing to the productive force of the nation and, consequently, are unable to stake a moral claim to membership of their communities" (76). In this way, asylum claimants, by being made to wait for gainful employment, and thus economically and structurally marginalized, are temporarily (and sometimes indefinitely) produced by the state as non-contributors to the nation. Asylum claimants find this not only unjust but confounding. As Sharon told me one afternoon as we tried to develop a budget for the small allowance her brother was giving her, "you know, in this country everyone says to work hard. 'Work, work,' they say. But right now, the only way I'm allowed to work is to ask, to beg, to borrow."

Sharon laid bare the cruel ironies and paradoxes confronting asylum seekers about their economic rights. In the eyes of the public, asylum seekers are morally suspect because of their perceived lack of economic contribution, but their inability to contribute is dictated by the state as a way, in part, of delineating their deservingness of protection (are they a genuine humanitarian migrant who needs political—not economic—protection?). Moreover, asylum claimants must contend with conflicting public rhetoric that represents them simultaneously as economic threats—taking jobs away from hardworking Americans—*and* economic siphons—noncontributors who unfairly benefit from material and social resources in the United States. Such paradoxes are in part a consequence of the bureaucratic policies of asylum.

Mayblin (2020) helps provide some insight into the routinization and legitimation of these paradoxical and ultimately deleterious asylum policies. Her work has richly analyzed the systematic impoverishment of asylum applicants in the United Kingdom, premised on the observation that asylum has shifted from a political and humanitarian issue to an economic one. In defining asylum seekers as "undeserving poor," Mayblin (2020) argues, the state implements policies that restrict their access to both legal and economic protection. As I noted in the introduction, key to Mayblin's (2017, 2020) theorizing is her argument that the policies that impoverish asylum seekers constitute a form of necropolitical, slow violence that is critically informed by hierarchized categories of humanity established by colonial histories. In the United Kingdom, asylum applicants are denied the ability to work but are provided housing and welfare assistance by the government—a system, Mayblin (2020) argues, that works to systematically exclude asylum seekers while simultaneously allowing the state to claim its adherence to its human rights obligations.

In contrast, the United States provides the opportunity of employment for affirmative asylum applicants while barring them from other sources of governmental support. This provides the United States, like the United Kingdom, with the ability to fulfill humanitarian obligations while also marginalizing and excluding asylum claimants, particularly as this policy approach aligns with and is justified by the logic of interrupting the puta-tive "pull" factor that economic rights would generate. Of course, during the often-protracted period of waiting for an EAD, asylum applicants are provided no economic rights at all, justified by the same logic that assumes humanitarian migrants are categorically different than "economic" ones. The everyday violent effects of asylum seekers' economic marginalization or exclusion are both intentional and normalized by these state policies and their associated bureaucratic logic.

I have been considering how the double binds of limited economic rights—where one is subjected to the mandates of economic-productivity-as-moral citizenship while being closed off from the opportunities to fulfill this—have personal and intersubjective consequences as well as significant material effects. How, then, do asylum claimants get by? As noted, among my interlocutors, the fear of jeopardizing an asylum claim by engaging in informal or irregular work meant that many shunned such opportunities, leaving them to rely on support from others. Asylum claimants who were more isolated and disconnected from a specific ethnic or religious com-munity seemed particularly wary of considering any kind of informal labor. This was the case not only because of the fear of losing their asylum case, but also because without social connections and networks, opportu-nities for informal work did not readily present themselves.

Among my Cameroonian interlocutors, however, informal paid labor was not uncommon, especially among women. Female asylum claimants, including Ruth and Louise, would periodically cook and prepare meals for others for a fee, and much of my co-cooking in their kitchens was dedi-cated to these efforts. Ruth, who had been a professional seamstress in Cameroon, had a steady stream of Cameroonian clients for whom she would alter clothes. Several of my female Cameroonian interlocutors also collected fees for braiding hair, sometimes spending all evening or week-end plaiting friends' hair in small, cramped rooms. Others received small fees or prepared meals in exchange for childcare services. Such informal work was not exclusive to women, however. Eric, who had volunteered to DJ for a couple of parties, quickly realized he could charge a modest fee for his services and began to be regularly booked for birthdays and other celebrations. And Albert, who we met in chapter 1, had established a rep-utation as a videographer within the Cameroonian community, recording weddings and parties. The informal labor of these asylum claimants was at once a survival strategy within a context that economically marginalized or excluded them *and* a set of creative and agentic acts that helped restore meaning and connection amidst an institutional regime that socially and politically worked to alienate them.

While the institutional barring of asylum claimants from work or structural factors promoting asylum claimants' underemployment have been shown to compel asylum seekers and irregular migrants into an exploitable pool of labor (Burnett and Chebe 2010; Smit and Rugunanan 2014; Waite 2017), my Cameroonian interlocutors who worked informally did so largely on their own terms. However, the need to engage in informal or irregular work can be considered "forced" or coerced, in that asylum seekers without an EAD are not given the option to engage in the formal economy as a means of survival (Allsop, Sigona, and Phillimore 2014; Lewis et al. 2014). Importantly, though money from informal jobs helps to pay bills and mitigate financial stress, my Cameroonian interlocutors told me that it was "never enough." Though vital for their lives, these funds remain largely supplemental. And if asylum claimants struggle to support themselves, what does this mean for their loved ones in their countries of origin, many of whom look to these claimants for support from afar? Ahmed's story begins to bring this into view.

TRANSNATIONAL EFFECTS OF ECONOMIC EXCLUSION

Ahmed was an ethnic-Somali asylum seeker from Ethiopia in his late twenties. The oldest of four children, he described a happy and relatively peaceful childhood within a close-knit middle-class family. His father was a businessman who owned a small but successful jewelry store. After graduating from university, Ahmed was hired as a translator for the United Nations and other international organizations, working in English, Somali, and Amharic (one of Ethiopia's principal languages). Most of this work was near his hometown on the Somalia-Ethiopia border, where violent conflicts had broken out between the Ethiopian government and rebels fighting for the self-determination of Somalis in the region. Despite his political neutrality, Ahmed was abducted by Somali rebel forces, who accused Ahmed of sympathizing with the Ethiopian government. They took him to a remote campsite where he was deprived of food and sleep and routinely beaten over several weeks. After a harrowing escape, Ahmed made it back to his family's home, where he learned that his uncle had been murdered, presumably by rebel forces. Ahmed's father frantically began to look for a way to get Ahmed out of Ethiopia, with the goal of getting him to Minnesota, where Ahmed's sister, Bilan, had been living on an employment-issued green card. Because it was too risky to seek a visa or other travel documents, Ahmed's father used part of the family's savings to hire a smuggler to take Ahmed on a long and circuitous journey from Ethiopia to South America, through Central America, and then into the United States via Mexico—a journey that took over five months.

Shortly after finally arriving in Minnesota, Ahmed learned that his father had been killed by the same people who had detained and tortured Ahmed—a fact that would continually haunt him. He was flooded with guilt that he and his international work might have indirectly been the impetus for his father being targeted. Compounding his grief and self-blame was his economic struggle in the United States. His lack of work authorization was a significant challenge to Ahmed, particularly when Bilan was laid off from her job as a cashier at Target. "I want to work. If anybody could give me a job, I would work," Ahmed stressed. "That is no question. But I have no document. So the cruel thing is, how can I survive? Before you win your case, you are nothing. And the government is not helping me, and now my sister and I, we are both suffering here very bad. Really very, very bad situation."

Ahmed felt a responsibility to help support Bilan. In addition, he also keenly felt his new role, in the absence of his father, as caretaker for his two younger brothers and his mother back in Ethiopia. Without access to employment, Ahmed was unsure how to navigate this. "This my life now," he reflected. "I lost my uncle and my father now. According to my religion, according to my culture or my people, the first child, he should be like the father. My younger brothers, they need a father, so I should replace my father. I should provide help for them. But I can't even help myself. So how can I help them?" Ahmed, at least in the beginning stages of his asylum process (it would take many years for his claim to be adjudicated), fixated on the EAD delay specifically rather than on the uncertain timeline of his asylum claim, both because his immediate existential concern was employment and because he could not imagine how protracted the adjudication of his claim would become. Reflecting on his capacity to endure elements of the asylum process, Ahmed declared: "Maybe I can find the patience to wait for the [asylum] hearing, but I need work. My family needs me. I can't handle not being able to take care of my family."

Things only got worse. By 2011, Ahmed's EAD application had been pending for two years. His sister, Bilan, had been supporting the two of them with her full-time cashier wages and money was tight, especially as Bilan tried to send some money to their family in Ethiopia each month. When Bilan took on a second part-time job, Ahmed was filled with shame about his inability to assist in financially supporting them. Feeling unable to fulfill his familial role as the newly appointed patriarch in the wake of his father's death, Ahmed was racked with guilt and humiliation. "I cannot talk to my mother knowing that she sees me as the only person who can help, but I can't help," he told me through tears. When I asked Ahmed if he had explained to his mother that his lack of employment is no fault of his own, but a result of the laws governing the asylum process, he shook his head: "She doesn't understand my situation. She will never understand asylum, immigration. She just keeps asking me when I am going to get my papers and work, but she doesn't understand asylum. She doesn't understand the system."

Though Ahmed's familial role as eldest son also meant helping his sister in Minnesota, Ahmed's primary concern was for his family in Ethiopia. Ahmed felt not only the financial struggle caused by a delay of a work permit, but also the emotional burden of this, pained by his inability to fulfill his gendered and cultural role as family provider. If obligations and commitments to others are, as Bourdieu (1997) has argued, "continuous justification for existing," then asylum seekers' inability to meet the expectations of their loved ones is demoralizing and deeply distressing (240). That is, rather than becoming reasons for existence, in the context of asylum seeking, familial expectations, pleas, and solicitations of support contribute to asylum seekers' sense of suffering. These cultural and gendered expectations function as "both as an anchor for resilience and an anvil of pain" (Eggerman and Panter-Brick 2010, 81). In my conversations with asylum claimants, I found that they were just as focused—and often even more so—on how their lack of work eligibility impacted their loved ones as they were on how it impinged upon them personally. Because their "identities were constituted through their relationships to other people," asylum claimants' struggle to orient themselves within the onerous asylum system was therefore always shaped by their sense of self as it related to others (Besteman 2016, 210).

In the previous chapter I discussed the intense pain caused by family separation—prolonged and made uncertain by the sense of limbo generated by the bureaucratic control of time. Waiting, I noted, was transnationally embodied, as its effects stretched across the globe. So, too, were the effects of asylum claimants' economic exclusion/marginalization. We see this in Ahmed's interactions with his mother, who looked to Ahmed for economic support. If bureaucratic opacity prevented Ahmed from understanding why his EAD application had not been processed, he certainly could not explain this to his mother. As we saw in the previous chapter, avoiding phone calls with family was one way that my interlocutors evaded the pain of family separation and the relational strains this sometimes produced. Ahmed identified his inability to work as the driving factor in avoiding these interactions, noting that he could no longer talk to his mother if he could not fulfill his duties as a breadwinner, given the shame and confusion it caused them both.

While Ahmed's struggle with feelings of failure over fulfilling his economic expectations had specific gendered and cultural contours, it was not only men who felt the relational effects of economic exclusion. For many female asylum seekers, economic support of loved ones, especially children, was simultaneously a form of affective labor (Mahler 2001; Baldassar 2007, 2016; Grace 2019; Bryceson 2019). Moreover, if, for instance, monetary donations to the SCNC could help Cameroonians feel connected to homeland and assuage feelings of guilt or moral failing, so too could economic remittances help to maintain family ties in both tangible and intangible ways (Castañeda 2019; Yarris 2017). Scholars of transnational mothering have suggested that financial support takes on additional meaning when a parent is physically absent (Dreby 2010; Horton 2009). For asylum claimants, financial remittances can become an "exchange" when unable to be there physically, at once providing tangible support to family and mitigating their sense of guilt and shame over leaving their children (Horton 2009, 30). However, asylum claimants' explicit political and economic exclusion—in theory temporary but in practice sometimes indefinite—means that the very possibility of offering financial remittances is often out of reach, promoting a painful sense of "moral failing" (Horton 2009, 28).

THE PROMISES AND LIMITATIONS OF A WORK PERMIT

One breezy spring afternoon, I received a call from Ahmed. "You are the first person I am calling," he exclaimed in an almost breathless voice, announcing that he had at last received his work authorization in the mail. He recounted to me, in detail, coming home from a walk and seeing the mail from "immigration." "Right away," he said, "I thought it was a deportation letter. I became paralyzed when I saw the mail. I mean, I could not even move. I became so weak, my body so heavy. It took me five minutes until I was able to open it." Ahmed was eager to find a job and start working. "I think," he declared, "the work authorization can change my whole life now. Now I am eligible. I am eligible." Ahmed laughed, adding, "I ask myself, why has my life here been dependent on this little card, this little piece of paper? But I cannot deny the system. That is the reality of the system." I acknowledged that being able to work would be a welcome change. "Yes," Ahmed said, "but it's more than that. I can wait for my [asylum] case with more patience now. And I will have something to do, somewhere I have to be," he said gleefully. He paused. "And, Bridget, I can help my family now. And I can help myself." He let out an audible sigh. "Now I can talk to my mother again. Before I couldn't say anything to her because I was not able to work and help my family and she didn't understand this process, the rules. But now we can talk again as mother and son. I am so happy about that."

Heath Cabot (2012) writes compellingly about the "life of documents" in her analysis of the "pink card," a temporary residence permit issued to asylum seekers in Greece. Her work illustrates how the pink card, by marking asylum seekers as temporary Others, symbolizes the vulnerable, oppressive, and limbo state in which these migrants live. Yet, she argues, asylum seekers attribute to the permit a sense of freedom, belonging, and access to rights, "thus reinterpreting both the pink card and the condition of limbo that it consigns" (2012, 17). In an analogous way, Ahmed imbued the EAD with meaning beyond its primary legal meaning of authorizing employment. For Ahmed, the EAD did not just usher in urgent and vital economic opportunities, but it also had profound non-material meanings. First, the document had the potential to reorient his relationship to temporal uncertainty, where he could more "patiently bide time" (Chua 2011). Indeed, as Sharon too noted, work permits could help to allay the sense of anxiety and uncertainty that infused my interlocutors' lives as asylum claimants.

Second, the work permit represented the potential for social connection, for reducing social isolation. The idea of a job as not just offering financial security but, as Ahmed puts it, "having somewhere to be," was salient across my conversations with asylum claimants who waited for their EADs. This struck me when one evening I arrived to dinner at Emmanuel's home much later than I had originally planned. I apologized, explaining wearily that I had had a long day with research interviews and appointments. "Why are you complaining, Bridget?" Emmanuel lightly reproached me, adding: "You don't know how happy I would be if I could be going from appointment to appointment all day, working all day." As noted earlier, the inability to work can have emotional and mental health consequences on asylum seekers, in part because work plays an important role in promoting self-identity and social connections that are crucial to well-being (Fleay and Hartley 2016; Hess et al. 2019). Indeed, many asylum claimants told me that getting a job helped them to feel better not only because they could start to better provide for themselves and their families, but because it prevented them from sitting at home, which often meant worrying and thinking too much.

Finally, Ahmed critically underscored the perceived potential of the work authorization to restore important social and familial connections. Viewed this way, his repeated exclamations of "now I am eligible" take on added meaning. With this declaration, Ahmed seemed to be not only claiming his legal right to employment, but also reinstating his legitimacy and worthiness as a son and a provider. The demoralization and shame Ahmed felt at not being able to provide for his family, both in the United States and in Ethiopia, had prompted him to withdraw from family interactions—a tactic that others adopted as well. Now, with the promise of work eligibility, Ahmed saw a way to repair these feelings of moral failure and to restore his filial duties to his family, even if his asylum case remained pending.

But to what extent are EADs able to fulfill the promises that asylum claimants like Ahmed find inherent in them? It is certainly true that asylum claimants' access to employment provides them with a means of survival. This cannot be overstated and has important policy implications. The economic barriers placed in front of asylum claimants have serious consequences, both tangible (poverty, homelessness, hunger) and intangible (demoralization, shame, anxiety, ruptured social and familial relations). With jobs made available through a work permit, many asylum claimants are able to pay their bills, move into their own or shared apartments, buy food and winter clothing, and sometimes even put away small amounts of money for family abroad. Yet, the promises of the EAD are often not fully realized, for several reasons. First, an EAD does not always translate into a viable job for asylum claimants; this was perhaps especially the case during my initial years of fieldwork, when the United States was just beginning to rebound from the Great Recession. Even with a work permit, many asylum claimants I knew remained unemployed, underemployed, or in jobs where they were subjected to discrimination and harsh working conditions (Collins 2016).

Trouble finding a job was not ubiquitous among my interlocutors. When Sarah, the Zimbabwean asylum seeker we met in the previous chapter, got her EAD, she received many offers for minimum-wage positions with the help of the social worker who ran the shelter where she was then staying. She was, however, indignant at the types of jobs being offered, which were mainly housekeeping or home health aide/nursing assistant positions. Sarah, who worked for two decades as an executive assistant in Zimbabwe, decided to try her hand at finding a job that matched her expertise and experience. She applied to numerous upper-level positions for executive assistants at various businesses and organizations across the city, but was rejected again and again. Explaining her frustration to me one afternoon, she explicitly pointed to racism as the reason for her applications being rejected. "They see a black person, an African, and they don't want me in their office. I know that is why I cannot get a good job." Sarah also understood her employment opportunities to be thoroughly gendered as well. The fact that most of my female interlocutors worked as health aides or nursing assistants must be understood in the context of racialized and gendered forms of labor and labor hierarchies. Underscoring the idea of intersectional, or "conjugated" oppression (Bourgois 1988; Holmes 2007), Sarah expressed her outrage that as a black, African female, she saw very little opportunities for meaningful employment:

> It's like the only option people like me have is to go into nursing aid or housekeeping but . . . they don't have passion for it. They are there only for money. And then the money is not even good. I'm not sure how to survive on that pay. So is that the only thing I can do to get money?! But it's not in me, Bridget, it's not! I've not got passion for that. Why should I be forced to do something that I don't have the passion for? I have qualifications. I have twenty-one years working experience. Why can't that mean something here?! I don't understand.

Sarah rightfully pointed out how these gendered and racialized forms of labor offer low pay and often evoke low employee morale. She was also correct in suggesting that her black, African, female asylum claimant status would make her appear a willing candidate for a position as a nursing aide. Many of the female Cameroonian asylum claimants I knew had these positions, and they complained of their low pay, abrupt docking of hours by their employers, and lack of health care benefits. This was not specific, however, to the health aide/nursing assistant industry. Other asylum claimants who had low-wage positions in places such as fast-food restaurants, hotel housekeeping, and janitorial services, also complained about their minimum wages, particularly when employers would cut their hours week to week without notice. Unsurprisingly, asylum claimants found this challenging, primarily in the threat posed to their ability to provide for family back home. Moreover, many told me that relatives in Cameroon or other home countries assumed that everyone was rich in the United States and pressed my interlocutors to send more money. Their hope that an EAD would help them fulfill their role of provider is not realized for many asylum claimants, as they struggle to support themselves and save money for their families. The disillusionment stretches across borders.

Beyond the poor wages, Ruth and Louise also faced deplorable forms of discrimination at work. I witnessed firsthand Louise's treatment at work. Because for a short time she was renting a room in the group home where she worked, I would often visit her there. Mostly this was after work hours, but sometimes she would invite me to stay in her room while she finished up work. One evening I heard an elderly client hurling vicious racial epithets and anti-immigrant slurs at her. I darted out of the room, ready to defend Louise, but she immediately shot me a look that clearly communicated I stay quiet. "It's okay Bree, go back to the room." I later asked her if that had ever happened before. "All the time," she said. I was aghast. I suggested that she report this to her boss, stressing that this was a hostile work environment, and she shouldn't have to put up with it. "Bree, I have no choice," she said to me, resigned. "I just try to ignore it and put it out of my head, because what can I do?"

I had had similar conversations with Ruth after she told me about the racial and xenophobic slurs her charges launched at her on a regular basis. Both Louise and Ruth explained to me that they were certain that they would be fired if they were to report the incidents, and they desperately needed the work. Plus, they added, their precarious legal status made them even more afraid to draw attention to themselves, emphasizing the ways in which asylum claimants straddle the line between "legality" and "illegality." These violations of dignity endured by Louise and Ruth draw attention more generally to gendered and racialized hierarchies of the labor market in the United States, "in which Latinos, African Americans, and 'immigrants' fall to the bottom" (Sargent and Larchanché 2011, 347). I hasten to point out, however, that a sense of demoralization about work was not shared by all the asylum claimants I knew. Some took great pride in obtaining minimum wage jobs. And some asylum claimants found work that they enjoyed and found fulfilling. Overall, however, while my interlocutors were quick to say that they were grateful for any job, their lower-class position within the labor force continued and exacerbated their sense of vulnerability and marginalization.

This brings us to a second, and related, reason that EADs do not always fulfill the hope of being transformative: the persistent and pervasive impact that "legal liminality" (Menjívar 2006) has on asylum claimants' lives. That is, although employment can help asylum claimants more patiently bide time, asylum claimants' precarious status and protracted uncertainty often ultimately trumps this sense of patience. Ahmed, for example, got a job on a factory assembly line and was initially elated. He worked full-time and took any overtime shift he could, allowing him to finally save money, support himself and his sister, and send money to his mother in Ethiopia. He was grateful for the ability to work. Yet, as his case remained pending and suffered numerous delays and rescheduling, Ahmed started to feel more and more despondent, an experience that I found common among asylum seekers.

Asylum seekers also have to contend with how their liminal status is interpreted by current and potential employers. Asylum claimants told me that in job interviews employers sometimes expressed wariness about hiring someone who, although legally eligible to work, was nonetheless categorized as a non-citizen. While not undocumented, asylum claimants, like irregular migrants, are often viewed as potentially temporary and therefore disposable labor (De Genova 2002). Several of my asylum-seeking friends reported being fired from their jobs after they were denied asylum, despite having submitted evidence to their employers of their intent to appeal their denials. Given asylum seekers' ambivalent status, employment, though critical, was often experienced as only a partial sense of security in their lives. My interlocutors looked to an asylum decision, decided through the legal adjudication of their claims, for the fuller resolution of their existential insecurity. This is where we next turn our attention.

*   *   *

This chapter has continued to build an understanding of the multiple forms of violence within the asylum system by focusing on how asylum claimants' socioeconomic exclusion and marginalization has myriad effects. The potential material effects of the systemic socioeconomic violence of the state are significant and cruel, including homelessness or housing instability and food insecurity. Yet, the state's socioeconomic violence against asylum claimants has effects beyond the material, indelibly transfiguring social and family relations in ways that could be a source of pain and demoralization. Work permits, when eventually issued, help to restore stability and repair social ruptures, but the often-hoped-for promise of an EAD to change asylum claimants' lives is not always realized. Within this context, asylum claimants adopt strategies that work to keep intact, or restore, meaningful connections to others, as well as recuperate their own identities and sense of dignity and purpose in their lives.

4 Epistemic Violence in Asylum Adjudication

The hopeful granting of asylum status is the ultimate object of asylum claimants' waiting, perceived as a much-desired end to the multiple forms of violence imposed on them, as discussed in the previous chapters.[1] For my interlocutors, asylum status represented a sense of present and future security. Within this broader context of waiting for an asylum decision, asylum claimants anticipate—with concomitant hope and fear—the legal procedures that bring them closer to a final decision. While asylum claimants often live many years in legal limbo, their asylum cases are heard and assessed in only a few instances during that time, namely in asylum interviews and court hearings. I was able to see various legal proceedings and their effects up close. I accompanied asylum claimants to meetings with their *pro bono* legal counsel and went with many of them to their hearings in immigration court. (Unlike immigration court, where observers can attend, an asylum interview conducted by USCIS restricts attendance to the asylum claimant and, if applicable, their legal representative and interpreter.) In total, I observed almost two dozen court hearings.

In addition, I also conducted interviews with fifteen immigration attorneys and advocates and went to numerous legal immigration conferences and training sessions. These activities provided me with important insights into the legal procedures surrounding asylum determination. However, I was also eager to understand this process from the perspective of asylum adjudicators themselves—the ones who make determinations on asylum claims. To this end, I spent months calling and emailing officials at the Chicago asylum office, one of the eight USCIS asylum offices in the country,[2] to ask permission to interview asylum officers as part of my research. Asylum claims filed in Minnesota fell under the jurisdiction of the Chicago asylum office, and asylum officers based in the Chicago office would routinely conduct "circuit rides" whereby they traveled to other regional USCIS field offices, like the one in Bloomington, Minnesota, to conduct asylum interviews. Circuit rides to Bloomington happened about twice a year. The director of the Chicago asylum office submitted my request for permission to conduct interviews with his staff to his superiors at DHS. I followed up weekly for months, and after submitting copies of various identity documents, I was finally granted permission by DHS to interview asylum officers who heard and made decisions on initial (affirmative) asylum interviews.

In this chapter, I focus on yet another site of bureaucratic violence within the asylum system: the legal arena. This is not to say that all adjudication proceedings (asylum interviews, court hearings) involve forms of harm. Yet, I do consider how the context of asylum adjudication often engenders forms of epistemic violence, as asylum claimants' understandings and articulations of their experiences may be effaced, devalued, or manipulated. In other words, asylum claimants' experiential knowledge is often subordinated to bureaucratic or legal interpretations. In its broadest sense epistemic violence, a term originating with postcolonial theorist Gayatri Chakravorty Spivak (1988), characterizes the pernicious effects of silencing or ignoring the voices of marginalized groups. It is a form of violence that denies the Other—whether an individual or community—the status as a *knower* or holder of legitimate knowledge. Epistemic violence serves to reinforce and reproduce the dominance of those in power (see also De Sousa Santos 2014; Dotson 2011; Fricker 2007). What I describe in this chapter as epistemic violence is also aptly understood as "epistemic injustice" (Fricker 2007). Indeed, it was often through the frame of (in)justice and (un)fairness that my interlocutors expressed the effects of such violence upon them.

As I show, forms of epistemic violence have not only material effects—
impacting whether one is granted asylum status or not—but also psychological, emotional, and social consequences as well. To explore this, I put
into dialogue my interlocutors' experiences of the legal system with interview and observational data collected among institutional actors, including attorneys, advocates, and asylum officers. I draw most heavily on data
collected with asylum officers to illustrate the bureaucratic logic and forms
of "moral reckoning" that undergird the asylum regime more broadly
(Willen 2012, 805). The juxtaposition of bureaucratic reasoning with asylum seekers' own perspectives of asylum adjudication reveals critical dis-
junctures between how asylum seekers understand themselves as morally
deserving subjects and the logic and grammar of the legal system that
assesses this claim.[3]

BUREAUCRATIC ENCOUNTERS

Having finally secured permission to interview asylum officers, in early
2010 I traveled to the Chicago asylum office, where I interviewed a dozen
asylum officers over two days. When I arrived, Bill, the director of the
office, greeted me with a welcoming handshake in the lobby. Prior to starting my interviews with asylum officers, Bill wanted me to "meet some of
the team" and talk briefly about my research. We entered a brightly lit
conference room, where Bill urged me to help myself to coffee and bagels
arranged neatly on a table against the wall. Six USCIS staff, mostly asylum
officer supervisors, sat around the table and offered friendly greetings
when Bill introduced me. I gave a brief spiel about my research, basically
reiterating the information that I had already communicated to Bill in my
emails to him and the more official letters I had submitted to be forwarded
to his bosses at DHS. I was careful to stress that I wanted to hear from
asylum officers because I thought that their perspective on the asylum
process was important and would offer a point of view that perhaps dif-
fered from that of asylum applicants themselves. The supervisors in
the room were polite but I could tell from their questions that some
of them were a bit skeptical of my intentions. Several supervisors wanted
to impress upon me the difficulty of asylum officers' jobs, the rigorous

training they received, and the strong sense of ethical duty that their supervisees demonstrated. Perhaps positing my primary research goal as understanding asylum claimants' experiences of the asylum system made them feel uneasy. I did my best to assure them that I came with no biases or preconceived notions, that I was appreciative of the challenges of their jobs, and that I valued the insights that their staff could offer.

Before Bill took me to the room where I'd be interviewing asylum officers, he asked that while on the premises, I should refrain from looking into any interview rooms in order to protect the confidentiality of the asylum applicants on the premises. To minimize this risk, Bill had scheduled me to be in an available conference room for the entire day, where asylum officers would join me. While this was all understandable from the standpoint of confidentiality, it was nonetheless a striking contrast to the fieldwork I had been conducting thus far. The sterility and quiet of the asylum office, the closed doors, the fluorescence of the conference room lights, the tailored and starched clothes of staff members—these signaled that I was in an altogether different site. The intimate spaces of homes, yards, parks, and churches, with their amalgam of scents and sounds, that I had been sharing with asylum claimants, all seemed far away. I knew that my interlocutors had been or would be in a similar office in Minnesota, being questioned about their reasons for seeking protection in the United States. Yet, my visit here was so different than theirs. I was the one who would be asking questions of the asylum officers. I would be able to probe the nuances of asylum officers' decision-making process and bureaucratic rationales—aspects of the asylum system that are largely opaque and illegible to asylum claimants, whose very lives are the subject of these deliberations.

The first asylum officer I interviewed was Richard, who had been with the USCIS asylum office for six years, after having worked for a decade as a border patrol agent near the US-Mexico border, first under INS and then the Customs and Border Protection (CBP) branch of DHS. He was attracted to the asylum officer position because of the "high level of responsibility" that it required. Richard thought that his diverse work experiences, not just with INS and DHS, but also his time in the Army and his work in the financial sector (he had an MBA) was proof of his sharp analytic skills—essential for asylum officers. He also cited the fact that he was a religion major as an undergraduate and was a devout Christian, both of which, he stressed, "evidences my interest in human values." Richard clearly recognized the depth of responsibility that adjudicating asylum claims entailed. "This is a very important job," he declared. "I mean, this is not making widgets, you know. It can make a big, big difference. Not only to the applicant but to their families back home and their families near at hand. I mean it's a huge thing." This was a responsibility that Richard welcomed: "I love the responsibility. I love having been chosen for this task because I believe I am doing the job right." While Richard recognized his responsibility to the asylum applicants he interviewed, he acknowledged that his professional allegiance was to his country. "It's the federal government, the USA, that we work for, though," Richard asserted. He continued:

> You know, in the final analysis, my take is, that's the community that we work for. Yeah, we work for the applicants, okay, but they're just applicants. Until they've demonstrated they're true refugees, then we will accord them the benefits they seek. Until then, they're coming to us, and they want something from us. So, my biggest challenge has always been granting somebody who ought not to be granted and referring or denying somebody who should be granted.

Richard made clear that the responsibility for proving one's deservingness of asylum sits squarely with the applicant. Looming large in this narrative is the representation of the United States as the benevolent host bestowing its hospitality on the guest who demonstrates themself worthy of such a humanitarian gesture. Like Richard, the other asylum officers with whom I spoke framed their role as a negotiation between protecting the state and protecting deserving applicants. In this way, asylum officers conceived themselves as *moral gatekeepers:* caught between the humanitarian imperative to grant refuge to those in need, on the one hand, and the duty to protect the security of the nation, on the other. Here, I take my cue from Heyman (2009) who has described immigration officials on the US southern border as "guardians of a restricted good" (381). Additional narrative excerpts from my interviews with asylum officers highlight this sense of moral gatekeeping or guardianship:

> You know, you just hope that you do right by the applicant. And you hope you do right by your country. Because, you know, we were hired by the coun-

try to protect the citizens of the United States. And so, at the same time we want to be humanitarian and extend the helping hand of the country to the people that deserve it. You're just constantly doing a balancing act and you're hoping you're getting it right. (Male asylum officer, mid-forties)

Certainly, you don't want to make a decision where you're sending someone into harm's way, but at the same time you don't want to disrupt the integrity of the program and just kind of find everybody eligible that may not deserve it, may not need the same kind of protection as somebody else. So, it's just kind of [a] hard balance sometimes. (Female asylum officer, early thirties)

Asylum officers explicitly and repeatedly engaged the concept of "deservingness" to discuss the asylum system. Key to asylum officers' moral gatekeeping is the presumption of asylum seekers as already-constituted subjects with regard to their deservingness of legal protection. For example, Richard spoke of wanting to grant asylum to "people who are deserving." Other asylum officers framed their primary goal conversely: as one senior asylum officer put it, "to not bestow a benefit on somebody that's not deserving." Deservingness in this context is not something that is produced, performed, or co-created, but rather inherent to an asylum claimant. Asylum officers saw (un)deservingness as something that might be hidden, but was discoverable by their trained eyes. Such a view, however, dangerously obscures the ways in which the asylum system in fact produces these categories of deservingness. In her parsing of the "everyday politics of recognition" in the Greek asylum system, Cabot (2014) underscores this point, noting that "recognition is performative . . . in that it both produces and enacts that which it signifies: the process of being recognized itself makes the refugee real" (146).

Two key questions emerge from the above asylum officers' narratives. First, *who* is understood to be deserving of asylum? And, second, *how* is deservingness demonstrated? To the first question, from the perspective of asylum officers we can see how the broader distinction between a presumed economic migrant and a "true refugee" is mobilized in local adjudicatory settings. While concerns over terrorism and threats to national security were a significant impetus for increasingly restrictive immigration measures (particularly post-September 11, 2001), the asylum officers I talked to seemed confident that the numerous screening measures would prevent terrorists or other persons who posed a national security threat from getting through the system. Rather, asylum officers saw the potential economic motivation of applicants as a key concern.

When I asked Richard what he meant by "somebody who ought not to be granted," he quickly responded, "Look, I don't want you to think this is all one big candy cane factory situation." He stared at me intently, and continued:

> We get the embellishers. We get the liars. We get the people with fraudulent intent. We're very generous and we try to be very fair. But the reality is we deal with a lot of economic refugees and that separates them from other refugees as a group. So, we get a lot of people that, in my opinion, are without a doubt, economic refugees who are trying to convert that into a claim that will pass muster.

What is important, and troubling, to note here is the conflation of fraud with the claims of so-called "economic refugees." This is not an issue of eligibility for Richard. That is, he was not suggesting that economically motivated migration simply does not fit the definition of a refugee under international and domestic law and for those reasons, he cannot grant asylum. Rather, Richard implies that "economic refugees" are deceptive, purposively trying to manipulate their testimonies to gain status. Such a reductive representation assumes that migrants recognize themselves as a member of one of these dichotomous categories in the first place—an assumption that has been shown to be false. Instead, migrants and refugees often experience their mobility in ways that defy the forced/voluntary or political/economic binary; they have multiple and overlapping reasons for migration (Vogt 2018; Yarris and Castañeda 2015). Moreover, Richard's emphasis on economic migrants' *intentional* manipulation of the asylum system reinforces broader institutional and discursive frames of "true" refugees as its counter: passive and without agency (Malkki 1996; Nyers 2006). Finally, Richard's narrative reveals a moral evaluation concerning forms of mobility—that there are "right" (political/humanitarian) and "wrong" (economic) reasons for crossing borders, and that these subsequently inform migrants' perceived moral status.

Richard's concern about fraud was echoed by the other asylum officers. They told me that "weeding out liars" was a necessary part of their job. Many, like Richard, viewed lying not just as indicative of immorality and lack of deservingness, but also as a personal affront and a threat to the asylum system overall. If asylum officers' point of departure is that there are fraudulent asylum seekers in their midst, this brings me to the second emergent question: *How* is deservingness demonstrated? Or, how do claimants prove they are not "bogus" asylum seekers (Ahmed 2004; Scheel and Squire 2014)? I have begun to sketch out thus far how a broader lens of suspicion becomes locally enacted (see also Haas and Shuman 2019). Below, I continue investigating this "evaluative gaze," the ways that adjudicators "engaged in processes of judgment, hierarchization and moralization," to probe how adjudicators assess (un)deservingness (Codó 2011, 738). Yet, I am simultaneously attentive to how asylum seekers *experience* this adjudicatory gaze. If asylum officers and other adjudicators grapple with issues of deservingness, truth, and suspicion, how do asylum claimants navigate these murky waters, and to what effects?

"CREDIBILITY IS EVERYTHING"

At a regional immigration conference, I attended a panel on preparing asylum cases. The first speaker, a seasoned immigration attorney, stood and without saying anything, advanced to the first slide of her powerpoint presentation. She let the audience sit in silence while we stared at the word "CREDIBILITY" projected on the large screen at the front of the room. "Credibility is the most important aspect of the asylum procedure," she announced solemnly. "If your client is not believable, then the whole case goes down. Credibility is everything." Indeed, many of my interlocutors had been given an adverse credibility decision, meaning that the asylum officer found them or their cases to be lacking credibility. And though credibility is not explicitly one of the criteria for refugee protection under international or domestic law, "in practice, being deemed credible may be the single biggest substantive hurdle before applicants" (Kagan 2003, 368; see also Thomas 2006, Coffey 2003, Rempell 2008). While credibility has always been a concern in asylum adjudication, with the passage of the REAL ID Act of 2005, an applicant's credibility was no longer to be presumed by adjudicators (Rempell 2008), thus generating a system in which asylum seekers are, in effect, guilty until proven innocent. To explore the issue of credibility further, I turn to the case of Patrick, an asylum seeker from Rwanda in his early twenties.

Patrick had arrived in Minnesota only a couple of months before I met him and had been working with CHR staff to file his asylum application. Patrick had been a university student in Rwanda when he was arrested by police. Though Patrick was not politically active, his professor and mentor was a prominent and vocal critic of the government at the time, led by Paul Kagame. When police stormed the classroom one afternoon, they grabbed Patrick, his professor, and several other students. Patrick was taken to a prison outside of Kigali where he was kept in isolation and severely beaten. After several days, officers took Patrick back to Kigali. As they kicked him out of the truck, the officers issued a clear warning that if they saw Patrick again, they would kill him.

Patrick made his way to his aunt's house, where she tended to his wounds. Patrick learned that his brother, who had recently gotten involved with a political party opposing Kagame, had also been threatened by police. Most frightening for Patrick was the fact that his father, too, had been followed by police officers, who had asked him questions about Patrick and his imputed political activism. He and his aunt decided that it was too dangerous for Patrick to return to the family's home, lest his presence put his parents in any danger. Patrick called his father, who was fearful that Patrick would be killed if he didn't leave Rwanda. He gave Patrick the name and contact information of a family acquaintance living outside of St. Paul. If there was a way to get to the United States, Patrick's father urged, he would surely be safe there until it might be possible to return. His father thought Patrick might even be able to continue his studies there, something that was important to both Patrick and his father. Patrick's aunt had enough money in the bank to pay for a plane ticket. She also worked for the ministry of justice and arranged to take Patrick there the next morning, where they were able to secure a visa.

Within weeks of arriving in Minnesota, the family acquaintance with whom Patrick had been staying referred Patrick to a local center that assisted survivors of torture, who then referred Patrick to CHR for help preparing his asylum application. They also found a volunteer family, the Larsens, who offered to house Patrick, provide him with meals and transportation, and provide additional support to him while he sought asylum.

Patrick was settling into his new home and had just started seeing a counselor at a local mental health center when he received a phone call from his aunt with devastating news. Patrick's father had been found dead outside the family's home, from what appeared to be severe head trauma. The family speculated that it was the police who murdered him, though they were never able to prove this. When I first met Patrick, it was hard for him to get through a conversation without breaking down in tears. He felt an acute bitterness toward his country: "I hate my country. I never want to go back there," he told me repeatedly. Patrick feared for the rest of his family in Rwanda. "What is their fate, now?" he wondered anxiously. He hoped that his asylum case would be processed quickly and that he would be able to bring his mother and younger siblings to the United States.

Over the course of several months, Patrick's mood grew a bit lighter, and he was more hopeful when he received a date for his asylum interview. Talking to him the evening before his interview, he said he was confident and relaxed. His lawyer had assured him he had "a really good case." But when I checked in with him the day after his interview, he seemed troubled. It had not gone the way he had expected. Patrick wanted to wait until he received the asylum officer's decision to discuss the interview further. He was just too worried about it, he said. One month later—much quicker than any of my other interlocutors—Patrick received a notice that his case had been referred to immigration court. We discussed his asylum interview soon after.

BRIDGET: How did you feel going into the interview?

PATRICK: Well, first I had expected to start my interview at 9, but I started my interview at 11:40.

BRIDGET: 11:40?!

PATRICK: Yeah! And I was there at 8:15. And at 8:30, I said to myself, 'okay in thirty minutes I should start my interview.'

BRIDGET: Why so late?

PATRICK: I don't know. They don't explain it.

BRIDGET: Did anyone apologize?

PATRICK: Noooo! You just have to wait. You have to be in the waiting room and when they call you, you have to be there to go in. And you can't ask why they're so late. And when you're nervous, it's hard to be waiting a long time. But when I got into the room I was feeling confident. I wasn't scared anymore. I was expecting the room to be a big room, but it was a small room and it seemed like an office, like a job interview. So I felt calmer.

BRIDGET: How long did the interview last?

PATRICK: About one hour.

BRIDGET: Can you tell me about it?

PATRICK: Well, there were things that she [the asylum officer] kept asking about because she was comparing my application with the US Embassy and what I said here [on the asylum application]. So, I tried explaining everything but it wasn't helping. So it was just, like, a lot of misunderstanding. And I just kept trying to explain everything.

BRIDGET: Like what kind of things?

PATRICK: Okay, so before I got the visa [in Rwanda], I had to get [security] clearance. So she [the asylum officer] asked me how I got clearance if I was a target of the police. I explained how you get clearance. Usually in my country, to get the clearance it's not the police that give you the clearance. It's the ministries of justice. So I didn't go to the police, I went to the ministries of justice. And it's only if you are in jail for, like, three or six months that the police will report it to the ministries of justice. So when the ministries of justice looked into their computers and records of files, it showed I didn't have a police record because I was only in jail for less than a week and it had just happened. So that's why I got clearance.

BRIDGET: Okay, and did she seem to understand that?

PATRICK: No, because she kept asking me 'why would they give you clearance if you were in trouble with the police?' She kept saying that I went to the police to get clearance but I told her I didn't go to the police. It was the ministries of justice. But she was like, 'Uh-huh. Okay.' [using a dismissive tone]

BRIDGET: Were there other misunderstandings?

PATRICK: Yeah, so because in my [asylum] application, I say I don't have a brother. And in the application with the US Embassy in Rwanda it says I have a brother. So she asked me about that. I explained that in order for me to get a visa I had to say that I had a brother here [in the United States]. But really, it was a friend of my father's, that was going to help me. I don't know him. He sent his friend to come pick me up at the airport and take me to his house. But he told me that I should be on my own after that and I went to [CHR]. But if I said I was meeting a guy that was a friend of my father's, I wouldn't have gotten the visa. So to get the visa, I said I had a brother here. So now if you compare my application with the Embassy and my [asylum] application, it doesn't match. And for her that was a big problem. Even though I explained everything.

BRIDGET: Do you think she believed you?

PATRICK: No, she didn't believe me. She didn't get it. I kept trying to explain. Even, I mean, if I had a brother here why would I move in with a white family, you know? So I tried to explain again and she was like [imitates putting up a hand] 'okay, let me ask you the next question.' So it was just like that.

BRIDGET: How did you feel during those interactions?

PATRICK: Well, when I started talking about everything, like, all the bad things that happened and how my dad was killed, that's when it was very, very hard. It's kind of like your mind, your brain, just opens something up that's been stuck somewhere and it just goes 'pshhhhhh' (makes a soft exploding sound). It comes up and you see everything in your face in front of you.

BRIDGET: That sounds difficult.

PATRICK: Yes, and there were times at first when I tried to speak up, like to say more about my father, but it [words] didn't come out. It was just so hard. But she [the asylum officer] said it was okay, she could tell it was hard for me. But then I was so surprised when later she asked if I have proof that my father is dead. And it just, it took me a while to even answer because I don't even know how to answer that. I mean, he's dead. He's gone. He passed away. My aunt told me. Why wouldn't I believe my aunt? But she [the asylum officer] was saying I should have a death certificate. But this isn't something I ever heard about. So, when she kept asking me about my father's death and how can I believe my father is dead, like asking 'where is the proof?' That, that hurt me very, very much. I mean, maybe that's her job but it made me feel really bad. My father is dead.

BRIDGET: So, at the end of the interview, how were you feeling?

PATRICK: My feeling was that it wasn't fair. I didn't get a chance to say what I wanted to say. I mean, I guess that's her job, that you have to keep things going and have more people [asylum applicants] coming, but it was a bad experience for me. I didn't get the chance to say a lot of things. It was like she wanted certain answers. Like she wanted me to just say 'yes' or 'no,' but I couldn't just say 'no' because sometimes there was more that I needed to say in order to explain myself.

BRIDGET: What did the decision letter say?

PATRICK: It just said nothing specific. Just that you are being sent to an immigration judge. You are a citizen of Rwanda and you can be deported. And then on the bottom they explain why you didn't get granted. Just two lines. About not having evidence and things not matching up and things I said not making sense.

BRIDGET: How are you feeling about your case now?

PATRICK: At first, it was very hard. I was feeling so bad and confused about how things [the interview] went. But now I am feeling better. I realize I can't do anything about my case. It's not under my control. And my lawyer told me not to worry, at the next step you'll be granted. And I have decided that when I am in front of the judge of immigration, this time I am going to say what I want to say even if they stop me. I will explain *everything*. And I will say 'I still have more, please let me explain.' Then they will understand. They will see the truth.

Patrick very clearly felt unable to exert control over both *what* he wanted to say and *how* he wanted to say it. The state's power was demonstrated even before the interview started, by making Patrick wait hours past his scheduled start time, without explanation or apology, which is not uncommon. The waiting in the asylum office lobby is a microcosm of the broader "struggle for ownership over time" within the asylum system (Eule et al. 2019, 178; see also chapter 2). Yet, the manipulation of time as a technology of power did not only manifest in a slowing down of time; asylum officials could also weaponize time by accelerating it or foreclosing it (Griffiths 2014; Rozakou 2021). We see this in Patrick's experience of feeling rushed and not being given the time to fully explain himself. This bureaucratic control over time was simultaneously a control over meaning. Patrick's story contains multiple examples of epistemic violence, where his experiential knowledge was delegitimated, subordinated to the bureaucratic logic of the asylum officer.

Patrick recounted numerous misunderstandings, disconnections, and frustrations in his asylum interview. Ultimately, these resulted in the asylum officer's mistrust of his testimony and a failure to grant him asylum. Inconsistences between older and newer documents were an obvious problem for the asylum officer. And when Patrick attempted to provide details that would explain these inconsistencies, she cut this additional informa-tion short, seemingly having already interpreted them as a "red flag" for lack of credibility. His experience raises numerous issues surrounding cred-ibility and eligibility that emerged in my research among both asylum claimants and asylum adjudicators, though in often conflicting ways. If, as the seasoned immigration attorney stressed in her talk, "credibility is eve-rything in an asylum case," it was also a slippery concept, conceptualized by different stakeholders in shifting, contested, and often frustratingly obscure and sometimes seemingly arbitrary ways. Without exception, asylum offic-ers identified credibility assessments as the biggest challenge of their jobs, namely because, as one senior asylum officer put it, "It's just impossible to tell if someone is really telling the truth." Yet, even if impossible, credibility assessments were a key aspect of asylum adjudication.

Assessing and Performing a Narrative of Persecution

When I asked asylum officers how they assessed credibility, they told me that they relied on factors such as detailed descriptions of events, consist-ency between the written application and oral testimony, and the per-ceived plausibility or logic of past events or experiences. Asylum officers especially focused on an applicant's ability to consistently recall dates and names (Jacquemet 2019; Schuster 2018). These are all aspects of credi-bility determinations that are outlined in USCIS training manuals and disseminated through initial and ongoing asylum officer training. While the asylum training manuals outline these factors—consistency, detail, and plausibility—as a sort of straightforward checklist, in practice both interpreting and performing these domains were rife with challenges and paradoxes. For example, officers claimed that vagueness or lack of detail could be read as a lack of credibility, but *too much* detail was often viewed as suspect. Consistency was understood as a sign of truthfulness, but if a testimony appeared memorized this could serve as an indicator of inau-thenticity. Internal consistency and a linear narrative are often given significant weight in a credibility determination (Sorgoni 2019). Yet, applicants should also be able to move around chronologically in their narrative. The murkiness of credibility assessments reveals the "indeterminate forms of knowledge production" in the context of asylum adjudication (Cabot 2014).

So, barring inconsistencies within testimonies or between forms of testimony, how do asylum officers judge the credibility and legitimacy of an asylum applicant's claim? "They [asylum applicants] just really have to be honest. I mean that's gonna be the biggest thing," Danny, an asylum officer, told me. This was a shared view, as asylum officers repeatedly told me that successful claimants need only to "just tell the truth" or "just tell [their] story." Yet these appeals to "just be honest" or "just tell your story" obscure the crucial fact that an asylum seeker's story needs to be performed in a specific way to be recognized as deserving and legitimate. Here, *believability* is not the same as truthfulness. So, it's really not just "telling your story." Instead, applicants need to tell their stories in a way that aligns with the narrative culture of immigration institutions (Coutin 2001; Danstrøm and Whyte 2019; Bohmer and Shuman 2008, 2018; Giordano 2008; Holland 2018). That is, they must present detailed, chronological, individual-focused, fixed narratives. This form of narrating persecution and fear, however, often contrasts with asylum seekers' own personal and cultural ways of articulating suffering. While asylum officers told me that they relied on their own sense of plausibility or logic of the events being described to them, this could be a point of contention between adjudicators and asylum seekers. For Patrick, the fact that security clearances were obtained from the ministry of justice and not the police was a logical and credible explanation in reply to the officer's questioning of how Patrick had been able to evade police surveillance to leave Rwanda. Here, Patrick was, in fact "telling his story." Yet, his explanation did not fit the perceived logic and model of plausibility of the asylum officer. This reflects Shuman and Bohmer's (2012) observation that "asylum seekers and asylum officials operate within different vernaculars, different conceptions of what counts as normal," but "asylum seekers are subject to an asylum official's assumptions about what is credible" (205).

As I talked with asylum officers, it became clear that there were additional elements that contributed to the construction of a more privileged narrative. Gary, an asylum officer who had been with USCIS for several years, noted that "some applicants make it easier for me to see their story." He continued:

I've noticed a better educated asylum seeker has a much easier time telling me what happened. . . . It seems like people who aren't well educated have a hard time telling a story. They're all over the place. But people who can tell me the story in order have a lot easier time. Or I have an easier time understanding them than someone who's all over the place. And it might be education. It might be some cultures. . . . But if they can go a, b, c, d, e, then that's really nice.

Failing to articulate a privileged coherent, linear narrative could result in the delegitimation of the claim. If Gary recognized the structural factors and forms of cultural capital, such as education, that inform narrative coherence, these were not necessarily factors or differences that he or others accommodated in their interviews. Bureaucratically-imposed time constraints within the asylum interview made being narratively "all over the place" a liability. However, David, a relatively new asylum officer, noted: "I think what makes something convincing is if someone can tell the story without it feeling like they're just re-reading the affidavit all over again. So, I think when somebody can jump around in the story, that to me is more convincing." Thus, counter to Gary, David saw the ability to depart from the chronological written narrative as an indicator of credibility, not its opposite. Asylum officers also noted that people who are reticent or only answer "yes" or "no" may seem less credible. At the same time, some officers also expressed frustration at applicants who are too verbose. Thus, asylum claimants must negotiate competing—yet illegible—narrative mandates.

This ambiguous line between saying enough and not too much was visible in Patrick's recounting of his asylum interview. Patrick was unable to talk much about his father because of the painful feelings it awoke in him, something that may have worked to his detriment, as the asylum officer was skeptical about his father's death. Patrick was not my only interlocutor who told me that they left their interview or hearing feeling like they had much more to say. Asylum officers' attempts to control the narrative within the interviews not only contradicts the putative goal of allowing an applicant to "tell their story"; such epistemic violence profoundly effaces and delegitimizes what really matters to an asylum seeker. Patrick's insistence that in immigration court he will ignore requests to stop talking was, above all, a refusal to abdicate the meaning of his testimony.

Prepping and Translation: The Making of a Good Witness

Asylum claimants, then, had to learn what constituted a good perform-ance or "good speech" in the legal context (McKinnon 2009, 209). My interlocutors had the advantage of being connected to *pro bono* legal assistance through CHR. Overall, the lawyers and legal advocates I met emphasized the importance of crafting a coherent and concise written tes-timony, as well as preparing clients to ensure that they "testify well." One lawyer summed up his role as "preventing my client from hanging him-self." Lawyers noted that their job required a fair amount of "guiding" cli-ents on what and how to say things. As a seasoned immigration attorney told me: "I don't tell them [asylum applicants] to bury things, but I'll direct them to talk about certain things and not others. I guess my job there is to get them to focus on stuff that really matters."

An asylum applicant's performance in interviews or court hearings was the area in which lawyers found they had the least amount of control. Verbose clients were often the most worrisome for attorneys. And while attorneys' attempts to constrain talkative applicants was often a strategic move with the aim of securing legal status, this did not preclude asylum claimants from feeling frustrated by such constraints. Just as Patrick felt anger and frustration at being silenced during his asylum interview and aggravated by what he sensed was the asylum officer's desire for yes-or-no answers, several of my interlocutors told me they had similar grievances with their legal representatives. For example, one asylum claimant, whose lawyers told him he talked too much and instructed him to "give straight answers," responded: "I don't have straight answers. I have *explanations*. And I have to put these things into perspective."

Asylum claimants' discussions of the political histories of their home countries is often cited by asylum officers as an example of extraneous information in immigration hearings. But while the imparting of geopo-litical histories is seen as irrelevant, if not bothersome to adjudicators, for asylum claimants the distinction between the political and the personal is often blurred at best. Even legal personnel aiding asylum claimants often urge them to focus on their personal stories and exclude information about geopolitical situations, as this information will be submitted as sup-plemental evidence with the asylum application (via country conditions reports or news articles). But for asylum seekers this information is an essential part of their personal stories (see Coutin 2001). For my Cameroonian interlocutors, for example, the answer to the question of how they came to be in the United States did not begin with the precipitating act(s) of persecution that eventually prompted their flight but rather with the oppression and violence rooted in complex (colonial) histories that made them feel like an Other in Cameroon. Collective political histories are a key resource through which asylum claimants make sense of their displacement and claims for protection. Adjudicators' attempts to partition the political from the personal in the asylum process disrupts the meaning that asylum seekers make of their experiences.

Given this complex and often illegible process, legal representatives see their duty as one of translation—of converting their clients' stories into narratives that can be recognized as credible and legitimate, and thereby deserving of legal status. What I am describing here as prepping and translation may be understood as what Coutin (2003) terms "procedural subjugation" (108). By this, Coutin calls attention to "the ways that legal personnel and legal proceedings discipline their subjects" by crafting personal stories to conform to "prototypes of deservingness" that fit with legal criteria and convention (107; see also Bohmer and Shuman 2008; Statz 2018). This becomes a tricky bind for attorneys and legal aid staff. As Coutin (2003) importantly adds: "Despite the seeming cultural and political hegemony involved in producing asylum narratives, to not render clients' life stories as instances of a prototype would be to do clients a disservice, because it is only as 'prototypes' that these people can obtain political asylum" (99). Certainly, asylum claimants often come to understand that simplistic answers are a strategic maneuver used to successfully navigate the asylum adjudication process. Yet, a simultaneous consideration of what else is produced through the enactments of these prototypes is critically important. That is, asylum advocates and attorneys, in helping to craft affidavits and prep claimants for their hearings, risk enacting a similar kind of epistemic violence that I have traced among adjudicators, like the officer interviewing Patrick. In addition, attorneys' reproduction of such prototypes of deservingness means that "their constructions win asylum for some, while excluding others unable to fit imaginaries of victimhood" (McGuirk and Pine 2020, 3).

TRAUMA AND ADJUDICATION

The asylum officers I talked to often posited asylum claimants' trauma as "evidence" of their experiences of persecution, thus making their eligibility more visible. Here, the traumatized or suffering body is subjectified as authentic and deserving (Fassin 2008; Fassin and d'Halluin 2007; Ticktin 2011). At the same time, officers acknowledged that claimants' trauma could interfere with credibility assessments, given that manifestations of trauma include problems with memory recall, flat affect, nervous demeanor, confusion, and comprehension issues (Cohen 2001; Paskey 2016). This paradox was acutely articulated by Eileen, who had been an asylum officer for just over a year and a half:

> We get a couple of trainings about dealing with trauma survivors. It's tricky for credibility because if we want to get people who are detailed and consistent and then you have somebody who doesn't remember well. Sometimes that makes them more credible. . . . But one time I had a man, this poor guy, he was getting his dates all confused and he was all over the place and I was, like, gosh this guy is so making up this story. And then he described going to jail and I asked what did they do to you and he said 'they hooked me up to some wires.' And I said 'then what happened?' And then he said 'then I got really hot.' And I was like 'oh, my god, you were electrocuted.' Your brain's scrambled eggs, you can't give me dates. But unfortunately because the guy was not represented and had no medical evidence I couldn't say he was credible because his dates were a mess. So, there's some conflict there with trauma survivors.

This narrative excerpt illustrates Eileen's knowledge and recognition of the links between trauma and cognitive impairments such as memory recall deficits and incoherence. However, rather than bolster her interviewee's claim that he was imprisoned and tortured, these manifestations of trauma interfered with Eileen's ability to grant him asylum due to his inconsistencies in other areas of his testimonies. Eileen's final judgment of denying credibility comes not from her *subjective* disbelief of the claimant's story, but rather from the institutional disciplining of adjudicators that requires "subjective" evidence (e.g., personal testimony) to be corroborated by other putatively more "objective" elements (e.g., medical evidence, legal argument, expert testimony) (Good 2007; Berger et al. 2015; Haas 2019).

"You Don't Know What's Real": The Role of Psychiatric Evaluations

Lawyers worked with psychological professionals and organizations to produce psychiatric evaluations that could be submitted as supporting evidence with an asylum claim. Attorneys whom I interviewed during my fieldwork expressed ambivalence about the weight that psychological or psychiatric evaluations played in asylum claimants' cases. While almost all lawyers I talked to told me that they submit a psychological evaluation if they have one, they sometimes wondered about their efficacy. Susan, a senior staff member and legal advocate at CHR opined, "I think the psychological stuff has weight, but I think that there may be some level of PTSD fatigue going [with adjudicators]." Other immigration attorneys and advocates agreed with these assessments, suggesting that psychological evaluations may, as one lawyer put it, "begin to seem too subjective."[4]

Many asylum officers found psychiatric/psychological evaluations helpful for two primary reasons. First, some officers noted that they could compare what was written on the psychiatric evaluation to the written testimony of the asylum application, thus uncovering any inconsistencies that might indicate a lack of credibility. Many others found evaluations helpful as evidence of psychological injury. This sentiment is supported by the work of Fassin and Rechtman (2009) who have examined the devaluation of asylum seekers' personal testimonies within the political asylum process in France, arguing that the diagnostic category of post-traumatic stress disorder (PTSD) may mark "an end to suspicion" and a medical certificate attesting to an asylum seeker's PTSD may constitute "proof" of persecution (2009, 77; see also Fassin and d'Halluin 2005, 2007).

Yet, perhaps reflecting the "PTSD fatigue" the CHR staff member noted, ultimately some asylum officers were ambivalent about psychological evaluations. For example, one asylum officer acknowledged that applicants have often endured horrendous acts of violence and suffering, but she nonetheless voiced skepticism surrounding psychiatric diagnoses. "It seems like everybody says they have PTSD and depression," she told me with a slight sigh. "So, it's kind of like 'meh,' you don't know what's real, what isn't." Other officers told me that though they did not deny the possibility of psychiatric disorders, they feared that applicants might deploy a PTSD diagnosis to paper over aspects of their testimony that were vague or inconsistent, as a kind of *post hoc* rationale for credibility lapses. Thus, although the frequency with which asylum seekers exhibit symptoms of PTSD, depression, and anxiety is well established in the psychological literature (Hall and Olff 2016), in practice the perceived ubiquity of such diagnoses may actually lessen the import of these categories within the asylum interview. For asylum claimants, there was also the risk that a submitted psychological evaluation could be a source of inconsistencies and thus used to weaken or even disprove credibility, as the following case illustrates.

Daniel

Daniel, whom I first met in 2010, was a twenty-year-old asylum seeker from Liberia. Daniel had grown up in Monrovia, where he and his three sisters were raised by a single mother. Daniel had a close relationship with his mother and sisters, a bond that grew closer as they spent more and more time inside their home during the second civil war that began in 1999. His mother made ends meet working as a secretary and earning extra money on the side as a part-time seamstress out of the family home. The family had been increasingly concerned about being victimized by the Taylor regime, which had been violently targeting people sharing their ethnicity, Krahn. In 2003, when he was months shy of his thirteenth birthday, these fears were realized. Soldiers raided his family's home. He was forced into a closet, and alone in the dark could hear a chaotic and terrifying scene unfolding throughout the house. After the screams of his family, the booming voices of soldiers, and the harrowing sounds of gunshots finally gave way to silence, Daniel emerged from the closet to find his mother's and sisters' lifeless bodies, draped haphazardly in sheets and curtains that had been pulled down from the windows. Utterly horrified, Daniel ran to the house of a neighbor. The neighbor, too scared for Daniel to stay with her for long, arranged for him to accompany a family member of hers who was planning to travel to Senegal. Once in Senegal, Daniel was left on his own and forced to fend for himself for the next five years. "I just felt trapped there because there was no one to take care of me but I wasn't able to go back to Liberia. So, I just survived." Daniel lived in a makeshift shelter on the beach that he shared with other homeless adolescents like himself. He and the others survived by working odd jobs and finding temporary work in hotels that catered to tourists. Yet, as Daniel told me, "life there was so hard." He was routinely arrested and abused by the police.

In 2007, Daniel was approached by an American missionary, who, after hearing Daniel's story, secured a falsified passport, travel documents, and a plane ticket for Daniel. He first arrived with this American missionary family at their home in Nebraska but soon found his way to Minnesota, taking the advice of a friend on Facebook. When I first met Daniel, he had been in Minnesota for over a year. He had been living in a homeless shelter since his arrival and, after having a Liberian acquaintance help him file an asylum claim, he had been referred to an immigration judge following an unsuccessful USCIS asylum interview. A case worker at the homeless shelter where he was staying had introduced him to CHR, which was assisting him with his asylum case.

Daniel had his asylum hearing in immigration court in 2010. I was present, along with Lisa, a case worker from the shelter who had become Daniel's close confidant and ally. Daniel testified, consistent with his prepared written statement, that soldiers forced him into a closet while his family members were murdered in the main room of the house. A mental health clinic had prepared a psychiatric evaluation which was submitted with his application, with the intent of supporting Daniel's credibility and adding weight to his claim of persecution. The evaluation outlined Daniel's high levels of PTSD. The rest of the psychiatric evaluation was largely consistent with Daniel's asylum testimony except for one seemingly small detail. In the clinic's evaluation, the psychologist had written that Daniel claimed he "hid" in the closet, rather than was forced into the closet. In court, the immigration judge quite pointedly pressed Daniel on this issue. "[The psychological evaluation] says that you hid," the IJ said to Daniel. "But you are saying that you were forced into the closet. Which is it?" he demanded. Daniel, reacting to the judge's abruptness, shifted uneasily on the witness stand, and insisted that he was forced into the closet and that clinician must have written down the wrong information.

Daniel's psychiatric evaluation also noted that Daniel had been detained and beaten in Senegal, and thus labeled Daniel as a "victim of torture." Daniel had not mentioned this in his written or oral asylum testimony, though he did not deny it when the IJ raised the issue in court. Again, he was pressed by the judge. "Why didn't you tell me that? Why wasn't that in your application?" he asked Daniel sternly. "I don't know," Daniel responded, in a shaky voice. Daniel was visibly upset after the hearing. His lawyer had tried to assure him that the IJ might still grant him asylum despite his terse demeanor. They would just have to wait until the IJ issued his decision, the timeline of which was not clear. Daniel told me and Lisa that he didn't bring up his detention in Senegal to his lawyers because they never asked about it. "They only asked me questions about Liberia, about what happened to me there." Daniel didn't think that this incident was pertinent to his claim of persecution in Liberia, and his lawyer had made clear that the points Daniel should focus on centered around his ethnic identity as a target of persecution in Liberia. Yet applicants' omissions of information in a legal context are often interpreted as deliberate withholding of information or even lying. The IJ used the information that the psychiatric evaluation revealed about the abuse Daniel endured in Senegal as evidence that he was withholding information, thus impugning Daniel's credibility. But this was not the only instance in Daniel's hearing when elements of his story were challenged in painful and dehumanizing ways.

Before being questioned about his omission of his abuse in Senegal, Daniel had to testify about what happened in Liberia. Lisa and I looked on as Daniel, slightly hunched in an oversized suit on the brightly lit witness stand, choked back tears while recounting the details of hearing his family murdered. The DHS attorney stood up for cross-examination and asked Daniel if he had the death certificates of his family members. When Daniel, looking confused, replied that he did not, the DHS attorney proceeded with a line of questioning seemingly aimed at eliciting some sort of proof of his family members' deaths, just as the asylum officer in Patrick's interview had done. He pressed Daniel: "Did you actually see the faces of the bodies under the blankets?" "How did you know they were the bodies of your family?" Daniel struggled to explain that they were the only ones in the house prior to soldiers entering. "Who else would be under them [blankets]?" Daniel retorted. Daniel reiterated, "I saw their hands and legs sticking out. It was my family." The DHS attorney nodded. "But no faces?" he asked again. Daniel, completely bewildered at this point, weakly uttered "no," confirming that he, a twelve-year old boy at the time, had not lifted up the blood-soaked cloth to look at the faces of his murdered mother and sisters. The DHS attorney ended this line of questioning by asking Daniel if he had ever attempted to get a death certificate for his mother or other family members. "No," Daniel said. As Daniel began to say something more, the DHS attorney turned to the IJ: "I have no further questions."

Like Patrick, Daniel experienced the adjudicator's skepticism of his family's murder as an assault on his dignity. "It just hurt me so much," Daniel reflected, when I asked him how he felt about the DHS attorney's questioning. "I mean, why would I lie about that?" For Daniel, the loss of his mother and sisters had been a profound existential rupture. His embodied grief was his continuous evidence of their deaths. Yet, even though asylum can be granted on testimony alone, the DHS attorney made clear that without some sort of external "proof," Daniel's claim remained suspect. While the DHS attorney's request for a death certificate fits a (purportedly amoral/apolitical) bureaucratic logic in which putatively "objective" data are used to corroborate "subjective" personal testimony, its effect is emotionally wounding.

It was not just that the request for a death certificate constituted a moral indignity, but, as Daniel stressed to me, it was also unreasonable. "He [the DHS attorney] shouldn't have asked me that question, 'why didn't I have a death certificate?' Why would he ask that? I guess he wanted proof. But Africans don't know about that. No one knows about death certificates. They don't even have birth certificates unless they're traveling. Most of them don't even know their ages."

CORROBORATING ONE'S STORY: EVIDENCE AND DOCUMENTATION

Though academic and policy literature points to the difficulties and risks inherent in procuring corroborating documentation, as well as the cultural differences in the issuance of documentation (see Bohmer and Shuman 2018, 39), it was striking how often I observed or heard about requests for such corroborating evidence. Corroborating evidence refers here to a variety of external documentation that may be used to support an asylum claimant's testimony. This includes not only death and birth certifications, but documents such as political membership cards, affidavits from witnesses attesting to the applicant's persecution, police records and arrest warrants, as well as the psychiatric/psychological evaluations discussed above. Adjudicators engage with these forms of documentation to "produce and reinforce hierarchies between what is 'knowable' and what is not" (Merry and Coutin 2014, 1). And though external documentation and evidence supporting asylum seekers' testimonies were not legally required, almost without exception every lawyer and advocate I talked to stressed that, in practice, it is hard, if not impossible, to win your asylum case without it.

The REAL ID Act of 2005 made changes to documentation requirements; section 101(a)(3) allows adjudicators to require that asylum applicants submit corroborating evidence for otherwise credible testimony if the judge decides that such evidence can be "reasonably obtained." A key issue here—unaddressed by the Act itself—is what constitutes "reasonably obtainable." Indeed, legal scholars have pointed to the fact that discerning what kind of evidence can be reasonably obtained is subjective and open to abuse by adjudicators (Cianciarulo 2006). Daniel's accurate assessment of the impossibility of obtaining death certificates for his family, then, would be rendered moot in the face of a judge's request for such evidence. Several attorneys told me that they frequently deal with what they view as judges' unreasonable requests for documentation from asylum claimants.

The demand for documentation is even more problematic when we consider the ambivalence with which adjudicators themselves approached documentation. When I first asked asylum officers about corroborating evidence, they endorsed it as a positive element to a case. Yet as our conversations continued, it was clear that the assessment of documents was imbued with paradoxes and gray areas. As one asylum officer explained: "I mean sometimes the more documents you have the less likely it might be to believe a story. Like, if someone says that the militia came and set fire to her house but then you have all these documents, I'm going to think 'Well, how'd you get these documents if your house was on fire?'" Documents and other kinds of material evidence may be requested by adjudicators, and yet that same evidence may then be viewed as suspect.

Suspicion of documents can be acutely problematic given the circulation of false documents that proliferates in the migration industry. Gregory, an asylum officer with three years at USCIS, explained how the known existence of fraudulent documents in certain countries complicates his ability to assess their validity. "It's more challenging to be from a country where fake documents are readily accessible because you just can't believe them," he pronounced. "And they might have perfectly nice documents but we're going to be like 'yeah, but you're from Cameroon.' You know. It's more suspect. So, I think they have a harder time proving their case." Notably, Gregory did not frame this as a problem for *himself*, as an asylum officer, but rather for the asylum applicants from Cameroon—*they* will have a harder time communicating their legitimacy because of the larger political landscape in which the circulation of fraudulent documents is embedded.

Indeed, it was my Cameroonian friends who were often targets of adjudicators' suspicion about documents. Eric, whose case took almost six years to be fully adjudicated, ran into difficulties when the DHS attorney questioned the validity of his SCNC membership card, which was submitted as supporting evidence. As the request of DHS, Eric's case, like Louise's, was put on hold while the government conducted an overseas investigation to verify Eric's membership card. After nearly thirteen months, during which Eric was placed on an ankle monitoring bracelet for a second time, the DHS team concluded that the authenticity of Eric's card could be neither proven nor disproven since, the report indicated, "fraudulent membership cards are easily manufactured and sold throughout Cameroon." Eric, who found the purported need for an investigation ridiculous, let out an embittered laugh when telling me about the DHS report. "Well, thank you very much, I could have told you that! Without two years overseas investigation," Eric said sarcastically. He added, no longer laughing, "So, I'm being punished because my country is corrupt? That doesn't make any sense. That is why I'm here in the first place!" Though Eric was, in fact, eventually denied asylum, in her written decision, the IJ did not cite the DHS report. Though it did not work to ultimately discredit (or support) Eric's testimony, it did result in almost two years of additional waiting.

Photographs emerged as an especially fraught object of suspicion among my Cameroonian interlocutors' claims. Ruth's case illustrates the detrimental consequences of this. While I met Ruth after her initial asylum hearing, she granted me access to her files, including the court transcript and the supporting documents. The primary issue in her hearing, and the reason for the IJ's adverse credibility finding, surrounded discrepancies with her SCNC identification card, which the IJ interpreted as altered. The issue date on her SCNC card was several years before she had received the beating to her face that produced a thick scar across her jawline. In the affixed photo, however, her scar was visible. Both the DHS attorney and the IJ pointed to this in their assertion that Ruth had either altered the card or that it was fraudulent. Yet Ruth consistently, in both court records and in her conversations with me, maintained the same explanation. She had originally been issued the card without a photo on it, as many other SCNC members had been. In fact, this was not unusual. As one of my Cameroonian friends explained to me, photos are risky in Cameroon. "Many cards don't have pictures on them," he elaborated, "because that picture identifies you. Pictures connect to a person. They [government] can search for you with pictures, so people will have their membership card and pay their dues, but they will only have their name on it, no picture or birthdate."

However, because Cameroonian asylum claimants had run into trouble without photographs, some advised fellow asylum claimants to affix a photo on the membership card before submitting it as evidence in their asylum case. This is exactly what Ruth did. Because Ruth did not initially see her decision to affix a photo on her SCNC card as problematic, it was only after the DHS attorney brought it up that she offered an explanation. Because Ruth's SCNC card was deemed to be altered or possibly fraudulent, the IJ argued that "this consequently casts doubt on the whole of her testimony." The IJ also cited the fact that Ruth offered only a *post hoc* rationale for the affixed photo, thus making her doubly lacking in credibility. This was the case even though Ruth's attorneys submitted additional forms of proof attesting to her SCNC membership, including receipts for paid dues and a letter from the leader of her local SCNC party. Ruth was baffled and outraged at this:

> What has a picture got to do with the whole case!? Because it seems very unfair because the judge says that you took a new picture and put it on an old card. And so, you are refusing all what I have been through and hang the whole case on this card just because I put a new picture on it. It just doesn't make sense. Does that make my medical problems or being in prison a fraud

or lies? They didn't say I'm inconsistent. All the problems that I laid out that made me leave my county, none of those things were found to be a problem. Then why can't they give me asylum? So, it's just the picture. But what importance is that picture to all of the persecution that I've gone through!?

The staggering disconnection between Ruth's logic and the bureaucratic logic of adjudication has multiple layers here. First, the adjudicators failed to consider the shifting and contextual meaning of a photograph. In Cameroon, a photo can be an existential liability, but in US immigration court it represents a form of proof and legitimacy. Second, the punishment of Ruth for not *proactively* explaining that she affixed the photo on the card at a later date only makes sense if such a move is understood to be problematic in the first place. That is, because Ruth did not see this as an "alteration of evidence," but, ironically, a way of strengthening the validity of the card, it was not in her purview to offer an explanation upfront. And finally, what Ruth came to understand, in hindsight, as a singular misstep—the act of adding a photo to her membership card—was extrapolated by adjudicating bodies to produce Ruth as wholly lacking in credibility, to cast doubt not just on this piece of paper but on Ruth as a legitimate asylum claimant.

WHEN CREDIBILITY IS NOT THE ISSUE

This chapter has thus far concentrated on the suspicion and delegitimating of asylum claimants' stories based on their perceived lack of credibility. However, some of my interlocutors were denied asylum not for lack of credibility but because adjudicators found that their cases did not meet the necessary criteria for asylum status. The case of Miriam demonstrates that forms of epistemic violence within the asylum system are not only related to denials of credibility.

Miriam was an asylum claimant from Kenya who had been targeted by the Kenyan government for her HIV/AIDS activism. She had waited over two years to have her hearing in immigration court. When the hearing finally arrived, she was relieved. Miriam thought her hearing went well and even her volunteer lawyer, a corporate law attorney who was new to *pro bono* work for CHR, went out of his way to assure Miriam that he thoroughly expected her to be granted asylum. After an agonizing six month wait for the IJ's decision, Miriam tore open the decision letter she received in the mail. It was a denial. Sick and panicked, she called her lawyer, who had already received a copy of the letter and was prepared to appeal the decision to the BIA. When I visited Miriam during a return field visit in 2015, her appeal had been submitted and she was, again, waiting anxiously. We sat together in her small, dimly-lit living room over tea as I asked her questions about the hearing. "I'm just really, truly shocked, Bridget," she told me. "And I'm also disgusted at the judge." In Miriam's view, the case was straightforward and her fear of returning to Kenya was clear. "I just really felt in my heart that I was going to get asylum, you know. I had given her [the IJ] all the facts. What else does she need from me!?"

In her testimony, Miriam had detailed years of verbal abuse, insults, and threats against her life from both civilians and government officials in Kenya. She had also been accosted and severely beaten one evening while doing outreach and advocacy work in a rural area surrounding Nairobi. When she went to the police, instead of taking her criminal report, they detained Miriam without food and without access to her HIV medication for days. She was verbally and physically abused by police while in prison, ridiculed and spit upon because of her HIV status. Without her medication and not knowing how long she would be detained, Miriam feared for her health and, ultimately, her life. When she left prison, she fled to her sister's home where she stayed for months, afraid to go out for fear of more abuse or imprisonment. She was finally able to secure a temporary visa and a plane ticket to the United States with the help of her family, who urged her to flee the country.

According to the IJ's written decision, which Miriam watched me read and then had me read again, Miriam's testimony was credible, but the IJ determined that Miriam had failed to establish that she had been persecuted or that she demonstrated a well-founded fear of future persecution. I read the IJ's words aloud: "brief periods of detention, ethnic conflict, or isolated violence do not necessarily constitute persecution." Miriam swatted the paper. "What is persecution to her then!?" Miriam cried. "What is being locked up without food and medication? Does she not know what being beaten means!?" The IJ also suggested that internal relocation—

moving to another location within Kenya—would be possible, a suggestion that Miriam adamantly refuted. To this end, Miriam showed me a newspaper article that her lawyers had submitted as evidence with the asylum application, arguing that 80 to 90 percent of persons with HIV are abused in the areas throughout the country. The IJ also suggested that Miriam could have gone to the Kenyan government with her complaints, emphasizing that the police should not be considered government agents. Miriam countered this: "well, she has most certainly never been to my country because they [police] absolutely are [government agents]!"

A large part of Miriam's frustration and disgust concerned what she saw as the IJ's over-reliance on external documents in discerning whether Miriam's claims of persecution and fear of further persecution were "objectively reasonable" in the eyes of the law. The IJ and the DHS attorney, throughout the hearing and in the IJ's written decision, referred to country conditions reports, especially US State Department reports, as evidence that contradicted the concerns or fears that Miriam expressed. For example, the IJ indicated that country conditions reports indicated that there were laws protecting HIV-positive individuals in Kenya from abuse. Yet this putatively objective evidence was at direct odds with Miriam's experiential knowledge. "Well, then, they need better research," Miriam exclaimed to me. "She needs to research [about Kenya] to see how it really is, to really come up with the truth, to see that the laws are not enforced. The judge says that there are laws to protect, but she doesn't know that nothing is enforced . . . Laws are on paper only; they don't have any meaning there." The DHS attorney arguing the case against Miriam had also seemed to rely on a notion of what Miriam identified as "laws on paper." He had emphasized to the IJ that there were no police records to corroborate Miriam's testimony that she had been targeted and abused because of her HIV status and activism or that she had been arrested and detained. Miriam found this incredible, as she had stated all along that in the past police had failed to file any of her grievances and that during the time she was detained the police were the actual perpetrators of her abuse. "So why would they ever report that!?" Miriam wondered to me, eyes wide, shaking her head in dismay.

The reliance on country of origin information (COI) or country conditions reports was not unique to the judge presiding over Miriam's case. All of the asylum officers I interviewed stressed the importance of country conditions research, particularly US State Department reports, for testing, establishing, or refuting an applicant's credibility or eligibility. While the use of resources such as State Department reports on country conditions could be seen as a way to triangulate data, officers instead framed this as the need to affirm or negate a claimant's *subjective* testimony of suffering and persecution with a putatively *objective* source (see Lawrance 2019). Moreover, legal scholarship has pointed to the "wildly varying degrees of deference" given to State Department country reports by immigration judges (Walker 2007, 4; Miller, Keith, and Holmes 2015). Critics of the overuse of State Department reports argue that these reports have been problematically used "as dispositive rejections of the asylum applicant's admittedly credible personal testimony" (Walker 2007, 4; see also Schuster 2018; van der Kist and Rossett 2020).

As Miriam and I wrapped up our conversation, the day had given way to dusk. Miriam stared down at the two sets of documents on the table in front of us. One was the IJ's written decision letter, spelling out her denial. The other document was Miriam's personal testimony, in which she had written, in much detail, about her experiences of struggle as a HIV-positive person in Kenya, the police abuse she had endured, the fear she felt for her life. "This," Miriam said, picking up the judge's decision and waving it in the air, "this is denial. This is the judge's words forced into my mouth." She tossed it on the table disdainfully and then smoothed out her written testimony on her lap: "But this," she said softly, "this is *my* experience. This is the truth." I nodded, acknowledging these two disparate renderings of Miriam's story. Miriam's gesture and words exposed the epistemic violence of the asylum process, in which "officials possess all the textual resources to impose their version of events as the legitimate one" (Jacquemet 2009, 277).

But the judge's version made no sense to Miriam. "Why would I come and sit here with this dirty carpet, in this dark room, and I can't see my daughter or my granddaughter, why would I be here if I was free in Kenya?" Miriam asked. It was a question that captured the deep divisions between asylum seekers' conceptions of themselves as deserving refugees and the institutional logic that requires that "deservingness" be performed and proved in ways that are often experienced as punitive, arbitrary, or simply confusing or illogical to applicants. For Miriam her presence in that dim and musty living room outside of St. Paul, Minnesota was a testament to her legitimate need for protection. She emphasized the sacrifices she had made and the violence she had endured in search of legal protection—the anguish of limbo and family separation, economic precarity, social isolation. For Miriam, and my other interlocutors, this served as an irrefutable form of evidence of their legitimacy as deserving subjects.

ASYLUM DENIAL AS MORAL ASSAULT

The consequences of having a figure of authority cast doubt on and delegitimate your story and/or deem your fear or experiences of violence as not enough to warrant protection go beyond the material and legal. A denial of asylum takes a tremendous emotional and psychological toll on asylum claimants. A denial due to a lack of perceived credibility was uniquely wounding. Thinking back to Patrick's response to the asylum officer's doubt over his father's death, we can see how this mistrust of Patrick's testimony was bruising not only because it meant he was not granted asylum, but because of the moral assault it entailed. This was something I noted again and again. When Solange, a Cameroonian asylum claimant, received the IJ's decision that she was denied based on a lack of credibility, stemming from inconsistencies on the details surrounding her rape, she was devastated:

> It's hard for me to understand why she said that, that she didn't believe me. I don't know why she said that. I don't know—why would she say something like that? I would have been ten times happier if she just said 'I'm not going to grant you asylum.' You know, I'll take that, you know. Okay, you don't want to grant me asylum. Tell me no, but to give me a reason that, that breaks my heart, my soul. You know that just really deepens my wounds.

Striking here is how much Solange's initial reaction to her denial was not focused on the consequences of the denial—a removal order—but rather on the painful reason for the denial. Hassan, after his initial denial, mused aloud to me about what he would like to say to the judge:

I want to be like, 'You know what? You're a human being. How can you do this to another human being? God has given you a job that can destroy life, [or] you can make life. Your decisions are not just decisions. Your decisions are making life for other people. Your words that come out of your mouth can make a huge impact on somebody's life. And why are you just sitting there saying deny, deny, deny.

Reflected in these narratives is the awesome disparity of power within the asylum adjudication system. We see the making and unmaking of people's lives in the judge's refusal to legitimate Miriam's "truth" or in the heart-breaking mistrust of Solange's experience of sexual assault. Hassan was searching for a way to understand how asylum adjudicators make sense of the fact that they may make a wrong decision that could have severe consequences for an asylum seeker. I had, in fact, explored this very question with the asylum officers I interviewed.

"TWO BITES OF THE APPLE"

As my conversation with Bruce, a senior asylum officer, was wrapping up, I asked him if he ever worried about making a wrong decision by not granting asylum to someone who was truly in need of protection. And did he ever wonder, I asked him, if he found an applicant lacking in credibility when they had really been telling the truth? Bruce paused, then told me, "You know, I've come to realize that I don't really know. Bottom line, I don't *really* know. I believe I'm a perceptive person and I'm intuitive but, you know, I can't read a person's mind. . . . I'm not infallible. So, I live with it." Bruce was not alone in concluding that decision-making in asylum cases was, ultimately, indeterminate. Asylum officers often conceded, either explicitly or implicitly, that adjudication, in general, and credibility determinations, in particular, were fluid, subjective, and open to interpretive error, despite their attempts to make it as "objective" a process as possible.

Over the course of interviews, asylum officers would often concede that ultimately adjudication relies on one's "gut," as several officers told me, or is ultimately "always a judgment call," as another framed it. And yet, this subjective core is elided by asylum officers' simultaneous insistence that "objective" evidence is brought to bear on elements deemed "too subjective" (affective displays, psychological affidavits, and so on). The cruel irony here is that while the emotions of asylum seekers are often deemed too subjective—and, hence, suspect—to be counted as evidence, it is ultimately often the emotions of asylum officers that serve as a technology of constructing the "truth" about an asylum applicant. As Kobelinsky (2015) notes, asylum adjudicators use emotion both to dispel and create suspicion. Asylum officers' use of their "gut" or their intuition is problematic in that such modes of apprehending claims represent "hidden practices of decision-making that remain beyond scrutiny" (Puumula, Ylikomi, and Ristimäki 2017, 16). Moreover, the routinization of such hidden practices (e.g., the use of one's intuition or the reading of non-verbal cues) ensures that over time these practices gain legitimacy and are uncritically viewed as part of professional knowledge (Jubany 2017; Puumula, Ylikomi, and Ristimäki 2017).

So how do asylum officers like Bruce "live with it?" Given the impossibility of certainty when evaluating stories of others' pain and suffering, how do asylum officers subjectively and intersubjectively mediate the demands of their position? Asylum officers readily owned their decisions to grant asylum, especially to those whom they deemed to be what they often described as "genuinely deserving." They told me that part of their job as an asylum officer included "saving somebody's life" or "helping somebody in a very real sense." However, asylum officers would often distance themselves from cases that they denied or referred, thus demonstrating an ambivalent relationship to their own authority and power. A refrain I heard repeated from almost all the asylum officers was that claimants get "two bites of the apple." They were referring to the fact that most asylum seekers can have their case heard by an immigration judge if an asylum officer denies them. Asylum officers' emphasis on the "two bites of the apple" defense undermines their own authority as decision-makers by highlighting immigration judges as the definitive arbiters of asylum claims, and allows these officers to avoid taking the ultimate responsibility for denying someone asylum. In their examination of European asylum regimes, Eule et al. (2019) identify a similar pattern, what they term "passing the buck of responsibility" among institutional actors. As they note, the numerous persons and institutions involved in asylum determination create a situation in which "nobody feels either legally or personally responsible for legal outcomes" (207).

When I asked Rita, an asylum officer who was a returned Peace Corps volunteer, how she dealt with telling applicants that she was not going to grant them asylum, she said, "It's really hard sometimes." She described situations in which this was emotionally difficult for her: "Sometimes, they [applicants] beg. They're begging you, 'please, please.' I want to be like 'I'm not the queen,' you know, I have to follow the rules and whatever. It's not *me* giving it to you. It's *you* qualifying.'" Senior asylum officer Anthony likewise distanced himself from responsibility for the consequences of an asylum decision, though slightly differently than Rita.

> A lot of times I'll tell the new officers when they get here it's like you have to be able to divorce yourself if you want to be able to sleep at night. You make a decision. The best decision you can based on the information you have at hand. And you let it lie. You know, our job is to try to help the people. But we're not the ones who are harming them. . . . They still have the burden to make their case. And if we decide against them . . . alright, you can't sit there and second-guess yourself that they're going to be deported and go back and be killed. Because certainly that may happen. But you're still not the one killing them. Somebody else is.

Both Rita and Anthony engaged the implicit framework of asylum as service or benefit and emphasized that the burden is on asylum claimants to prove their case. This effectively shifts responsibility of a denial from adjudicators to claimants. Moreover, the legal framework of asylum that places the burden of proof on the asylum claimant facilitates asylum officers' moral distancing (Gill 2016), serving to divorce asylum officers from the visceral pain of asylum claimants and the powerful impact that their decisions have on claimants' lives. As Gill (2016) importantly notes, moral distancing can occur regardless of geographic proximity. Indeed, "the very unequal power relations of the hearing setting structure the transmission of the refugee stories in a way that often prevents an emotional encounter between decision makers and refugees" (Rousseau and Foxen 2010, 70). A denial of asylum, in Rita's narrative, is a result of asylum claimants' performance, not the adjudicator's interpretation. In Anthony's reckoning of the potential harm that may befall an asylum seeker who is denied and expelled, the fault is not with the adjudicators whose asylum denial results in deportation, but with the perpetrators who were the impetus for asylum seekers to flee in the first place.

On a final note, worth consideration is the role of "vicarious traumatization," a process parallel to countertransference in the therapeutic setting, where denial of refugees' testimonies is one response (Rousseau et al. 2002). As Rousseau and colleagues (2002) have argued in the Canadian context, adjudicators' vicarious traumatization in turn contributes to a collective "culture of disbelief" in which refugee claimants are denied at high rates because of a perceived lack of credibility. Ultimately, asylum officers' emotional and moral distancing may help them to accept the decisions they make about other people's lives amidst ever-present indeterminacy—it helps them to "live with it." Yet this, too, is part of the power of the adjudicatory gaze. Asylum claimants must also "live with" adjudicators' decisions, but in ways that are vastly different and often profoundly injurious—from further protracted waiting, family separation, and social-structural precarity to deportation and the threat of further harm or death.

5 The Aftermaths of Asylum Decisions

I had been keeping in touch by phone with Eric, who had, in legal termi-nology, "voluntarily departed" from the United States after the BIA upheld the decision to deny his asylum application. As specified in the Immigration and Nationality Act and its subsequent amendments, voluntary depar-ture, if "granted" to a migrant by the government, allows them to leave the United States of their own accord and at their own expense rather than be physically removed by a DHS agent to their country of citizenship. Legally speaking, voluntary departure is considered a form of relief *from* forced removal, or deportation. Yet, for most of my asylum seeker friends, it was experienced as an act *of* removal—an issue I return to shortly. The process of voluntary departure requires asylum seekers to return to their country of citizenship, but Eric knew that he and his family would not feel safe enough to stay in Cameroon. While still in Minnesota, Eric had been vir-tually introduced to a Nigerian pastor who had moved to the United Arab Emirates (UAE) to start a small church and school and extended an offer to Eric and his family to join him after they left the United States.

Before leaving the United States, Eric made plans to take himself, his wife, Victorine, and their two children immediately to Nigeria upon land-ing in Douala, Cameroon. After a two-day car trip, they arrived in Nigeria, where they stayed with Victorine's cousin for a few months. From there, Eric and his family moved to the UAE. For about the first six months after he arrived, Eric and I briefly talked every month or so. Sometimes during our phone chats, Eric would talk about his bitterness and sense of injustice about his asylum denial, or his ongoing concerns about the oppression of Anglophone Cameroonians. Other times, our conversations were lighter, and we'd talk about music and current events, or swap stories of our children's mischief and accomplishments.

On the phone one evening, Eric described the struggle he and his family were having settling into life in the UAE. Eric had been working part-time at the pastor's school, mostly doing afterschool programming. Victorine had not found work, and although the pastor rented them an apartment attached to the church at a modest rate, they were struggling to financially support themselves. He was also sending money to family in Cameroon. Eric had convinced Victorine to send their two children back to Cameroon to live with relatives until they could become more financially secure. Though Victorine had reluctantly agreed to this arrangement, she found the absence of her children too much to bear during the two months they were separated. "She doesn't like it here [in the UAE] and then when they went away, she started to have a mental breakdown, just crying all the time," Eric described to me. "So, we brought them back, and she's better but things are not easy here. It's like we're now starting all over again here. I just really hoped things would have ended differently [in the United States]." During our conversation that evening, I mentioned that I was continuing to work with asylum seekers and that I knew many who, like him, had been denied and removed from the country. Eric, too, knew many whose asylum claims were rejected, often after being in the United States for years. Eric speculated that perhaps what my research had been documenting all along was the "false hope" that the United States offers to asylum seekers. He hung up before I could press him on what he meant. But it resonated with me, as I had been grappling with how to understand hope—as well as despair—in this context. And I've returned to this concept of "false hope," or some version of it, myself over the years.

Throughout my years of research with asylum seekers, I have accompanied my friends on an array of journeys through the asylum process. These journeys have had disparate outcomes, with my interlocutors produced by the process as excludable or includable subjects. In legal terms, the adjudication of claims ends with a granting of asylum, voluntary departure, or deportation. The experience of each of these categories, or outcomes, however, are far from monolithic. This chapter traces the various aftermaths of asylum outcomes. I draw most heavily on conversations and interviews I conducted with my interlocutors in 2019, with the aim of understanding their life trajectories after asylum seeking. How, this chapter asks, do asylum seekers engage with and experience new subject positions generated by the asylum regime (asylee, deportee)? To what extent did asylum—the object of my interlocutors' waiting and hope—offer a resolution to their sense of existential limbo? Addressing these questions, I illustrate that the social and emotional effects of the asylum regime's continuum of violence are not bounded by the temporal parameters of the adjudication period. Rather, the experiences of asylum-seeking have consequences that outlast a granting or denial of asylum. I also explore how hope as both an analytic concept and a lived phenomenon shifts over time and place within the lives of my interlocutors, finding my way back to Eric's proposition about "false hope" in the asylum system.

"VOLUNTARY" DEPARTURE?

Asylum claimants facing removal proceedings may request and be "granted" voluntary departure by DHS or an immigration judge. As noted, voluntary departure is considered to be a form of relief from removal and allows a person to leave the United States at his or her own expense without incurring a final, formal removal order ("deportation"). The purported benefits of voluntary departure include not only the opportunity to leave on one's own terms rather than being formally deported but, importantly, also the ability to avoid a ten-year bar on re-entering the United States. Voluntary departure may be granted at the beginning or end of removal proceedings. If voluntary departure is requested from an immigration judge, as was the case among my interlocutors, the IJ has the discretionary power to grant or deny it, based largely on their overall impression of the asylum seeker and the case.[1] If granted by an IJ, an asylum claimant may re-enter after three years if they have been "unlawfully" present in the

United States for less than one year and after ten years if they have been "unlawfully" present for more than one year.[2] The IJ may allow a person up to sixty days to depart and has the authority to order detention as a condition of voluntary departure. In addition to coming up with the requisite money to travel—often a hefty sum for an international flight—those taking voluntary departure are, in most cases, required to post a $500 bond. Thus, my friends who "voluntarily" departed were often overwhelmed by the logistical and financial burdens that such a form of "relief" entailed. Moreover, my interlocutors interpreted and experienced voluntary departure in varied ways, as the cases of Eric and Miriam illustrate.

During the year when Eric's appeal of his asylum denial was pending with the BIA, he would often tell me he had a bad feeling about the outcome. Though Eric's volunteer lawyers told him they were "cautiously optimistic," Eric was familiar with the statistics that reflected a 10 percent success rate for BIA appeals. And though there was the legal option of appealing the BIA's decision to a US Circuit Court of Appeals, this was not something that was often encouraged by CHR staff and volunteers because of the time and money it involved, let alone the even slimmer chances of success at this level. Thus, Eric knew the BIA would be his final step in his long attempt to secure permanent refuge in the United States. He no longer shared his lawyers' sense of optimism, no matter how cautiously tempered. When the BIA, as Eric anticipated, upheld the IJ's decision to deny him asylum, Eric coordinated with his lawyers to request voluntary departure, which DHS granted. He was given two months to leave the country, and was ordered to wear an ankle monitoring bracelet until he left. It was a cruel irony that Eric's (hyper)visibility was now a way for the state to ensure his future *in*visibility, his erasure from its borders.

When I asked Eric how he was feeling about his impending departure, he said he had mixed feelings. He was feeling bruised and tired from his long legal battle and the criminalizing and demoralizing forms of governing to which he had been subjected. He had hoped—even when he started to know it was unlikely—that he would be rightfully given asylum and allowed to live in the United States, a place in which he and his family had already begun settling. "My son, he is a [US] citizen. We have friends here, a neighborhood. I have worked; paid taxes; given my blood, sweat, and tears to this country. For what? For them to say, 'well, forget it, you cannot be here.' They know I cannot go back to my country, that I will die if I go back to Cameroon, but they don't care." If asylum adjudicators, like the ones in the previous chapter, locate the responsibility for a failure to get asylum with the asylum applicant—who is unable to prove their deserv-ingness of protection—Eric rejected this narrative. He interpreted his departure not as a result of his inability to demonstrate his legitimacy to the state, but as the state's failure to justly recognize his legitimacy and need for protection.

In Eric's view, the injustices of the US government did not only subsist in the state's denial of his asylum claim. There was also a violence in the state's abrupt revocation of the life that Eric and his family had developed in the United States. His refuge in the United States had always been ambiguous, contingent, and temporally uncertain. The creeping doubt about a positive outcome of his case, which had increased as Eric contin-ued through the asylum process, helped to temper his disappointment at being denied asylum. On the other hand, uncertainty invites hope. It is precisely because the outcome is uncertain that a positive result—a grant-ing of asylum—remains possible in asylum seekers' imaginations (Eule et al. 2019). Here, hope also worked as a tool of government.

Eric also recognized the fiction of his "voluntary" departure. "They call this *voluntary* departure," Eric said acerbically, "but the choice is not leave or stay. Really, there is no choice at all. It's you-pay-to-leave or we take you across the line ourselves. Either way, I am being told to leave." I asked him why he requested voluntary departure, then. "Because fuck them," Eric replied, "because *I'm* done with *them*." By "them," Eric meant US immi-gration officials collectively. In this way, Eric instilled his departure with a sense of dignity and agency despite the state's constraints, making clear that he was accepting voluntary departure because he had had enough of the injustices and indignities he had endured as an asylum claimant.

Like Eric, Miriam had appealed the IJ's asylum decision to the BIA. Given her outrage at her denial and her volunteer lawyer's confidence in the merits of her case, Miriam held out hope for the BIA to reverse the judge's decision. When, in 2015, she received a letter notifying her of the BIA's decision to uphold the IJ's denial, Miriam felt crushed. "I thought my case was so strong. I really didn't expect that to be the outcome," she told me. When her volunteer lawyer recommended that she request voluntary departure, Miriam initially balked. "I was confused about the term. It sounds so bad, like I'm giving up," she recounted. "So, at first, I really wanted to keep fighting." Her lawyer explained that, unlike deportation, departing "voluntarily" would allow Miriam the possibility of returning to the United States, and that an additional appeal of her case was almost certain to be unsuccessful. "So, I thought about it and then decided that this was really the best option for me," she concluded. What made her departure even harder was the fact that she had started to date someone— a man she met through an online dating site. Although the relationship was only several months old, they had grown quite fond of each other.

Unlike the years spent waiting in a state of uncertainty, feeling the slow passage of time, Miriam was relieved to have two months to prepare for her departure. Whereas for years, she had lamented the excesses of time as an asylum applicant, she was suddenly left longing for more of it. Yet, there was something about the certainty of knowing when she would leave that gave her a small sense of peace, even though she had no specific future plan. "Leaving the US is not at all what I wanted or expected to happen, but at least there is some decision now, and I can move on." Just as Eric had formulated a plan to travel to the United Arab Emirates via Nigeria upon his departure from the United States, Miriam used the time before she left not only to shore up the money for a plane ticket and the $500 voluntary departure fee, but also to coordinate a safety plan for when she returned with her oldest daughter in Kenya. Miriam knew she could not continue her HIV/AIDS activism when she returned to Kenya, and she was likewise fearful of moving back to her hometown. Instead, she resettled with her grown daughter, her son-in-law, and her young granddaughter in another part of the country and lived a quiet life where she kept mostly to her home and small community. "It was a different kind of life, not like the one I was used to before," Miriam described to me in 2019. "I felt scared for a long time, being back there."

While Miriam eventually settled into this new life in Kenya, the necessity of inhabiting a different kind of life there—far from the one she had previously cultivated—speaks to the complexity of the notion of "return." Like other asylum seekers who leave their countries of citizenship, Miriam had fled Kenya because it was no longer a place where she could live securely. She was returning to a place not of safety but of threat. Here, the consequences of the disconnection between US asylum officials' under-standing of Miriam's experience and her own lived reality become evident. The fact that immigration adjudicators decided that Miriam's fear of returning to Kenya was unsubstantiated did nothing to allay her actual fear.

Miriam and the man she had been dating continued to keep in touch for several years while she was in Kenya. He visited twice, and during his second visit, they decided to get married in a small ceremony attended only by Miriam's daughter and son-in-law. A year later, Miriam joined her new husband in the United States. Talking to Miriam in 2019, I noted how much happier she sounded than when we had first met so many years ago. She recognized the contrast, too. "When I think back to that time [asylum seeking]," Miriam recalled, "it was just a very dark time for me. I was so lonely, so isolated. I didn't know where I was going. It was hard to have your mind straight." Then she added, "But things started to change toward the end, after I met [her now-husband]. So, now I often think, maybe that's the whole reason I was in Minnesota. Why God brought me there. To meet him." If Miriam's return to Kenya required her to live in her country of citizenship in a different way, she also returned to the United States with a transformed subjectivity. "I think I emerged from the whole [asylum] process as a better person in the end. I know my rights now. I am someone who knows my legal rights here [in the United States]."

For my interlocutors, the resolution of an asylum claim prompted a re-evaluation and reinterpretation of the years embedded within the asylum system. Time spent within the US asylum regime provided a space of tem-porary safety, removed from the existential dangers in the countries they fled, even for those denied asylum in the end. Yet, many asylum seekers recognize that the years spent on what would ultimately be a failed attempt to gain asylum could also foment risk. The (hyper)visibility of asylum applicants means that if they are denied asylum, the ability to then live clandestinely can be difficult (see Ordoñez 2008). Asylum seeking can be risky, as so many of my Cameroonian friends emphasized, because the governments of asylum claimants' home countries interpret asylum-seek-ing in the United States—which, by definition implicates their country of origin as being unable or unwilling to protect them—as acts of hostility, if not treason. This was particularly the case for asylum seekers whose claims were based on political opinion or activism that opposed ruling governments. For example, Eric knew that if he were to return to Cameroon, his status as someone who had fled and sought safety in the United States would, as he told me, "Put a target on my back."

Yet, even if not experienced as a "choice," asylum seekers made the legal category of voluntary departure meaningful. Though immensely powerful at structuring the material, structural, and geographic contours of present and future life for asylum seekers, the labels and identities produced by the asylum regime were not always internalized by asylum claimants, at least not always in the ways that the regime intended. For Miriam and Eric, an asylum denial set in motion the need for alternative visions for their futures—ones that were counter to what they had initially hoped for. Yet, it did not alter their subjective sense of fear, their assertion of need for protection, and their sense of deservingness. Though they were subjected to the conditions of being labeled a failed asylum seeker, my interlocutors refused to subjectively identify with this label.

Eric and Miriam came to understand and experience voluntary departure in disparate ways, especially as it related to the possibility of returning to the United States. Importantly, for Eric, the possibility of return meant he was able to assert his *refusal* to do so. Even when I talked to Eric years after his arrival in the UAE, when he and his family had begun to feel more settled and financially secure, and even though he had a US-citizen son, he was adamant he would never return to the United States. "How I was treated, I will never set foot in that country again," he repeatedly told me. Of course, it's impossible to say with certainty that Eric and his family will never attempt to find refuge in the United States again. Yet, this is beside the point. His disavowal of the option to return acts as an important form of critique, highlighting the "social and moral aspects of refusal" (McGranahan 2018, 370; see also El-Shaarawi 2021). Eric's refusal calls attention to his sense of injustice and the racialized forms of violence he was subjected to as an asylum seeker. His refusal of the possibility of return is also an example of what Sarah Willen (2019) eloquently terms "dignity in motion," an act of "dignity pursued, safeguarded, recuperated, reclaimed" (17).

In contrast, Miriam, though she initially resisted the idea of voluntary departure, eventually embraced the possibility of return that this form of "relief" entailed. While Miriam did, like Eric, feel a sense of injustice and anger about her denial of asylum, return, and not its disavowal, became an act of refusal. In returning to the United States, Miriam refused to be constructed as an excludable subject. She returned not as a "failed asylum seeker," but rather as a person "who knows my rights." In this way, the legal consciousness that Miriam developed as an asylum seeker allowed her to engage with the law creatively and meaningfully in ways that recuperated both her sense of dignity and her ability to envision a good life.

DEPORTATION: "THEN THEY SHOULD JUST PUT ME IN A BODY BAG"

Except for Ruth, all my interlocutors whose claims were denied eventually left via voluntary departure. It is notable, however, that many asylum claimants often colloquially refer to voluntary departure—their own or others'—as "deportation." The conflation of these categories underscores how much the expulsion of asylum claimants via their "voluntary" departure is interpreted and experienced as a form of violence. Ruth had appealed her case to the Circuit Court of Appeals, which meant she gave up any right to voluntary departure. Thus, when the circuit court issued its decision to uphold her asylum denial, she was issued a final removal order, or an order of deportation. Because Ruth had been wearing an ankle monitor while awaiting the appeal results, a CHR staff member told her it was unlikely she would be detained prior to deportation. Yet, another attorney who I took Ruth to see counseled Ruth that she should expect to be detained before being deported. Complicating Ruth's case was the fact that she had no Cameroonian passport (and thus no passport at all) and the Cameroonian embassy had refused to issue her a new one when US immigration officials requested it. So even though Ruth's deportation was certain, the timing and procedural aspects of it were unknown. Time, for Ruth, was no longer "sticky" but instead "frenzied" (Griffiths 2014, 1994), as the acceleration of time became a tool of governance (Rozakou 2020). The institutional logic behind governing through uncertainty and surveillance for deportees-in-waiting is that they may be a flight risk, finding ways to evade the state's gaze and remain within its borders. But, in the months leading up to Ruth's deportation, she was nearly immobilized with fear. I could not reconcile the government's positioning her as a "flight risk" with how frail and financially destitute she had become. The looming uncertainty about how and when she would be deported consti- tuted a startling "technology of cruelty" (Aradau and Canzutti 2022).

Ruth was taken into custody by ICE officials when she appeared at one of her regular weekly ISAP appointments. I was not in Minnesota when this happened, but I had talked to her a few days prior. During that con- versation, she talked to me about how much suffering she had been through, first in Cameroon and then as an asylum seeker in the United States. "But this is where I thought my suffering would end, in America." After a moment, she added "What has all this been for? Now I'm cast out, an old woman. I don't even recognize myself." It had taken almost six years for a final determination to be made on her asylum claim. Ruth was pain- fully aware of the creeping passage of time, in which she had become older and the stress of asylum seeking had made her a stranger in her own body. In asking "What has all this been for?," I knew that Ruth was not question- ing her choice to leave Cameroon, as she had consistently stressed to me that she would have been killed if she had stayed. With this question, Ruth was trying to find meaning in the years she had spent seeking refuge in the United States, the years she had spent separated from loved ones, the energy spent appealing her case, the humiliation endured because of the criminalizing tactics of the asylum regime. How, she seemed to be asking, was she to understand her temporary reprieve from the existential threats to which she was now being forced to return—threats that may have mag- nified in her absence?

I later spoke with her several times from the jail where she was taken by ICE agents, some seventy-five miles north of St. Paul, where she stayed for three weeks. Ruth held out hope that the Cameroonian government's refusal to issue her a passport would prevent her deportation, but ICE alerted her that she would be returning to Cameroon without one. During our last phone call from that jail, what would be the night before she was deported, Ruth implored me, "Please, write letters. Tell them that I am a sick, old woman. This isn't supposed to be happening. I've done nothing wrong." "To whom should I write letters? Who is the 'them?'" I asked her. She replied that I should write letters to the United Nations, to President

Obama, to ISAP, to "immigration," to her church. I could write the letters, I told her, but I didn't think it would change anything and I wasn't sure what to write. "Just tell them my story. Tell them the truth," she urged quietly before hanging up.

Days later, I received an alarming email message from Ruth's former volunteer lawyer, with a police report attached, per Ruth's request. The brief police report detailed an incident in which ICE agents had taken Ruth from the jail to the airport, with the intent of deporting her. According to the report, on the plane's jetway, Ruth became "agitated" and "attempted to physically assault" the ICE agent who was there to accompany her on the several flights overseas and across the Cameroon border. Ruth was handcuffed, taken away from the airport and transported to a new jail, about one hundred miles away. I had no way of reaching her so was relieved to get a call from Ruth about a week later. Through the scratchy phone connection of the jail, Ruth told me what happened. Walking on the jetway, she had panicked, her whole body feeling "on fire," and she attempted to return to the airport, feeling like she was having a heart attack. She remembered being thrown face-down onto the ground, in view of a line of people waiting to board the plane. Back in detention, she knew ICE was scheduling her for another flight in the coming days and she was terrified. "I can't go back there, to Cameroon! If they want to take me there, then they should just put me in a body bag. I'm not supposed to be deported, Bridget! I didn't do anything wrong. I'm not at fault. This shouldn't be happening." The line beeped loudly, signaling the end of time, and we eked out teary farewells before the phone cut out.

Several months went by before Ruth contacted me again. Since being deported, Ruth had been living in the capital city, Yaoundé, far from her hometown of Bamenda. A pastor of a church had taken her in and was allowing her to stay with his family in exchange for some light housekeeping. She liked the pastor and his wife but felt like a stranger in the Francophone capital. She was also feeling physically ill. "My whole body is hurting," she told me, her voice audibly weak. Things would only take a more tragic turn. Within a month of being back in Cameroon, her son was murdered outside the family home in Bamenda. Though the Cameroonian government concluded her son was a victim of a robbery and the crime was not politically motivated, Ruth was convinced her son's murder was perpetrated by government-backed military officials, either as a threat to Ruth or as retribution for her return. Ruth was distraught and too frightened to return to Bamenda for the funeral, so she had to mourn the loss of her son alone and from afar.

Over the next year or so, I called Ruth every couple of months to check in on her. She moved with the help of the pastor and his wife and rented a room in an apartment near the church. She had taken up sewing again and between housekeeping and clothing alterations, she was making enough to live. Yet she increasingly complained of a decline in her physical health, including the development of heart disease, which she attributed to the stress of her deportation and the ensuing isolation and fear she experienced as a deportee in Cameroon. Some of her children had come to visit her in Yaoundé since she remained afraid to return to the northwest region of the country, though she pined to go back there. What she seemed to long for the most, however, was an opportunity to return to the United States. Without fail, each time I spoke to her, Ruth asked me if I had written letters to the US government or the UNHCR, or if I might know of a lawyer who might take on her case. I tried, seemingly to no avail, to explain that deportations cannot be reversed and that she had taken her case to the highest level of appeal. But she seemed undeterred by this, only repeatedly responding that her case should not have been denied, that she shouldn't have been deported, and that she is still in danger in Cameroon.

"God Parted the Red Sea"

Ruth had experienced a range of violences as an asylum seeker in the United States, long before her final removal order was issued. The act of deportation itself was marked not only by emotional and psychological violence but also by brute physical violence. Once deported, frightened and isolated from her family and friends, and rejected both by Cameroon and the United States, the country in which she had hoped to find permanent refuge, Ruth became a "disintegrated subject," occupying "a space of legal nonexistence" (Reiter and Coutin 2017, 585).

Yet, despite the crushing effects of removal, Ruth repeatedly reiterated her hope to find a way back to the United States and to be recognized as an asylee. Ruth refused to internalize the asylum regime's construction of her as undeserving or failed. Surely, her desire to be back in the United States was also driven by her experience of Cameroon as one of existential threat. The more she and I talked, however, I began to find Ruth's continued hope to be given legal protection in the United States troubling. During one phone call with Ruth, when I again tried to tell her there was no legal path to overturn her deportation, she replied, "God parted the Red Sea, he will make a path for me, too." She had said this phrase to me before, when she was in Minnesota and preparing her appeal. As I recounted in chapter 2, at the time I interpreted this as an open-ended way of envisioning the future. Other asylum seekers had also suggested abstract desires such as these, which I found "constitute[d] hope for a less precarious future" rather than concrete plans or expectations (Parla 2019, 168). But hearing this from Ruth after her deportation, knowing the finality of this legal move as well as the fact that she lacked any means to travel, her use of this phrase felt charged with a different meaning. Her hope seemed to be singularly focused on a chance at gaining legal protection in the United States. The path that she hoped God would pave, Ruth seemed to now envision as a literal path to the United States. Using the phrase proffered by Eric earlier, I began to wonder if this was a story of false hope.

Whereas I had previously understood Ruth's hope for asylum as a vital strategy of endurance, I began to see this hope as potentially destructive to her well-being. This prompts questions about the fraught nature of hope. When and how might hope or hoping move from a practice of perseverance to an impediment to it? And how might the role and meaning of hope change over time and context? Recent theorizing on hope is instructive here. Georgina Ramsay (2020b) draws on Lauren Berlant's concept of "cruel optimism" to underscore the "destructive potential" of seeking resettlement, given the high probability of failure (110). Berlant (2011) describes cruel optimism as "a relation of attachment to a compromised condition of possibility ... of maintaining an attachment to a problematic object *in advance* of its loss" (21). Given that many asylum seekers do get granted asylum (unlike resettlement, for which far fewer refugees qualify), my argument is not necessarily that asylum itself is a form of cruel optimism. However, given the increased improbability of success at asylum at the BIA or the appellate court level, I would argue that in the case of asylum claimants such as Miriam, Eric, or Ruth, the attachment to a positive asylum outcome may begin to approximate a form of cruel optimism. Yet, the successes of asylum claimants at these levels are not aberrations; these positive outcomes are integral to the institutional maintenance of such attachments. They allow *all* asylum claimants to imagine the possibility, however slight, of obtaining asylum. Though Ruth's optimism or hope may have emerged as false or troubling, it was set in motion by the asylum regime's exploitation of both uncertainty and hope. In this way, then, though the pursuit of asylum on the surface may not be a form of cruel optimism, a belief in the asylum system's representation of itself as equitable, just, and humane does constitute such a form.

Importantly for Berlant (2011), what can make hope or optimism cruel is not only the improbability, if not impossibility, of attaining the desired outcome, but also the ways in which hope can work as "an obstacle to [one's] flourishing" in these contexts (1). While Berlant's conception of cruel optimism is political, as she critically ties optimism to the ethos of capitalism, psychological work on "false hope syndrome" (Polivy and Herman 2002) offers another way of understanding the potential destructiveness of hope. Developed through research on "self-change" programs such as addiction or weight loss treatments, the paradigm of "false hope syndrome" underscores the often damaging cognitive and emotional toll that investment in highly improbable outcomes have for people. In Ruth's case, her persistent attachment to returning and obtaining legal status in the United States was contributing to her declining mental and physical health, as well as her ability to imagine alternative visions of the future. Ultimately, then, hope is not a singular or monolithic concept. As Ayşe Parla (2019), positing an "equivocal approach to hope," argues: "hope has the potential to enable or to disable, to inspire or to obscure, depending on the context, its object, and its justifications" (26).

If hope for a particular outcome or future (gaining asylum status and settling in the United States) helped Miriam and Eric to endure the asylum process, it was the abandonment of this hope that allowed for different ways of confronting the future, even if these alternative visions were originally undesired (Feldman 2016). Though both Eric and Miriam could have chosen to continue their fight for asylum, their decision to leave constituted yet another kind of refusal, beyond their rejection to identify as failed asylum seekers. In proposing different encounters of the future among Palestinian refugees, Ilana Feldman (2016) argues that a "refusal" to engage with a particular vision of the future may be an agentic move whereby refugees "refus[e] to exhaust themselves, to be further depleted in and by their constricted present" (418). A disengagement from the investment in and hope for asylum allowed both Eric and Miriam to begin creating conditions for a new vision of the future, despite their disappointment, anger, and fear at the outcome of the asylum process.

FROM ASYLUM SEEKER TO ASYLEE

But what about those who were granted asylum? Fifteen out of my twenty-six interlocutors were eventually granted asylum, becoming, in legal terminology, asylees. It would be easy to assume that asylee status would symbolize a sense of refuge, an end to a long and painful process of obtaining legal protection. This proved to be more complicated, however. Before examining these complex stories of my asylum-seeking friends who have appeared throughout previous chapters, I want to underscore that being granted asylum did provide an immeasurable sense of relief. That my asylee interlocutors no longer needed to live a "deportable existence" provided a critical sense of existential security (Talavera, Núñez-Mchiri, and Heyman 2010, 167). Yet, more than this, being granted asylum also had important moral implications, as Sharon underscored.

One afternoon in 2011, Sharon called me, jubilant with the news she had just received a letter granting her asylum. I rushed to her apartment and as we embraced, she exclaimed, breathless from relief and excitement: "I feel I am worthy now." "Worthy?" I repeated. "Yes," Sharon continued, "having been granted asylum is having been appreciated." Her smile wide, she nodded slowly and looked around, as if taking in this newfound sense of worthiness. "It is finished. I don't need anything else. This is now the conclusion of all my sorrows and worries. And pains and suffering and everything. Before I would say I might be going . . . you know, I did not concentrate on good things. I was just thinking about my going. If I am going, if I would be told to leave. This was always on my mind. But now it is like . . . I look at everything differently. I feel I belong." Though others who were granted asylum likewise felt a sense of moral legitimacy associated with this legal decision, Sharon's response was remarkable in her declaration of asylum as the termination of suffering. In the week following her asylum decision, Sharon even decided to stop taking her anti-depressants and ceased counseling sessions, declaring these unnecessary because, as she put it, "asylum is the most powerful medicine" (see Haas 2021).

The first thing Sharon did after obtaining asylee status was file what is informally known as "follow-to-join" paperwork with USCIS. Once granted asylum, individuals can petition for a spouse or unmarried child under twenty-one years old to join them in the United States. This process can be long—sometimes taking years—and has myriad steps. Because Sharon's youngest daughter was under twenty-one at the time, she was eligible for the follow-to-join process. Sharon's three older children were, however, not eligible for this form of family reunification because they were over twenty-one and married. Sharon would have to first get a green card or US citizenship before she could even begin the petition for them to join her.

Sharon, like all my interlocutors who were granted asylum, quickly became oriented on how to obtain a green card, with the goal of eventually gaining US citizenship. My interlocutors saw legal permanent residence (LPR) and citizenship as providing another layer of security and protection. Yet, as I describe more fully below, the primary impetus for pursuing these additional legal statuses was the possibility of more expeditious family reunification. US citizenship would also provide my interlocutors the ability to visit their countries of origin should they feel they could safely do so in the future, given that as asylees they were prohibited from doing so. In this way, US citizenship would—and did—allow my interlocutors a way to both claim a sense of "stillness" in the US (Gill 2009) *and* allow them the option of mobility, two things denied to them by the asylum regime.

Ultimately, Sharon's initial interpretation of asylum as a panacea would prove illusory. Shortly after gaining asylum, Sharon moved away from Minnesota, wanting, she told me, "a fresh start." She settled in a New England community and became connected with a meditation center, where she felt welcomed and supported. "I am finding joy in life again," she told me, with an ease in her voice that I hadn't heard before. While she remained relieved at the sense of safety that asylum brought her, the resolution to uncertainty and distress that asylum had originally delivered began to wane. The uncertainty about how and when her asylum case would be decided was replaced by an uncertainty regarding when, and even if, she would be reunited with her children. She was waiting yet again. Then, after waiting almost two years, Sharon's daughter, then in her early twenties[3], arrived in the United States to live with Sharon, which rejuvenated Sharon's joy and sense of peace. Waiting for other things would be easier now, she thought.

Sharon also had to wait for extended periods to achieve her goal of obtaining first a lawful permanent resident (LPR), or green card, and then US citizenship. Asylees can apply for a green card if they have been physically present in the United States for at least one year after being granted asylum. After a green card, asylees must wait an additional four years to apply for citizenship.[4] Importantly, these required wait times do not include the time—months or even years—that it takes for these applications to be processed and issued. In 2018, Sharon's daughter moved to a city several hours away from Sharon to begin attending college. They had developed a close relationship—the kind of relationship that Sharon had always longed to have with her children—and Sharon was sad to see her move but immensely proud of her. Though Sharon struggled financially, finding that the recurring symptoms of her past trauma, such as memory problems, pain and fatigue, prohibited her from working, she felt emotionally and socially supported within her local community of Buddhist practitioners. By this point, Sharon had also received her green card and had filed paperwork in hopes of having her three adult children join her in the United States.[5] Even if the application was successful, this would entail a significant wait time: at the end of 2019, the average processing time for PLRs' filings for adult unmarried children was 58 months (USCIS n.d.).

The paperwork, though, would be rendered painfully moot. During the same year that Sharon's youngest daughter went off to college, Sharon's two sons were killed in Kenya, one in a hit-and-run automobile accident, the other one shot to death while he walked home one evening. Neither of the perpetrators of these senseless, violent acts were ever found. Sharon bitterly placed blame for her sons' unsolved murders on what she viewed as endemic violence and corruption in Kenya. Because she was not yet a US citizen, she could not travel to Kenya for their burials.[6] After such a long separation and years maintaining the hope that she would someday be able to bring all her children to the United States, Sharon, in her grief, was denied even the opportunity to touch her sons again before they were interred. This lack of closure would continue to haunt Sharon. By 2019, she had gotten her US citizenship, about which she felt very proud. The sense of belonging she had experienced upon first being granted asylum, but which had waned over the years, was brought to the fore again. Her happiness would be tempered by her sons' death and the absence of her oldest daughter, whose application for reunification remained pending. Sharon mourned not only the physical loss of her sons but also the loss of her hope at providing them, even after they had entered adulthood, a chance to pursue an alternative vision of the future. "There are so many good things about life here [in the United States]," Sharon told me. "You have the ability to speak your truth, to be safe, to be free. My sons never got to experience that." She paused and added, "but my daughter is here, and she has opportunities that I never dreamed of. She is my hope for the future."

Sharon's story reveals many aspects of the aftermath of a positive asylum decision that were shared among others who are granted asylum. First, Sharon's immediate response to obtaining asylum highlighted the sociomoral implications of this new legal status. Although she was relieved for the existential safety inherent in asylee status and the potential material benefits that came with it (such as access to government financial and housing assistance), Sharon's emphasis was on the sense of belonging the status conferred. The moral terminology with which Sharon framed the granting of asylum status importantly brings into relief the critical link between legal recognition, moral deservingness, and the legitimation of suffering (Cabot 2012, 2014; Holmes and Castañeda 2016; Ticktin 2011; Willen 2010). Second, Sharon's experience illustrates that although she and other granted asylum claimants no longer wait for the adjudication of their claims, waiting, as a lived phenomenon, nonetheless continues to have a significant presence in their lives. In the aftermath of an asylum decision, however, there is a shift in both *what* asylum seekers wait for and *how* they wait. Moreover, if asylees focus on new objects of waiting, these are likewise new objects of hope. And hope itself among asylees takes on new contours, not just in terms of its objects, but also its enactment and its meaning.

Third, and intimately tied to waiting, is the central role that hope for family reunification plays in the lives of asylees. The hope and goal of bringing family, particularly children, to the United States is always present for asylum claimants throughout the asylum process, but being granted asylum frequently catalyzes this as a primary object of waiting. Sharon's indefinite and uncertain waiting for her children, mired as it was in an opaque and onerous bureaucratic process, challenged her ability to fully embrace the initial sense of belonging and joy her asylee status brought her. Like Sharon, asylum claimants' conceptions of the good life and their ability to flourish were thoroughly relational. That is, if asylees like Sharon can ostensibly begin the hoped-for-process of gaining US citizenship and establishing their place in the United States, without their families with them, such efforts often hold limited meaning. Finally, as Sharon would come to realize, despite the initial feeling that asylum was the end to all her suffering, the desired promises of asylum are not always actualized. In suggesting this, I am not minimizing the continued relief asylees feel at being granted protection, secure in the fact that they themselves will not be forced back to a situation of existential threat. Yet, for many asylees personal safety in the US does not insulate them or their families from the effects of violence, both near and far. For many asylees, then, legal status and even US citizenship cannot fully guarantee them a sense of peace, security, or a place of belonging.

Ahmed: "Asylum takes so much of you"

Ahmed was finally granted asylum in 2015, after having waited almost six years for the adjudication of his case. He continued to live with his sister Bilan, who was preparing to apply for US citizenship. Since getting his EAD Ahmed had been working multiple, mostly entry-level, jobs including stocking shelves at a big box store and working for a moving company. He worked up to twelve hours a day, going weeks without a day off. Ahmed was relieved and gratified to be able to fulfill his self-described duty as a provider for his family, both for Bilan in the United States and for his mother and brothers back in Ethiopia. In previous chapters, I traced how the asylum process took an emotional and physical toll on Ahmed, from his sense of hopelessness to his perceived declining health. When he was finally granted asylum, Ahmed felt an immediate and enormous sense of relief, not only because he knew he no longer faced the threat of forced removal but because he could begin to envision and plan for the future.

When I visited Ahmed in 2019, I was overjoyed to see him in good health and living in a well-appointed apartment. He had started his own transportation business, owning a fleet of vans that worked mainly to transport elderly and infirm individuals. He had other business plans in the works and attributed his entrepreneurialism to his father, who had been a successful businessman in Ethiopia. In chapter 2, I noted that Ahmed found that the existential limbo of asylum seeking prohibited him from hoping and dreaming of a future. During our visits in 2019, it became clear that his ability to "encounter the future" changed after he was granted asylum (Feldman 2016). He told me, "When I got [asylum] status and then I got my green card [in 2017], I could finally think about other things. So once all my asylum was settled, I could shift my mind and think about my health, my future. Now I am settled. Now I can say that I live in America."

Ahmed knew his best chance at getting his mother to the United States would be to file paperwork after getting his US citizenship.[7] Given that he got his green card in 2017, Ahmed hoped to be eligible to apply for citizenship in 2021. In the interim, he had taken action to ensure his mother's safety in Ethiopia. By the time that Ahmed got his green card, he had saved enough money to purchase a small property in the capital city, Addis Ababa, and have his mother relocated there, far away from their hometown in the Somali region, where ethnic and political tensions remained. "That was the last thing that was preventing me from having a totally free mind," Ahmed reflected. "Now that I know she is safe, I am really able to think about my future." I remarked that he seemed to have made some real accomplishments toward his goals and that he'd already achieved so much. "Yeah," he agreed, with a blush. "I think the only thing left now is to find a wife." Although he was laughing when he said this, Ahmed went on to explain that this would be an important next step in his life. Marrying a Somali woman would be imperative, he explained, because his mother does not speak English and, moreover, he would want to meet familial and cultural expectations as a Somali man. Meeting with Ahmed in 2019, I realized that I had never had this kind of conversation with him, with his talk of the future, his elaboration of concrete plans and goals, his sharing with me his vision for realizing "possible selves"—reconfigured notions of potentiality for himself and his social world (Parish 2008).

Ahmed's use of "settled" as it relates to post-asylum life implicitly positions life during asylum-seeking as *un*settled. This unsettlement was evident in what I have described as asylum claimants' challenge of temporally and spatially situating a life trajectory in the context of limbo. Yet Ahmed's ten years in the United States before he was granted asylum included activities and the cultivation of attachments that subsequently facilitated his ability to successfully feel settled. For example, Ahmed had amassed significant savings through his multiple jobs and had been educating himself on starting his own business. These would help him to achieve his vision of the future once he obtained asylum. "Settled," for Ahmed, signified a sense of permanence and security. If asylum seeking meant only partially and ambiguously inhabiting a place in the United States, with asylee status Ahmed could lay claim to "living" in America.

As we talked over the course of the afternoon, however, our conversation turned toward what Ahmed saw as the lingering effects of the trauma he associated with asylum seeking. It was a contrast to the optimism he exhibited when he discussed his future plans. Turning a bit somber, Ahmed reflected on what he saw as irreparable changes in himself:

AHMED: You cannot recover from that [asylum] process.

BRIDGET: How so?

AHMED: I mean, I still think that if I got asylum ten years ago, like after six months, I think about what could I have done. What could I have done? Would I have been a father, with kids of my own? What would have been different? Asylum [seeking] takes so much of you. It's just gone and it never comes back. Half of your life. I'm not talking about the number of years, but part of yourself. Like, you become like very weak. Vulnerable. You feel worthless. Just like you're nothing. And you can't recover from that, those feelings.

BRIDGET: And that has carried on?

AHMED: Yes, I mean, it's still to me, like I always believe that so much of me went away with that process. Like a lot of my thinking, my attention, my life, myself. I still every now and then have dreams of being a refugee. I just had a dream a few weeks ago that I was paperless.

Somebody was asking me for ID and I didn't have it. I don't know who I am and then I just woke up. It's still right there. The process causes a lot of damage. . . . I don't think there is any other kind of torture. And some people can never recover. I still believe that there is a lot of me that has gone. Time has gone. My love of life has gone. Like since the time of asylum, I haven't changed. I still live that way in life where asylum put me. Isolated. Like I don't want to go out. . . . If I got asylum right when I came here, if I could connect with people, I would be maybe the same man that I was. But I was so isolated when I was seeking asylum. For years I was alone.

Ahmed vividly described how the asylum system's techniques of governing "get into inward parts" (Willen 2019, 87). The afterlife of an asylum decision carries with it the psychological and emotional debris of the asylum regime. Thus, although Ahmed imbued his asylee status with a sense of potentiality, he had to contend with the enduring impact of this process on his psyche and sense of self. In contrast to Sharon's experience of asylum status as a conferral of worthiness, Ahmed—despite being deemed a legitimate, deserving claimant—internalized, to some extent, the "undeservingness" which he often felt as an asylum seeker. For Ahmed, the embodied consequences of withstanding the bureaucratic violences of the asylum regime were inextricable from the subject-position of "asylee." Being granted asylum meant that Ahmed recuperated hope for a better future, but it could not erase the injuries the asylum process had inflicted. Ahmed was not alone in observing the enduring lived consequences of the asylum system's continuum of violence.

Louise: "My biggest problems are gone but I still feel stuck in the middle"

Because Louise's youngest daughter was under age twenty-one at the time that Louise filed for asylum, she was able to petition for her, as well as Louise's husband, to join her in the United States immediately after being granted asylum. Her daughter was living with Louise within a year. Louise's husband, however, had been growing increasingly ill over the previous several years, and did not want to come to the United States. "He wants to die in Cameroon, not America," Louise told me. Though Louise was wracked with grief, particularly as it became clear she would not be able to physically see him again, she understood the journey would be too much for him. Louise's husband passed away just months after her daughter arrived. In 2014, Louise's middle daughter, Elisabeth, and her husband came to the United States, living several states away. Louise's son-in-law had a brother who had migrated to the United States over a decade earlier and, because he was a US citizen, was able to petition for his sibling (Louise's son-in-law) to join him. The process itself had taken a decade and Louise was grateful that Elisabeth had found an alternative way to the United States, given that reunification through Louise, if even possible, would have taken an inordinate amount of time.

Louise got her US citizenship at the end of 2015 and filed for her oldest daughter and her son, both married with children, to come to the United States. In 2017, Elisabeth gave birth to twin boys and came to Minnesota to live with Louise, who would help to care for the boys so Elisabeth could work. Elisabeth's husband continued to live in a separate state to keep his job, but he visited Elisabeth and the boys as often as he could. Louise had continued to work as an aide in a nursing home, though she completed her certified nursing assistant (CNA) certificate after getting asylum, which entitled her to a small raise. The job was relatively low-paying, and Louise sometimes had to put up with difficult co-workers and clients. Her boss was a particular source of headache, often belittling her or threatening to dock her hours if she asked for time off. But unlike her years of working as an aide while seeking asylum, Louise felt more emboldened in her job. Previously, even though Louise had a work permit, she had worried about "making trouble" at her job, lest her employer somehow jeopardize her asylum case—a concern that was highly unlikely to be realized but that was nonetheless powerful in constraining her voice and actions. "But I'm a US citizen now," Louise declared. "She [Louise's boss] can't treat me that way. Now I know I don't have to put up with that and I say something back to her." Like Miriam's assertion of knowing her rights upon returning to the United States, Louise embraced the sense of political subjectivity that she found through US citizenship.

On a return research visit in 2019, I spent a lot of time with Louise, her daughter Elisabeth, and the twin boys, who were now living in a spacious condominium in a quiet suburb of St. Paul. Her youngest daughter lived in an apartment just a ten-minute drive away. One afternoon, Louise and I sat together on her sofa, looking through photo albums of her family. She also showed me on her smartphone a long video of her mother's funeral in Cameroon; Louise was unable to attend, but had sent money to ensure that the church had enough flowers, food, and music to provide her mother with a beautiful ceremony. As the video ended, our conversation quickly turned to the heightened violence in the western (English-speaking) regions in Cameroon. Though this was not often mentioned in newspapers in the United States, I had been following the conflict through international and alternative news sources, as well as text and phone communications with my Cameroonian friends. A nonviolent strike by Anglophone teachers and lawyers in November 2016 had quickly escalated into an armed conflict in the English-speaking regions of Cameroon when secessionist groups, including the SCNC, took up arms in response to the government's violent repression. In October 2017, following separatist groups' declaration of independence for "Ambazonia"—the self-declared nation of Anglophone Cameroon, the government, still being led by Paul Biya, initiated a violent crackdown and an armed insurgency ensued. In November 2017, Biya made the SCNC and other secessionist groups illegal, labeling them terrorist organizations. Since then, secessionist groups have continued to fight for the independence of Ambazonia, an end goal that they will not concede. The Cameroon government agreed to give the two English-speaking regions "special status," but has refused to give up any sovereignty and has continued its violent crackdown on separatist groups.

By the time I found myself sitting with Louise on her sofa that afternoon in 2019, over two thousand people had been killed and scores displaced in the recent conflict, almost exclusively in the northwest and southwest regions of Cameroon (Amin 2021). Louise turned again to her smartphone, but this time it was not to show me another celebration. As she pressed play on a video in her library, grainy footage of a charred car, all but its main frame melted away, appeared on the small screen in front of me. The camera panned to the street and zoomed in on a dead body lying supine in the mud, his face covered haphazardly with a blood-stained t-shirt. "Oh, my God," I reacted. "What is this?" "This is what is happening right now in Cameroon!" Louise cried. Perhaps I had become accustomed to the more sanitized photos of the Cameroonian violence on the BBC news website, as my reaction to the gruesome images on Louise's phone screen was visceral. Louise continued to show me videos of the death and destruction in Cameroon—some sent to her by friends and family in Bamenda and Buea, others she retrieved from Facebook. As we viewed these together, she noted how technologies over a decade ago did not allow for so much visual evidence of the violence in Cameroon. Louise connected these images to her personal difficulties in seeking asylum:

> When I was going for my asylum, they [immigration officials] never believed me. They said Cameroon was in a good state. If they had believed me before, they would have granted my asylum quickly and things would have been better. But it was very long, many years. That time was too hard for me. And now Cameroon is in the worst stage, but that is how it was when I came. What I wrote in my asylum case is the same thing that is going on now. But they wouldn't believe us! I remember the judge told me that we [Cameroonian asylum seekers] are coming here and lying. I don't think that a woman of my age would run and abandon my whole family to come and lie to America. That is why it was so painful. I need to keep looking forward . . . [but] that [asylum] process really hurt me. I cannot look back to that time. And now the truth is coming out. Everyone is seeing it because those things are on the internet now and this can speak for us. They prove what Cameroon is going through for all these long years.

I asked Louise if the fact that she was eventually granted asylum helped to heal the pain of being disbelieved. "There will always be so much hurt," she said shaking her head, "because for so long they didn't believe me, they said I was lying. That will always hurt me." "But," Louise added, "with getting asylum, I can say that things really changed for me." She elaborated:

> LOUISE: The biggest change is that I can have hope. Before I got asylum, I was not that well. But then getting asylum I could have hope and think that things could get better. And they are so much better. I am free. I'm a free citizen. I can speak out if I see something that is not right. Before I couldn't do that because I was a nobody. But now, after asylum, I can. Also now I have a home of my own. I have an address, under my own name since I got asylum. That is a good achievement. My daughter is here. We have two grandkids who are citizens. I have opportunities here that I never had in Cameroon. At my age.

BRIDGET: What kind of opportunities?

LOUISE: I never even went to school. But when I came here, once I was granted asylum and I had my green card, I went to some evening classes and then finally I enrolled in the CNA school for the nursing assistant. So now I am a nursing assistant. And the government has given me insurance, and they give me transportation to [medical] appointments. All these things I can do because I got asylum. America is my country now. I love it.

At this point, Louise paused, glancing at the framed portraits of her son and oldest daughter that hung on the wall of her living room. "Having my kids here, the two that are here now, it has made things much, much better for me. I'm really relieved. But if I could have all my children with me, I would be complete. That would make life complete for me. The other ones couldn't get visas. We are still working on it. I am just praying every day that they will get them. That the government will give them a chance to come. I would be very, very happy. Because when you can be with your family, only then you can move on." Louise paused, her eyes dampening with tears. "My biggest problems are gone but I still feel stuck in the middle. My son is not safe in Cameroon. All that is happening, what you saw [on the videos], he is right there! I get so worried I cannot think, I cannot sleep. The other day, after I talked to him, I felt myself having a heart attack. I really thought I was having a heart attack. Elisabeth took me to the hospital, and they checked me and said I was ok, but my worry, it's too much." Our conversation was interrupted by the twins arriving home from daycare, bursting loudly through the door—a welcome distraction. Louise excused herself to finish dinner while I played with the boys and talked to Elisabeth and to Louise's youngest daughter, who had also arrived. At the feast that evening, the table spread with all the Cameroonian food Louise knew I loved—n'dole, rice, koki beans, fish rolls—Louise's son Derrick joined us via FaceTime from Cameroon. He made funny faces at the twins and joked that he wished he could taste his mother's food over the phone. The jovial atmosphere allowed us all to temporarily suspend the reality that Derrick was far away, surrounded by danger.

If Ahmed had internalized the demoralizing and isolating effects of the asylum system, lamenting what he understood as lost time and opportunities, it was the institutional disbelief of her story that had gotten under

Louise's skin. That she was labeled as not credible—a potential liar—for so long during the asylum process was an enduring wound for Louise, despite her ultimate approval. Moreover, as Louise astutely articulated, asylum adjudicators' original disbelief of her story critically patterned the waiting and structural vulnerability that she faced as an asylum seeker. It was because the government doubted her that her case was protracted, moving from asylum interview to immigration judge, then a lengthy overseas investigation to interrogate aspects of her claim. This protraction meant prolonged family separation and a continuation of what she described as a sense of "homelessness." Here, we see the inextricability of an institutional ethos of suspicion and forms of temporal governance. From this perspective, the videos of the violence in Cameroon—videos that Louise said can "speak for" Cameroonian asylum seekers—served as a kind of moral vindication for Louise, visual proof of the same violence she had fled years before.

Despite the enduring emotional effects of asylum, Louise, like Ahmed, saw asylum as establishing the "conditions of possibility for hope" (Jansen 2015, 47). That is, asylum—once the object of hope—also enabled new forms of hope and hoping. For Ahmed, this manifested in his ability to attend to aspects of his life that he felt were suspended during the asylum process: taking care of his health, owning a business, trying to find a wife. With asylum, Louise found new opportunities in employment, self-care, and homeownership that provided her with a sense of belonging and a hope for the future. For both Ahmed and Louise, asylum allowed a more general, affective freedom—freedom from the anxiety and uncertainty that could be immobilizing during the asylum process. Yet, the resolution of these "big problems" often did not result in a full sense of security or peace. Ongoing family separation, bolstered by a complex, opaque, and protracted family reunification system, challenges asylees' ability to fully move forward with their lives—to not just make life bearable but to flourish (Willen 2019). As Louise's experience reveals, it was not just the separation from family that challenged a sense of wholeness or forward trajectory, but also the knowledge that family left behind were still in harm's way. With no viable—or at least no immediate—way to get her remaining children and their families out of Cameroon and to the United States, Louise could not feel completely at ease. This tempered the hope and sense of belonging that she found with asylum.

In providing asylum seekers with individual security, asylum, as my interlocutors emphatically endorsed, provides an important end to pervasive fears about deportability and homelessness. However, Louise's declaration that she is "still stuck in the middle" speaks to a new temporal register and form of uncertainty that the separation from and worry about family generates. In this way, for Louise and many other asylees who await (often for years) reunification with family members and/or who remain fearful for family left behind, legal status, including US citizenship, is limited in offering a full resolution to uncertainty. Recent literature has importantly critiqued the notion that legal status and/or resettlement is a solution or end to displacement (Ramsay 2017; Brekke, Birkvad, and Erdal 2021; Tang 2015). Much of this scholarship emphasizes how conditions in so-called "host" countries often perpetuate refugees' structural vulnerability and prohibit their sense of belonging and potentiality. My argument here is slightly different. My asylee friends located their continued sense of displacement or unsettledness not in the material conditions of the United States, but rather in their ongoing separation from loved ones. The state is implicated in the production—and perpetuation—of uncertainty and unsettledness, given that family reunification entails an onerous and protracted process, undergirded by many of the same bureaucratic techniques that inform the asylum process (enforced waiting, multiple security screens/measures, lack of transparency).

The problem with understanding a grant of *individual* asylum as a solution to displacement or existential uncertainty is that it elides the fact that people are thoroughly relational. Asylum seekers' own subjectivities and wellbeing are inseparable from the important others in their lives. Thus, individual security, though it provides an overwhelming sense of relief, is not enough for people to, as Louise put it, feel "complete."

Emmanuel: "Even though you have asylum, you still cry"

During my 2019 research trips to Minnesota and the surrounding area, I found that any time I visited any of my Cameroonian friends or was among Cameroonians, someone—and usually multiple people—would pull out their phone or iPad to show me videos of the violence in Cameroon, just as Louise had. I offer one more story—Emmanuel's—to trace another experience of the aftermath of the granting of asylum. Emmanuel's story also highlights how the violence in Cameroon is inextricable from Cameroonians' lived experiences in the United States.

Emmanuel had been granted asylum in 2012 and within a year, his wife, Nafissa, and their four children, ranging in age from five to sixteen, were living with him outside of St. Paul. Emmanuel had found steady work at a manufacturing company, but his declining hearing and eyesight prevented him from working more than part-time. Luckily, Nafissa, who was trained as a nurse in Cameroon, was able to fulfill the necessary requirements to transfer her nursing license to the United States. By 2014, Nafissa was working full time and was the primary breadwinner. Both Nafissa and Emmanuel had become US citizens in 2018. When I visited them in 2019, their house was bustling with the energy of four boys. Nafissa, Emmanuel, and I sat at the large dining room table of the split-level house that they rented. Unsurprisingly, Emmanuel reached for his phone. "Don't show her those pictures," Nafissa scolded him. "Tsk, tsk," he murmured back, "no, she should see them." As Emmanuel scrolled through the grisly photos sent to him by friends in Cameroon or screenshots from the internet, he recounted to me—as he had on so many occasions over the years—the history of Cameroon, beginning with German then French and British colonial rule to the 1961 plebiscite that would deny Anglophone Cameroonians a right to self-determination. Emmanuel knew that I was familiar with the history of his country, but he was not telling me this as a history lesson. The visual evidence these clips and images provided pushed against the legacy of invisibility and marginalization that English-speaking Cameroonians had endured for decades. By couching the slideshow on his phone within an oral history of colonialism and neocolonialism, Emmanuel made certain I consumed these images through the lens of this legacy. Though legally asylum claimants must demonstrate that they have been an *individual* target of persecution, for my Cameroonian asylee friends, legal recognition in the United States was not just about their personal stories. Rather, legal recognition represented acknowledgment of a long, painful, and ongoing history of collective violence and oppression.

This embodied connection between, or even collapse of, individual and collective experiences of violence led Emmanuel to wrestle with being at peace in the United States. "I was able to escape," Emmanuel said about leaving Cameroon, "but it's not like you escape and then you now forget about everything. Anything that happens back there, it affects us here. Even if you have your family here, you will still have friends there. We still have our culture that we've inherited from our elders. Back there, they are not free. Then how are you free? How? They are not free, so you yourself you are not free. That is how it goes. So even though you have asylum, you still cry." I asked Emmanuel if being granted asylum and being reunited with his family had provided him any sense of peace or freedom. "Yes, yes, of course, so much." Echoing Louise's sentiment, Emmanuel asserted, "When you get asylum, you feel more hopeful about life. You are safe. You are here. You are legal. You can stand anywhere." He continued:

> With asylum, I was able to bring my family here. They are now with me. They are now free. So, even though you are crying so much for those back [in Cameroon], when you have all your people, your children with you, then [you] just have to say let bygone be bygone and you try to move ahead. Because if you are not able to bring your family, then your trauma, it will just multiply and multiply. Even though with all the hanging [waiting] with asylum, there are so many things that were left undone, disrupted. School, work. So many things. But you have to move forward and my kids, now they will not have all the problems I had.

Like Louise, Emmanuel saw family reunification as a requisite for moving forward. Emmanuel did not deny the abiding personal and social consequences of the asylum system. Yet his children's presence—a consequence of his asylum status—was both a balm to the wounds inflicted by past violences (both in Cameroon and the United States) and a source of envisioning the future. Here, as with other asylees, time spent within the asylum system—years waiting in a state of uncertainty and anxiety, and "longing for hope" (Jansen 2015)—were made meaningful. The positive outcome of his case meant that Emmanuel would be safe from the particular dangers he had fled. Thus, enduring the asylum process and its concomitant traumas ultimately meant that Emmanuel could see waiting as productive, a form of laboring that led to existential security. Since asylum is a conduit to family reunification, Emmanuel's waiting and enduring was also meaningful in the forms of opportunity it ultimately provided to his children. At the same time, though, Emmanuel points to the possible limitations of family for providing what Louise hoped would be a sense of "completeness," given the transnationally embodied suffering caused by the ongoing conflict in Cameroon, a country to which many of my friends were still deeply connected.

*   *   *

This chapter has followed the aftermaths of asylum decisions to illuminate the ways in which various legal outcomes are differentially experienced and made meaningful. Within the aftermath of an asylum decision, objects of waiting and hope shift with newly available subject-positions (asylee, returnee, deportee) and their material consequences. Often, my interlocutors engaged in a kind of triaging of hope. For many, it was not until they were granted asylum that they could begin to hope. In this way, asylum can be both an object of hope and a requirement for hope. Yet, it was not just those with successful outcomes who found meaning in the waiting, precarity, and pain of the asylum system. Some who were denied asylum engaged with their legal outcomes in ways that kept intact their sense of moral dignity, legitimacy, and deservingness. At the same time, the asylum system took a significant social, emotional, and physical toll, and its effects long outlasted an asylum decision, even a positive one. Compounding this for many asylees was the fact that family reunification as a hoped-for object entailed a new, but nonetheless protracted and opaque, bureaucratic process, exposing the somewhat illusory idea of asylum as the solution to suffering.

Conclusion

"I've lost my son." Louise's voice cracked, the rest of the voicemail message inaudible. I replayed the message, hoping that I hadn't heard it correctly. "I've lost my son." Her words were clear. I immediately called her back and left a message when she didn't answer. This was late November 2019 and I had just visited Louise months before, in the spring, when Derrick had joined us from Cameroon via FaceTime for a family dinner in her kitchen. When I had spoken to Louise a couple of weeks after that visit, she had told me that Derrick was planning to leave Cameroon. He had been unable to get a visa to come to the United States to join Louise and his sisters, but he felt he could no longer stay. The situation was too dire, and he was in serious danger.

When she called me back, Louise told me the story of Derrick's death. Derrick, a schoolteacher in Bamenda, had been living in fear since renewed violence had gripped Cameroon beginning in late 2016. Throughout 2019, the violence had escalated, and Derrick moved his wife and two small children to live with Derrick's sister, Louise's oldest daughter, and her husband in a safer neighborhood outside the city. Living alone in Bamenda, Derrick was being threatened by both armed separatists, dubbed "Amba Boys," and violent government security forces. Though he had long participated in nonviolent protests advocating for the right to self-determination for Anglophone Cameroonians, whom separatists identified as Ambazonians, Derrick was opposed to joining the armed insurgency. Waiting for years to no avail to get a visa to come to the United States to join Louise, he had begun to formulate a plan to leave Cameroon. He knew that going to Nigeria was risky, as the Nigerian government had begun to actively stop and return Cameroonians at the border. If he could get to the United States, Derrick thought, he could apply for asylum as his mother had done. Surely, the US government would recognize his need for protection, he told Louise.

Derrick was aware of many Cameroonians who were attempting to reach the United States via South and Central America. Friends of his in Bamenda were planning on taking this trek. He had enough money put away to support him while he traveled. When he told Louise that he was contemplating this journey, she was fearful but knew that his life was in danger in Cameroon, too. "I tried to tell him how dangerous it was, traveling that way," Louise recalled to me. "I know many boys who died on that route. But he was in so much danger there [Cameroon] so what could I say? And some people were making it to America." Though he promised Louise he would wait and think about the plan some more, the following day Derrick was terrorized by the beheading of his good friend and neighbor—a gruesome spectacle of violence that Derrick took as an ominous warning about his own fate. Derrick concluded that he could no longer wait and he, his cousin Francis, and several friends left that same day, traveling first to Nigeria. In Nigeria, Derrick and the other men found a network of smugglers whom they paid to arrange flights to Ecuador. From Ecuador, Derrick and the others paid another series of smugglers to take them across Colombia, Panama, Costa Rica, Nicaragua, then through Honduras and Guatemala to the Mexican border. They were able to reach Tapachula in Chiapas, Mexico—at the time a central gathering point for migrants trying to travel north to the United States—where they stayed for several weeks. Derrick knew that traveling through Mexico had become perilous due to the increased security and surveillance measures that the country had recently implemented, particularly near the Guatemala-Mexico border. While some of his friends decided to take their chances and head north on foot, Derrick and his cousin accepted an offer to join some others on a small fishing boat that would travel the Pacific Ocean along the Mexican coast, just far enough to avoid the most dangerous police checkpoints on the land route.

At this point Louise, in Minnesota, knew that Derrick and Francis had made it to Mexico. She had last heard from them weeks before when Derrick called from Tapachula. She did not, however, know that they were taking a boat. She would later learn that something went horribly wrong. What Derrick thought was a shortcut to a location a bit farther north in Mexico became a harrowing end to his life. The boat capsized, leaving the dozen or so people on board—too many to be accommodated by the small vessel—struggling to survive in the water. Several people, including Francis, were either able to swim to shore or rescued by local fishing boats, and notified the police of the accident and their missing fellow travelers. When Louise got a call from Mexican authorities that her son had died in a boat accident in Mexico she was confused. The police then emailed her a photo of a body that had been found near where the boat had capsized. To Louise's relief, it wasn't Derrick. But Francis had called Louise to tell her about the accident and that Derrick had not been found. Three days later, Louise got another call from Mexican police, letting her know that they had found her son's body in a sand dune on a beach thirteen miles from the accident, in a small coastal village in northern Chiapas. The police had been able to confirm Derrick's identity, as he was traveling with his passport. Kept safe inside it were two photos: one of his wife and children and one of Louise. A small, tattered prayer book was tucked into his underwear.

"Oh my God, Bree," Louise cried as she recounted the details of Derrick's death. "My soul feels empty now, I am so heartbroken. I feel hopeless. My world is collapsing." Louise's grief was so deep. She struggled to make sense of what had happened, as she had held out hope that Derrick would arrive safely. She had wanted to welcome him into the home she had made in this small corner of the United States where she had eventually found refuge. "Everything that I've worked for, everything that I've gone through, it's for what? I'm just so confused about my life now. I never thought I would see the day that I would bury my son." She told me again how long Derrick had waited trying to get a visa to the United States, to no avail. "In the end there was no other way for him to get here," Louise concluded. "How is Trump allowing this to happen?! Boys being killed trying to get to

America! Trump doesn't want anybody moving." But Louise could not see the logic in this when family and friends were suffering so horrifically across the globe: "You cannot imagine what is happening in Cameroon. Children are dying every day. People are being killed, burned because they are fighting against injustice." Louise spoke of a pain that stretched across borders, and her weeping turned to anger as we talked longer: "Now I am crying here and in Cameroon we have been crying and crying and nobody hears us. Nobody believes us. Biya doesn't want us. Trump doesn't want us. Nobody wants us!"

Entangled and Cumulative Violence

I have been grappling with the news of Derrick's death and my dear friend's staggering grief over his loss, struggling myself to make sense of all of it, or any of it. How might we begin to understand how Derrick's life met such a violent and sudden end? Who bears responsibility? Tracing his story's many roots and entanglements brings to light the myriad factors that shaped his trajectory and contributed to his death. It would be easy to frame Derrick's death as a tragic outcome of individual choice, arguing that he chose to leave Cameroon, make a risky trek, and ultimately made the decision to get on a boat that was unfit for the voyage ahead. Yet, such a framing reflects "misplaced autonomy," in which a focus on individual decision-making dangerously obscures the structural factors that constrain people's choices in the first place (Horton 2016, 3). This critique has been leveled at broader migration decision-making models that emphasize individual will or agency over political-economic and structural forces (Yarris and Castañeda 2015; Vogt 2018; Watters 2019). In Derrick's case, the terror surrounding him in Cameroon—epitomized by the hideous beheading of his friend—challenges the idea that his departure was a fully autonomous "choice."

It may be argued, then, that we can locate Derrick's death, at least partially, within the armed conflict in Cameroon, which drove him to flee his hometown of Bamenda. Certainly, my interlocutors throughout the years have often and repeatedly invoked Cameroon's government when narrating their displacement. Louise, in talking about Derrick's death, made this point with her declaration that "Biya doesn't want us!" Indeed, the tactics of the Biya regime in Cameroon explicitly marginalize and exclude Anglophone Cameroonians, clearly communicating this exact sentiment. Yet, the contemporary violence in Cameroon—the "Anglophone crisis"—is inextricable from the complex colonial history of the country, which has informed the neocolonial rule of the Biya regime (Amin 2021; Konings and Nyamnjoh 2019; Nwati 2021). Here, the "haunting presence of the colonial" incriminates these imperial powers in current political life, which is, in turn, inscribed on the bodies of those like Derrick (Good et al. 2008, 5). Emmanuel's narration of the (post)colonial history of Cameroon alongside images of destruction and carnage from 2019 (chapter 5) underscores this point.

I would also add that the invisibility of Cameroon's conflict to most of the world, including the United States, also contributes to and helps reproduce the suffering of those caught in this violence. Indeed, as many chapters of this book have addressed, my Cameroonian friends lamented what they saw as not only a lack of recognition but often a denial of their suffering, both within Cameroon and as asylum claimants searching for legal protection in the United States. In Louise's narrative this is unmistakable, as she proclaims that Cameroonians "have been crying and crying and nobody hears us." This assertion echoes her longstanding pain at being denied credibility and legitimacy for so long within the asylum system. The invisibility of Anglophone Cameroonians' plight is supported by empirical evidence that suggests that Cameroonian asylum claims have been consistently approached with particular suspicion among immigration officials, as the ethnographic evidence in chapter 4 also illustrated (Terretta 2015).

But even if the violent situation of Cameroon, past and present, was the impetus for Derrick's need to leave that country, his death was not inevitable. Rather, the conditions of his tragic death were produced and set in motion by multiple factors. First, as the previous chapter noted, Derrick had been trying to find a way to the United States through different channels. During his four years in office, President Donald Trump dramatically transformed the US immigration system, driven by a relentless focus on border enforcement and restriction of migration to the United States (Pierce and Bolter 2020). Derrick's inability to get a visitor visa to the United States was a direct effect of these policies. Though citizens of Arab and Muslim-majority nations saw the steepest declines in the approval of US visas, others were not immune to this policy change, and foreign visas overall plunged during the Trump era (Toosi, Hesson, and Frostenson 2018). Derrick and Louise felt hamstrung by these changes, as they blocked Derrick from the opportunity to seek protection in the United States in a way that they both interpreted as legal and safe. Derrick understood himself as fitting the legal definition of a "refugee," based on his knowledge of the status determination system and from what Louise had shared about the process. Thus, Derrick trusted that if he could just get to the United States and apply for asylum, he would be granted that protection. At the same time, although Louise had filed family reunification paperwork in hopes of having Derrick join her, this was a highly protracted and complex process. Indeed, they had already been waiting for years, to no avail.

Yet it was not just the increased border restrictions in the United States that informed Derrick's deadly journey. Rather, an entanglement of numerous border restrictions and the global rise of the criminalization of migrants constrained his options for a safe and viable plan. Derrick had known friends from Bamenda and other parts of Southwest and Northwest Cameroon who had made their way to Europe via Libya and across the Mediterranean Sea. While this had always been a dangerous journey—the Mediterranean crossing has led to more migrant deaths than any other route (International Organization for Migration n.d.)—by the time Derrick needed to leave Cameroon, this route had become even more perilous. In 2017, European Union leaders agreed to provide the Libyan government with €200m to reduce migrant flows crossing the Mediterranean from Libya to Italy (BBC News 2017), and the death toll of migrants attempting this journey subsequently rose. In addition, the fortified Mexico-Guatemala border that Derrick confronted on his journey was, in part, Mexico's response to pressure from Trump to prevent migrants from reaching the United States. Mexican president Andrés Manuel López Obrador, who came to power at the end of 2018, had initially promised a more humane approach to Central American migration but switched course when the Trump administration threatened to impose tariffs on Mexican imports should López Obrador's government fail to increase its enforcement capabilities on its southern border (Meyer and Isacson 2019).

Considering these multiple sites of militarization and border enforcement—from bureaucratic refusals to brute force—Louise's conclusion that Derrick had no other way of getting to the United States makes sense. Scholarship has shown that increasingly restrictive border measures fail to prohibit or lessen migration and border crossings; rather, they catalyze even more dangerous and deadly migration routes (Andersson 2014a; De León 2105; Khosravi 2010; Nyers 2015; Slack et al. 2016; Vogt 2018). It is not the case that migrants like Derrick fail to comprehend the risks involved with these dangerous journeys. Rather, the fact that people embark on these journeys despite the risk underscores migration as both "a strategy of survival" (Vogt 2018, 33) and a critical endeavor to pursue and create viable life projects (Nyers 2015; Tazzioli, Garelli, and de Genova 2018). As Louise reminded me, Derrick left knowing both that boys have died on that route and that some have reached America.

In my discussion of asylum adjudicators, I noted that moral distancing can occur even without physical distance. Yet, as Gill (2016) importantly argues, spatial distance allows for an especially pernicious form of indifference. The apathy of politicians and the public alike towards the injuries and deaths of migrants like Derrick is facilitated by their location in faraway and out-of-sight locations. Similarly, scholarship on the externalization of asylum has posited that the containment of refugees in camps or urban areas in the Global South helps to keep potential asylum seekers far beyond the borders of more affluent nations in the Global North (Hyndman and Giles 2011; Hyndman and Mountz 2008; Mountz 2010). The constellation of forces and policies that made Derrick unable to reach the United States worked to deny him the legal right to apply for asylum there—that is, to become an "asylum claimant." In this way, his asylum denial was not issued in an US immigration court but rather on a capsized boat in the Pacific Ocean.

My goal in tracing these various threads that patterned Derrick's catastrophic journey is to point to the complexity and interconnection of different legacies of violence and global antipathies towards migrants, manifest in various policies and legal procedures in disparate locations. These all come to bear on Derrick's decisions and lived experience of migration. Though the immediate cause of his death that autumn day was drowning, a much larger confluence of structural factors and forms of violence are critically implicated as well. But Louise was not thinking about these things. She had lost her only son and was struggling to recuperate meaning in the face of this tragedy. Derrick's death brought to the fore many themes that I have explored in this book. What does Louise's experience of loss tell us about the lived effects of her asylum seeking? First, Louise experienced the violence against Derrick as a violence against herself, illustrating the ways in which my interlocutors' subjectivities and senses of self are thoroughly relational and bound up with the significant others in their lives. If Louise's quest for asylum was not only about individual safety and protection but also about creating a future for her children, then Derrick's death meant that this would be forever unrealized. Listening to Louise's weeping when she recounted Derrick's death to me on the phone, I could not help but recall her words just months prior: that if she could get Derrick and her oldest daughter to the United States then her life would feel complete.

Second, Derrick's death painfully exposes the limitations of asylum status and even citizenship in enabling a sense of belonging. Despite her US citizenship, Louise was unable to successfully petition her grown children to join her, despite this being part of her impetus for gaining citizenship in the first place. Her legal status was unable to even obtain a temporary visa for him. But on an even broader level, Derrick's death and the circumstances surrounding it expose the "invisible walls" that constrained possibilities for Louise's belonging (Khosravi 2010). It is notable that as Louise told me about Derrick's death, she ended this with the proclamation that "Trump doesn't want us. Nobody wants us!" Here, the use of "us" is significant. In contrast to our conversations in earlier 2019, when Louise claimed that "America is my home" and articulated a sense of belonging and opportunity, in narrating Derrick's death, she expressed a profound sense of *un*belonging. By referencing not just Derrick but also her own collective belonging—*us*—as the object of Trump's rejection, Louise made clear the conditional hospitality she feels as an asylee in the United States. The racialized violence of the border is likewise a racialized violence of the interior. By the idea of conditional hospitality, I want to underscore how Louise's sense of belonging, despite her asylum status and subsequent citizenship, remains revocable; hostility and hospitality are intricately linked (Berg and Fiddian Qaysmiyeh 2018; see also Gill 2018).

The betrayal communicated by Louise's declaration of unwanted-ness suggests that for some asylees, a sense of belonging, despite their legal relationship to the state, may remain elusive. Louise's sense of *un*belonging also echoes the painful sense of homelessness (chapter 2) and a continued embodiment of the state's denial of recognition (chapter 5) that she experienced as an asylum seeker.

A Hierarchy of Deservingness

With Derrick's death, the violent effects of the border directly impacted Louise. For my other interlocutors, the southern border was more distant and abstract. Yet, when I returned to visit with my interlocutors in the spring and summer of 2019, talk of the US-Mexico border was abundant. This was the year that Trump had implemented the Migrant Protection Protocols, aka the "Remain in Mexico" program, which required many asylum seekers to wait in Mexico for the duration of their immigration proceedings. There was a seemingly endless stream of anti-immigrant speeches and rhetoric from the Trump administration, along with ample media coverage. Sometimes, my interlocutors would bring up the situation on the US-Mexico border organically, within our conversations, and other times they discussed this in response to my questions about how they thought asylum in the United States has changed over time. Though my interlocutors did not describe feeling personally targeted as a result of the increasingly xenophobic sentiments and policies of the Trump administration, they nonetheless conceded that this government hostility would make asylum seeking even more difficult. Many mentioned to me friends of theirs who had filed asylum claims and were facing even longer wait times than they themselves had faced as asylum seekers years ago. Indeed, the backlog of cases in immigration court approached 700,000 in 2019 and as this book goes to press, in late 2022, there are over 1.9 million pending cases (TRAC n.d.).

Many of my interlocutors expressed sympathy with asylum-seeking migrants at the border. "I keep hearing about the caravans," Emmanuel told me. "It seems everyone is running from trouble. Everywhere there is trouble. There is a lot of suffering in the world." Others recognized that the government's open hostility to immigrants, especially asylum seekers, made it an especially challenging time for potential asylum seekers. As one asylee friend told me, "People who seek asylum don't really have a choice, but I don't think I would ever encourage anyone to seek asylum. I would never tell them to despair, but I wouldn't encourage them to come here now." Princewill told me that "the way that the government talks about immigrants and refugees now, if it was me [as a potential asylum seeker] that would lead me to lose a lot of hope. Because they are really talking about you. It would be tough." When I asked Ahmed if he noticed a difference being a Muslim in America since Trump was elected, he responded: "No, not personally, but I see it in the news. It used to be that America was an example to the world, it used to be about humanitarianism, but it has changed. Now racism has a chance to thrive." He paused and added that the anti-immigrant and, particularly, anti-Muslim stance of the Trump administration did sometimes cause him to worry about his status in the United States: "I worry that when I try to apply for citizenship, they may make the process longer for me. They may think that because my name is an immigrant name and I get citizenship, I may vote for a Democrat so maybe they will delay my process." Ahmed had thought a lot about the situation at the US southern border and had a pointed perspective on it:

> The [Trump] administration is very hard, because they've kidnapped the [asylum] process. . . . The immigration process has come to be a major political crisis in America, beginning with the caravans, people from Central America. Saying, 'oh let's go to America.' But that's not how the process of how asylum is supposed to be. I mean, I know what asylum is. . . . But when ten thousand, one hundred thousand, twenty-thousand, people say let's walk three thousand miles and most of them are saying there's no jobs in my country so I have to go to the north, that's not asylum. Some of them are victims, real victims of gangs or government, or even religious persecution, sexual orientation and that's what asylum is supposed to be. Individual cases. Family cases. But not a group. Not ten thousand people to say we want to go to the same place. So the Republican party is saying these people are not asylum seekers. Look at me, over two hundred and fifty thousand people ran away from my own [Somali] region over the last ten years. But they never ran away all on one day. Everyone just ran for the safety of their own lives. So the asylum in America, the system has a problem now.

Ahmed's candid words here reflect the broader hierarchy of deservingness, or what Watters (2007) identifies as a particular moral economy that categorizes the legitimacy and illegitimacy of migrants globally. This moral economy of deservingness, moreover, as this book has discussed, maps onto the putative distinction between "economic migrants" and humanitarian/political refugees (Holmes and Castañeda 2016). The moral economy of deservingness that governs asylum is simultaneously a "hierarchy of suffering," in which some forms of migrants' suffering are more legitimated than others (Farmer 1996; see also Ticktin 2011). Though Ahmed concedes that some of the migrants at the US-Mexico border are "victims," his characterization of the "caravans" of thousands of Central Americans reproduces them as "economic migrants"—primarily looking for jobs that they are unable to find in their countries of origin. Ahmed's framing of "true" asylum seekers as those who travel individually or in families, rather than in large groups, also reflects broader ideologies and biases about what forms of mobility are legitimate. Here, Ahmed may have been reflecting broader public representations, driven home by the Trump administration's use of imagery of the border being "flooded" or overtaken by masses of foreign invaders (Astrada and Astrada 2019).

Many of my other interlocutors expressed a similar worry about how the arrival of thousands of migrants, mostly Central Americans, at the border could adversely affect the asylum system overall. For Louise, this was personal in that she had been trying to get her son to the United States to apply for asylum and knew many other Anglophone Cameroonians who had pending asylum claims or who were planning on applying for asylum. "I am not saying that they [migrants at the border] are not running from problems, but I don't want all this trouble about the border, these caravans, to make it harder for people who really need asylum." Like Ahmed, Louise did not want to fully discount the claims of Central American migrants at the border—using proxy language of "caravans" to distinguish this group from, for example, the many Cameroonian asylum seekers who were arriving at the same border—yet, she was wary of how this situation might impact the asylum system overall.

My interlocutors' narratives, however, are not just reproductions of broader circulating representations and ideologies surrounding asylum.

Their engagement with existing hierarchies or moral economies of deservingness surrounding migration also illustrate their knowledge and development of legal consciousness (Silbey 2005). That is, their deployment of
categories and representations of legitimacy reflects the creative and
agentic tactics they learned in maneuvering through the asylum process.
More importantly, what these narratives also bring to light is the way in
which asylum is conceived of and represented as a "limited good." If chapter 4 illustrated the ways in which adjudicators act as moral gatekeepers
or "guardians of a restricted good" (Heyman 2009), then here, my interlocutors reflect this sentiment. Though legally there are no quotas on asylum and asylum status is to be granted upon merit, the idea that asylum is
in short supply is nonetheless a lived reality. Ahmed's positing of his experience as one of "true" asylum seeking, or Louise's identification of
her Cameroonian asylum-seeking friends as people who "really need"
asylum—both, apparently, in contrast to the primarily Central American
migrants at the border—can be understood as attempts to stake a claim to
this limited good.

Even if my interlocutors' engagement with these categorizations of
migrant legitimacy were deployed agentively, this nonetheless also reflects
both their effective disciplining via the asylum system and the entrench-
ment of these categories in public and social life. There is potential danger
in my interlocutors' engagement of these hierarchical divisions of migrant
legitimacy. At the very least, it works to reproduce and reify these categories. The existing hierarchies of deservingness, and my interlocutors' reproduction of them, may potentially, even if inadvertently, work to foment
division rather than solidarity among migrant populations. Certainly, this
is not always the case, as evidenced by solidarity movements, protests, and
activism of migrant groups across the globe. Yet, as McGuirk and Pine
(2020) argue, "dominant narratives and taxonomies not only pit citizens
against migrants, they also pit categories of migrants against each other in
competition for resources that are only apparently limited" (10).

The experiences and narratives of my interlocutors support the significant body of scholarship critiquing both the "refugee" label itself and the
presumed dichotomy of economic vs. humanitarian migrants (Castañeda
and Holmes 2016; Crawley and Skleparis 2018; Erdal and Oeppen 2018;
Hamlin 2021; Yarris and Castañeda 2015; Zetter 2007). This critique is

important not only because of the potentially pernicious effects that the reproduction of these divisions or hierarchies of deservingness may produce, but also because these categories fail to map on to lived experience. Although my interlocutors, as I have traced throughout this book, identified with the label of "asylum claimant"—that is, they saw themselves as meeting the international definition of a "refugee"—my ethnographic data reveal that their lived experiences of seeking refuge were not fully contained by this category. By this, I mean that my interlocutors, even in fleeing situations of existential danger—death threats, detention, torture—over time came to envision and hope for a future beyond immediate security. For example, in chapter 2, we saw that they hoped for the opportunity to emplace themselves within the United States more permanently; they longed for a chance to envision a life that was not tentative or ambivalent.

In chapters 3 and 5, I showed how asylum claimants often view asylum status as a way to create viable futures for other family members. In this way, my interlocutors wished for—and waited for—both immediate existential security and safety and had "powerful aspirations of a better life" more generally (Watters 2019, 57). Derrick's case illustrates this as well. He had long wanted to reach the United States because of the oppression and marginalization he experienced in Bamenda. Though his impetus for his eventual flight from Cameroon was to escape the armed conflict that had arisen around him, refuge in the United States represented both protection from that immediate danger and a way to extricate himself from the structural violence that had constrained his life for years. As Charles Watters (2019) astutely observes: "Until it is recognized that monumental forced movements across continents are governed both by desires to escape danger *and* dreams of a better life, appropriate responses to migrants' plights will not be achieved" (58).

Implications for Change

The necessary dismantling of existing hierarchies of migrant deservingness is, no doubt, a formidable challenge. The ethnographic research reflected in this book, however, also raises additional areas of concern and may have particular implications for addressing—and changing—asylum policies and procedures. On the broadest level, we must end the criminalization of migration and asylum seeking. As I have shown, the ethos of suspicion that characterizes asylum shapes the lived experiences of asylum seekers beyond the border and in subtle but powerful ways. The illegalization and delegitimation of particular forms of mobility or claims for protection have resulted in an institutional system that presumes that people who assert their need for refuge are fraudulent and/or a threat to the security and integrity of the nation. As Vogt (2018) has importantly argued: "The violence of securitization will not end until there is a world in which human dignity and human life are valued more than national security" (209). Derrick's death epitomizes the violence of securitization and criminalization, but this violence impacts the everyday lives of affirmative asylum seekers like my interlocutors, as well, who are subjected to forms of disciplining and surveillance that have painful emotional and social effects. One particular insight from this book is that alternatives to detention (ATDs), like ISAP, are not necessarily experienced as a reprieve from this violence. Rather, asylum seekers experience them as a carceral technology, as one of many forms of violence that they confront within the asylum system's continuum of violence. Recent calls to redirect funds for personal surveillance technologies (ankle bracelets) to funding legal access and representation for asylum seekers are encouraging and offer important potential benefits (Betancourt 2021). Such a move would work towards de-criminalizing asylum by disengaging asylum seekers from the frame of criminality. It would also help to redress the troubling fact that asylum claimants who do not have legal representation face astoundingly high odds of being denied asylum.

A primary theme of this book, upon which I focused specifically in chapter 2, is the experience of waiting and the bureaucratic manipulation of and control over time as a specific form of violence within the asylum system. Asylum seeking is, above all, a time of protracted waiting, particularly for affirmative asylum seekers. The staggering backlog of cases pending with USCIS and in immigration courts means that asylum claimants face increasingly longer wait times, which in turn, means ever more protracted states of uncertainty and sustained family separation. Of the 1.9 million pending cases in immigration court, asylum cases made up over 670,000 of those at the end of 2021. The average wait time for an asylum hearing in immigration court is over five years (TRAC 2021). As of April 2022, there were 435,000 pending affirmative asylum claims with USCIS, translating to years of waiting time (Dzubow 2022). For those asylum claimants who are not granted at the interview (USCIS) level and are referred to immigration court, as many are, the waiting time is compounded. The violence of enforced waiting and its effects, which I have addressed in this book, are a growing and urgent concern.

Addressing the backlog of cases, however, should not come at the expense of expediting cases without proper deliberation. Additional asylum officers and immigration judges are needed to address this backlog in a way that ensures that asylum seekers are given a fair hearing (Berthold and McPherson 2016). In March 2022, the Biden administration announced a plan to overhaul the asylum process in the United States, including a policy that would allow asylum officers instead of immigration judges to evaluate defensive asylum claims (those pending in immigration courts), with the aim of mitigating the overwhelming docket of cases before IJs (Sullivan 2022).

Within the broader context of the asylum system, there are specific policies of enforced waiting that have clear deleterious effects on asylum seekers' ability to live humane and dignified lives, or to even meet their basic needs. In chapters 2 and 3, I outlined the ways in which my interlocutors experienced the required wait time in applying for an employment authorization document (EAD, or work permit) as not only a source of existential insecurity but also a threat to familial obligations and relationships. In June 2020, a final rule issued by President Trump went into effect that expanded this wait time from 180 days to 365 days. Fortunately, in his attempts to reverse numerous harmful Trump-era asylum policies, President Biden vacated this rule in September 2022, restoring the EAD wait time to 180 days. While this move is encouraging, it is not enough. Even a wait of 180 days is a punitive and demeaning policy that should be eliminated, returning to pre-1996 rules that allowed immediate access to employment for asylum seekers. Without immediate employment opportunities or governmental support, asylum seekers will continue to face numerous and potentially damaging barriers to their capacity to fulfill their basic needs.

Finally, my research suggests that there are several ways in which the experience of asylum adjudication can be improved. First, asylum adjudication must cease operating from a lens of suspicion, or by assuming asylum claimants' *lack* of credibility, as codified in the REAL ID Act of 2005. Second, and related, as Schuster (2018) has likewise suggested with regard to the UK asylum adjudication context, a move away from an adversarial approach is important. As evident in my ethnographic material, both the presumption of fraud or lack of credibility and the adversarial approach taken in immigration court—and even in asylum interviews, despite their designation as "non-adversarial"—have a profound impact on asylum claimants. Indeed, as I have traced, the experience of *non*recognition, or of being disbelieved, even if one's claim is eventually approved, has emotional effects that far outlive the adjudication period. Third, while my interlocutors were fortunate to have access to volunteer legal representation, this is not widely available to asylum seekers; yet it should be. As I have shown, the asylum process is a formidable challenge to navigate even for those with legal assistance. Given that asylum seekers without legal assistance face incredibly high odds of rejection, this is an urgent concern.

Finally, there should be concerted efforts on the part of bureaucratic immigration officials, from adjudicators to enforcement officers, attorneys, and legal aid advocates, to minimize the illegibility and opacity of the system. Asylum claimants' struggle to access information about their cases or to actively engage with immigration officials is dehumanizing and demoralizing. Asylum seekers need to be considered an integral part of the asylum determination process, so that they can actively speak and voice their concerns rather than being "spoken for" (see Statz 2018). Ultimately, the suggestions I've outlined above can begin to disrupt the invisibility and normalization of the everyday bureaucratic forms of violence inflicted on migrants within the asylum system.

*   *   *

Throughout this book, I have aimed to challenge the normalized processes of the asylum system—processes and policies that I have framed as comprising a continuum of violence. Indeed, this book has traced the often hidden and routinized effects of such a putatively "humanitarian" system. That my interlocutors were offered a partial and ambivalent form of refuge—not routinely detained, protected from deportation while their claims were pending, eventually afforded access to employment—allows the state to claim a fulfillment of its legal and ethical obligations to upholding the Geneva Convention and the rights of refugees, and to human rights, more broadly. Yet, as my interlocutors make clear, the US asylum system involves numerous forms of bureaucratic violences that not only exacerbate past trauma for those fleeing violent and oppressive situations, but also generate new forms of suffering and exclusion. This suffering, moreover, extends beyond the individual bodies of asylum seekers and the boundaries of the United States. Its effects are transnationally embodied, reverberating across oceans, leaking through borders. That asylum seekers like my friends endure this system and its everyday violences is a testament to their agency and their refusal to be reduced to passive victims or morally suspect Others. They creatively and forcefully navigate this landscape that works to restrict their lives and their senses of self. However, the very fact that they are forced to endure the system challenges the fiction of the affirmative asylum regime's purported benevolence. In this way, the pain and distress of my asylum-seeking friends powerfully critiques the asylum regime itself. In drawing attention to the suffering of asylum claimants, my goal has not been to fetishize suffering. Rather, this ethnography has revealed the mechanisms by which the asylum regime produces those forms of suffering. Asylum seekers' anxiety, grief, and fear, I have shown, are not inevitable features of displacement or of seeking refuge, but rather the lived effects of cumulative injustices and indignities at the hands of more powerful actors and regimes, including the one to which they turn for protection—the US asylum system.

Notes

INTRODUCTION

1. To protect confidentiality, all names in the book are pseudonyms.

2. Eric was an exception to this. Unlike most of my other interlocutors, he was active on social media and had established a social network among Cameroonian im/migrants in Minnesota and nationally. He recalled being warned by other Cameroonians about applying for asylum, given the possibility of denial and subsequent unavoidable deportation. Yet, he felt strongly he had "a good case" so decided to apply. While Eric had initial ambivalence, his decision underscores the understanding that he and my other interlocutors had about the legitimacy of their own cases.

3. Minnesota was one of twenty-two states that offered asylum applicants state-funded health care coverage at the time of my initial fieldwork (2010). Prior to 1996, asylum applicants in the United States were able to access federally funded forms of health care coverage—a benefit that was revoked for all noncitizens with the passage of the Personal Responsibility and Work Opportunity Reconciliation Act of 1996.

4. To this point, immigration attorney and advocate Jason Dzubow (2021) has recently argued that affirmative asylum claimants "represent a 'hidden asylum crisis' because their suffering is invisible to the general public and has thus far been ignored by lawmakers."

5. Of the twenty-six study participants, twenty-five were from African countries, including Cameroon (N=13), Liberia (N=4), Kenya (N=3), Ethiopia (N=3),

Rwanda (N=1), and Zimbabwe (N=1). One study participant was from Pakistan. Ten study participants were female and sixteen were male. Ages of study participants ranged from early twenties to mid-fifties. All identified English as a native language (Cameroonians) or were fluent English speakers.

6. These flyers stressed the confidential and voluntary nature of the study. Further, the flyer underscored that my study was separate from the activities of CHR, making clear that their clients' decision to participate or not in my study would in no way impact their asylum claims or the services they were receiving at CHR.

7. In her critique of humanitarian politics in France, Miriam Ticktin (2006, 2011) has argued that humanitarianism and anti-immigration politics are not conflicting sets of discourses and practices, but in fact often work together to advance restrictive immigration policies.

8. The fear and mistrust to which Eric alluded was not unique to asylum seekers from Cameroon. Indeed, the director of the legal aid program at CHR had anticipated that this would be an issue. Eric suggested that people might be much more willing to talk to me once their asylum case was resolved. To be sure, I had already found this to be the case. Several Cameroonian asylum seekers to whom I was introduced indicated that they would be willing to participate in my research study only after their case was adjudicated. Likewise, the CHR intern reported to me that several CHR (non-Cameroonian) clients had responded to a study recruitment mailing indicating the same stipulation.

9. "INS" refers to the Immigration and Naturalization Service, the US governmental agency of the Department of Justice that was responsible for administering federal immigration laws and regulations from 1933 to 2003. In 2003 (as a response to the terrorist attacks of 9/11) the INS was disbanded and its functions were transferred to three new entities: US Citizenship and Immigration Services (USCIS); Immigration and Customs Enforcement (ICE); and Customs and Border Patrol (CBP). It was not uncommon for research participants to continue to refer to "INS" or to use the broader term "Immigration" to refer to governmental organization(s) responsible for any immigration laws or policies.

CHAPTER 1

1. Ndolé is a traditional Cameroon dish made of boiled peanuts, bitterleaf, and fish.

2. While I did not learn of the specifics of the malfunction of this woman's electronic bracelet (EM), Martinez-Aranda (2020) has pointed both to the frequency of such malfunctions in EMs and the way in which such malfunctions serve to advance the state's criminalization of migrants. Malfunctioning technology, they write, "construct(s) immigrants as 'non-compliant,' an orientation

that blames immigrants, while off-loading responsibility from the state onto individuals and communities, thereby contributing to the criminalization of migrants" (76).

3. Unlike Maurice, most of my interlocutors were receiving *pro bono* legal assistance through CHR. Their legal representatives—namely volunteer lawyers who did not practice nor were trained in immigration law—were critical in getting my interlocutors' paperwork and documents filed and arguing their cases in court. Yet, in the protracted periods between asylum interviews, court hearings, and other necessary bureaucratic appointments, my interlocutors found that volunteer attorneys were not always helpful in navigating their concerns and confusion. This was not because they lacked commitment. Rather, these volunteer attorneys were often overloaded with their regular caseload; or themselves sometimes lacked or had trouble accessing information about asylum applicants' cases. At other times, asylum seekers told me that because they were receiving the legal aid for free, they were wary of seeming like a burden to their attorneys by calling them with too many questions.

4. At the time in Minnesota, asylum applicants, unlike undocumented persons, were eligible for MinnesotaCare, a state-funded health care program for Minnesotans with low incomes. The monthly sliding-scale premium per person whose income is at 100 percent of the federal poverty level was approximately $10. Some emergency care services were covered for asylum applicants under Medicaid's Emergency Medical Assistance program. While the monthly premiums were low enough that many of my interlocutors enrolled in MinnesotaCare, for those without work authorizations even this monthly payment could be challenging. As of 2018, asylum seekers whose cases had been pending for at least 180 days and who had received a work authorization permit were eligible for MinnesotaCare. All non-incarcerated noncitizens remain eligible for Medicaid's Emergency Medical Assistance program, which covers only health care emergencies.

CHAPTER 2

1. An earlier version of this chapter appeared as Haas 2017.

2. Unlike the United States, the United Kingdom does provide asylum applicants with housing and (albeit minimal) monthly cash assistance.

3. I recognized these moments in my fieldwork as serious mental health concerns for my interlocutors. During my fieldwork, I carried a list of local mental health providers and would encourage asylum seekers who were struggling with mental health issues to call and schedule an appointment. I also offered to call providers on their behalf and make an appointment—an offer that a few of my interlocutors accepted. I also sought out the assistance of psychological professionals in

responding to my interlocutors' expressions of suicidal ideation; they advised me to ask my interlocutors who expressed such thoughts/desires to verbally assure me that they would not harm themselves and that they would schedule an appointment with a mental health professional.

4. During my initial fieldwork and earlier follow-ups, FaceTime, Skype, and other video-calling platforms were not used by my interlocutors. This did change over time, and my later data (e.g., presented in chapter 5) reflect how these forms of media have begun to be used and experienced as part of social and familial connection.

CHAPTER 4

1. Portions of this chapter in an earlier form appear in Haas (2019).

2. In addition to Chicago, asylum offices are found in Arlington, Virginia; Houston, Texas; Los Angeles, California; Miami, Florida; Lyndhurst, New Jersey; San Francisco, California; and Rosedale, New York. Asylum office locations were chosen because of their proximity to where most asylum applicants reside.

3. For the asylum process in general, see "US Asylum Process" and figure 1 in the introduction to this book.

4. Interestingly, in contrast to her view on the potential subjective-ness of psychological assessments, Susan, along with other legal professionals I met, found other kinds of medical evaluations and records very helpful. When I asked Susan about this distinction, she explained, "Judges are much more swayed by it [non-psychiatric medical records/evaluations] because it's science. It's provable. It's concrete." Overall, medical evidence that could attest to phenomena like physical and sexual abuse, torture, or periods of detention has been shown to be more readily acceptable and legitimated than psychological evidence (Lustig et al. 2008). An important caveat here is that torture is often inflicted with the aim of not leaving scars or "evidence."

CHAPTER 5

1. In addition to these discretionary factors, a person must also meet the following procedural requirements to qualify for voluntary departure: has been in the United States for at least one year; has the necessary travel documents; shows financial means and intention to depart; has not committed an aggravated felony or been found removable on security-related grounds; and has demonstrated good moral character (INA § 240B(b)).

2. "Unlawful" time does not include time during which an asylum application is pending. Because there is a one-year filing bar for asylum, most of my interlocutors who took voluntary departure were eligible for re-entry after three years.

3. An I-730 form can be filed for a child who was under twenty-one at the time that the petitioner filed for asylum. Thus, although Sharon's daughter arrived in the United States after the age of twenty-one, she qualified because she was younger at both the time of Sharon's asylum and I-730 submission.

4. Technically, asylees must wait five years after receiving a green card to apply for citizenship; however, DHS counts one year in asylee status as permanent residence, thus making the actual wait time four years after getting a green card.

5. Her adult children were not eligible under the same procedures as her youngest daughter. For her oldest children, Sharon filed an I-130 form, "Petition for Alien Relative." Another available legal option for family reunification is an "Affidavit of Support" that could potentially allow a petitioner to sponsor a green card for a relative. However, this option was unavailable to Sharon because it is contingent on the petitioner to prove the ability to financially support the co-applicant. Sharon did not work and was dependent on government assistance, thus making far less than the required 125 percent over the poverty line.

6. Asylum seekers and asylees are prohibited from returning to their countries of citizenship.

7. Although asylees can petition to have additional relatives (that is, other than a spouse or child under twenty-one) join once they have a green card but not US citizenship, the processing times are considerably longer. It is often advisable to get US citizenship before petitioning for additional relatives.

References

Abarca, Gray Albert, and Susan Bibler Coutin. 2018. "Sovereign Intimacies: The Lives of Documents within US State- Noncitizen Relationships." *American Ethnologist* 45, no. 1: 7–19.

Ahmed, Sara. 2004. "Affective Economies." *Social Text* 22, no. 2: 117–39.

Allsopp, Jennifer, Nando Sigona, and Jenny Phillimore. 2014. *Poverty Among Refugees and Asylum Seekers in the UK: An Evidence and Policy Review.* Birmingham: University of Birmingham, Institute for Research into Superdiversity.

Amin, Julius A. 2021. "President Paul Biya and Cameroon's Anglophone Crisis: A Catalogue of Miscalculations." *Africa Today* 68, no. 1.

Anderson, Bridget. 2013. *Us and Them?: The Dangerous Politics of Immigration Control.* Oxford: Oxford University Press.

Andersson, Ruben. 2014a. *Illegality, Inc: Clandestine Migration and the Business of Bordering Europe.* Berkeley: University of California Press.

———. 2014b. "Time and the Migrant Other: European Border Controls and the Temporal Economics of Illegality." *American Anthropologist,* 116, no. 4: 795–809.

Aradau, Claudia, and Lucrezia Canzutti, L. 2022. "Asylum, Border, and the Politics of Violence: From Suspicion to Cruelty." *Global Studies Quarterly* 2: 1–11.

Armenta, Amada. 2017. *Protect, Serve, And Deport: The Rise of Policing as Immigration Enforcement.* Berkeley: University of California Press.

———. 2016. "Between Public Service and Social Control: Policing Dilemmas in the Era of Immigration Enforcement." *Social Problems* 63, no. 1: 111–26.

Asad, Talal. 2000. "Agency and Pain: An Exploration." *Culture and Religion,* 1, no. 1: 29–60.

Astrada, Scott B., and Marvin L. Astrada. 2019. "Truth in Crisis: Critically Re-Examining Immigration Rhetoric and Policy under the Trump Administration." *Harvard Latinx Law Review* 22: 7.

Baldassar, Loretta 2016. "De- demonizing Distance in Mobile Family Lives: Co- presence, Care Circulation and Polymedia as Vibrant Matter. "*Global Networks* 16, no. 2: 145–63.

———. 2007. "Transnational Families and the Provision of Moral and Emotional Support: The Relationship between Truth and Distance." *Identities: Global Studies in Culture and Power* 14, no. 4: 385–409.

Baugh, Ryan. 2020. *Annual Flow Report: Refugees and Asylees: 2019.* Washington, DC: US Department of Homeland Security (DHS), Office of Immigration Statistics. https://www.dhs.gov/sites/default/files/publications /immigration-statistics/yearbook/2019/refugee_and_asylee_2019.pdf.

BBC News. 2017. "Migrant Crisis: EU Leaders Agree to Plan to Stop Libya Influx." https://www.bbc.com/news/world-europe-38850380. Accessed May 18, 2019.

Berg, Mette Louise, and Elena Fiddian-Qasmiyeh. 2018. "Introduction to the Issue: Encountering Hospitality and Hostility." *Migration and Society* 1, no. 1: 1–6.

Berger, Iris, Tricia Redeker Hepner, Benjamin N. Lawrence, Joanna T. Tague, and Meredith Terretta. 2015. *African Asylum at A Crossroads: Activism, Expert Testimony, and Refugee Rights.* Athens: Ohio University Press.

Berlant, Lauren. 2011. *Cruel Optimism.* Durham, NC: Duke University Press.

Berthold, S. Megan, and Jane McPherson. 2016. "Commentary: Fractured Families: US Asylum Backlog Divides Parents and Children Worldwide." *Journal of Human Rights and Social Work* 1, no. 2: 78–84.

Besteman, Catherine. 2016. *Making Refuge: Somali Bantu Refugees in Lewison, Maine.* Durham, NC: Duke University Press.

Betancourt, Sarah. 2021. "'Traumatizing and Abusive': Immigrants Reveal Personal Toll of Ankle Monitors." *The Guardian,* July 12, 2021. https:// www.theguardian.com/us-news/2021/jul/12/immigrants-report-physical-emotional-harms-electronic-ankle-monitors.

Bialik, Kristen. 2019. "Border Apprehensions Increased in 2018—Especially for Migrant Families." *Pew Research Center* (blog). January 16, 2019. *https://*

www.pewresearch.org/fact-tank/2019/01/16/border-apprehensions-of-migrant-families-have-risen-substantially-so-far-in-2018.

Biehl, João, and Peter Locke. 2010. "Deleuze and the Anthropology of Becoming." *Current Anthropology* 51, no. 3: 317–51.

Biehl, Kristen Sarah. 2015. "Governing through Uncertainty: Experiences of being a Refugee in Turkey as a Country for Temporary Asylum." *Social Analysis* 59, no. 1: 57.

Bigo, Didier. 2007. *Policing Insecurity Today: Defense and Internal Security.* London: Palgrave MacMillan.

———. 2002. "Security and Immigration: Toward a Critique of the Governmentality of Unease." *Alternatives* 27: 63–92.

Bohmer, Carol, and Amy Shuman. 2018. *Political Asylum Deceptions: The Culture of Suspicion.* New York: Springer.

———. 2010. "Contradictory Discourses of Protection and Control in Transnational Asylum Law." *Journal of Legal Anthropology* 1, no. 2: 212–29.

———. 2008. *Rejecting Refugees: Political Asylum in the 21st Century.* London: Routledge.

Boss, Pauline. 2009. *Ambiguous Loss: Learning to Live with Unresolved Grief.* Cambridge, MA: Harvard University Press.

Bourdieu, Pierre. 1997. *Pascalian Meditations.* Stanford, CA: Stanford University Press.

———. 1977. *Outline of a Theory of Practice.* Cambridge, UK: Cambridge University Press.

Bourgois, Philippe. 1988. "Conjugated Opression: Class and Ethnicity Among Guaymi and Kuna Banana Workers." *American Ethnologist* 15, no. 2: 328–48.

Brekke, Jan-Paul. 2010. "Life on Hold: The Impact of Time on Young Asylum Seekers Waiting For a Decision." *Diskurs Kindheits-und Jugendforschung/ Discourse. Journal of Childhood and Adolescence Research, 5,* no. 2: 159–67.

Brekke, Jan-Paul, Simon Roland Birkvad, and Marta Bivand Erdal. 2021. "Losing the Right to Stay: Revocation of Refugee Permits in Norway." *Journal of Refugee Studies* 34, no. 2: 1637–56.

Broeders, Dennis. 2007. "The New Digital Borders of Europe EU Databases and the Surveillance of Irregular Migrants." *International Sociology* 22, no. 1: 71–92.

Broz, Ludek, and Daniel Münster, eds. 2016. *Suicide and Agency: Anthropological Perspectives on Self-Destruction, Personhood, and Power.* New York: Routledge.

Brun, Cathrine. 2015. "Active Waiting and Changing Hopes: Toward a Time Perspective on Protracted Displacement." *Social Analysis* 59, no. 1: 19–37.

Bryant, Rebecca. 2016. "On Critical Times: Return, Repetition, and the Uncanny Present." *History and Anthropology* 27, no. 1: 19–31.

Bryceson, Deborah Fahy. 2019. "Transnational Families Negotiating Migrration and Care Life Cycles across Nation-state Borders." *Journal of Ethnic and Migration Studies* 45, no. 16: 3042–64.

Burnett, Jon, and Fidelis Chebe. 2010. "Captive Labour: Asylum Seekers, Migrants and Employment in UK Immigration Removal Centres." *Race & Class* 51, no. 4: 95–103.

Butler, Judith. 1997. *The Psychic Life of Power.* Stanford, CA: Stanford University Press.

———. 1992. "Contingent Foundations: Feminism and the Question of 'Postmodernism'." In *Feminists Theorize the Politics,* edited by Judith Butler. London: Routledge.

Cabot, Heath. 2019. "The European Refugee Crisis and Humanitarian Citizenship in Greece. *Ethnos 84,* no. 5: 747–71.

———. 2014. *On the Doorstep of Europe: Asylum and Citizenship in Greece.* Philadelphia: University of Pennsylvania Press.

———. 2012. "The Governance of Things: Documenting Limbo in the Greek Asylum Procedure." *PoLAR: Political and Legal Anthropology Review* 35, no. 1: 11–29.

Calavita, Kitty. 2007. "Immigration Law, Race, and Identity." *Annual Review of Law and Social Science* 3: 1–20.

Campbell, Nancy D. 2004. "Technologies of Suspicion: Coercion and Compassion in Post-disciplinary Surveillance Regimes." *Surveillance & Society* 2, no. 1: 78–92.

Campesi, Giuseppe. 2018. Seeking Asylum in Times of Crisis: Reception, Confinement, and Detention at Europe's Southern Border. *Refugee Survey Quarterly* 37, no. 1: 44–70.

Carswell, Kenneth, Pennie Blackburn, and Chris Barker. 2011. "The Relationship between Trauma, Post-Migration Problems and the Psychological Well-being of Refugees and Asylum Seekers." *International Journal of Social Psychiatry* 57, no. 2: 107–19.

Castañeda, Heide. 2019. *Borders of Belonging: Struggle and Solidarity in Mixed-status Immigrant Families.* Stanford, CA: Stanford University Press.

———. 2010. "Deportation Deferred: 'Illegality,' Visibility, and Recognition in Contemporary Germany." In *The Deportation Regime: Sovereignty, Space and the Freedom of Movement,* edited by Nicholas P. De Genova and Nathalie Peutz, 245–61. Durham, NC: Duke University Press.

———. 2009. "Illegality As Risk Factor: A Survey of Unauthorized Migrant Patients in a Berlin Clinic. *Social Science & Medicine* 68, no. 8: 1552–60.

Cervantes, Andrea Gómez, Cecilia Menjívar, and William G. Staples. 2017. "'Humane' Immigration Enforcement and Latina Immigrants in the Detention Complex." *Feminist Criminology* 12, no. 3: 269–92.

Chavez, Leo R. 2008. "Spectacle in the Desert: The Minutemen Project on the US-Mexico Border." In *Global Vigilante*, edited by David Pratten and Atreyee Sen, 25–46. New York: Columbia University Press.

———. 1998. *Shadowed Lives: Undocumented Immigrants in American Society.* Second ed. Orlando: Harcourt Brace College Publishers.

Chiatoh, Valerie Muguoh. 2019. "Recognition of Minority Groups as a Prerequisite for the Protection of Human Rights: The Case of Anglophone Cameroon." *African Human Rights Law Journal* 19, no. 2: 675–97.

Chua, Joclyn Lim. 2011. "Making Time for the Children: Self-temporalization and the Cultivation of the Antisuicidal Subject in South India." *Cultural Anthropology* 26, no. 1: 112–37.

Cianciarulo, Marisa Silenzi. 2006. "Terrorism and Asylum Seekers: Why the Real ID Act is a False Promise." *Harvard Journal on Legislation* 43, no. 1: 101–43.

Codó, Eva. 2011. "Regimenting Discourse, Controlling Bodies: Disinformation, Evaluation, and Moral Categorization in a State Bureaucratic Agency." *Discourse & Society* 22, no. 6: 723–42.

Coffey, Guy. 2003. "The Credibility of Credibility Evidence at the Refugee Review Tribunal." *International Journal of Refugee Law* 15, no. 3: 377–414.

Cohen, Juliet. 2001. "Questions of Credibility: Omissions, Discrepancies and Errors of Recall in the Testimony of Asylum Seekers." *International Journal of Refugee Law* 13, no. 3: 293–309.

Collins, Kendall. 2016. "Rethinking the Employment Status of Refugees in the United States." *Columbia Journal of Transnational Law* 55, no. 1: 1519–48.

Conlon, Deirdre. 2011. "Waiting: Feminist Perspectives on the Spacings/ Timings of Migrant (Im)Mobility." *Gender, Place & Culture* 18, no. 3: 353–60.

Coutin, Susan Bibler. 2011. "The Rights of Noncitizens in the United States." *Annual Review of Law and Social Sciences* 7: 289–308.

———. 2005. "Contesting Criminality: Illegal Immigration and the Spatialization of Legality." *Theoretical Criminology* 9, no. 1: 5–33.

———. 2003. *Legalizing Moves: Salvadoran Immigrants' Struggle for U.S. Residency.* Ann Arbor: University of Michigan Press.

———. 2001. "The Oppressed, the Suspect, and the Citizen: Subjectivity in Competing Accounts of Political Violence." *Law & Society Inquiry* 26, no. 1: 63–94.

Crapanzano, Vincent. 1985. *Waiting: The Whites of South Africa.* New York: Random House.

Crawley, Heaven, and Dimitris Skleparis. 2018. "Refugees, Migrants, Neither, Both: Categorical Fetishism and the Politics of Bounding in Europe's 'Migration Crisis.'" *Journal of Ethnic and Migration Studies* 44, no. 1: 48–64.

Cwerner, Saulo B., 2004. "Faster, Faster and Faster: The Time Politics of Asylum in the UK." *Time & Society, 13,* no. 1: 71–88.

Dahinden, Janine. 2005. "Contesting Transnationalism? Lessons from the Study of Albanian Migration Networks from Former Yugoslavia." *Global Networks*, 5, no. 2: 191–208.

Daniel, E. Valentine, and John Chr Knudsen, eds. 1995. *Mistrusting Refugees.* Berkeley: University of California Press.

Danstrøm, Matilde Skov, and Zachary Whyte. 2019. "Narrating Asylum in Camp and at Court." In *Asylum Determination in Europe*, 175–94. London: Palgrave Macmillan, Cham.

Das, Veena. 2004. "The Signature of the State: The Paradox of Illegibility." In *Anthropology in the Margins of the State*, edited by Veena Das and Deborah Poole, 225–52. Oxford: Oxford University Press.

Das, Veena, Arthur Kleinman, Pamela Reynolds, and Mamphela Ramphele, eds. 2000. *Violence and Subjectivity*. Berkeley: University of California Press.

Darling, Jonathan. 2011. "Domopolitics, Governmentality and the Regulation of Asylum Accommodation." *Political Geography* 30, no. 5: 263–71.

Dauvergne, Catherine. 2004. "Making People Illegal." In *Critical Beings: Law, Nation and the Global* Subject, edited by Peter Fitzpatrick, 83–100. Hampshire, England: Ashgate.

Davis, Duane. 2019. "The Phenomenological Method." In *50 Concepts for a Critical Phenomenology*, edited by Gail Weiss, Ann V. Murphy, and Gayle Salamon, 3–10. Chicago: Northwestern University Press.

De Genova, Nicholas. 2020. "The Convulsive European Space of Mobilities. *Political Anthropological Research on International Social Sciences (PARISS)* 1, no. 1: 162–88.

———. 2018. "The 'Migrant Crisis' as Racial Crisis: Do Black Lives Matter in Europe?" *Ethnic and Racial Studies* 41, no. 10: 1765–82.

———. 2017. "Introduction: The Borders of 'Europe' and the European Question." In *The Borders of "Europe": Autonomy of Migration, Tactics of Belonging*, edited by Nicholas De Genova, 1–36. Durham, NC: Duke University Press.

———. 2013. "Spectacles of Migrant 'Illegality': The Scene of Exclusion, the Obscene of Inclusion. *Ethnic and Racial Studies* 36, no. 7: 1180–98.

———. 2007. "The Production of Culprits: From Deportability to Detainability in the Aftermath of 'Homeland Security.'" *Citizenship Studies* 11, no. 5: 421–48.

———. 2002. "Migrant 'Illegality' and Deportability in Everyday Life." *Annual Review of Anthropology* 31: 419–47.

De Genova, Nicholas P., and Nathalie Peutz, eds. 2010. *The Deportation Regime: Sovereignty, Space, and the Freedom of Movement.* Durham, NC: Duke University Press.

De Haene, Lucia, and Cécile Rousseau, eds. 2020. *Working with Refugee Families: Trauma and Exile in Family Relationships.* Cambridge, UK: Cambridge University Press.

De León, Jason. 2015. *The Land of Open Graves*. Berkeley, CA: University of California Press.

De Sousa Santos, Boaventura. 2014. *Epistemologies of the South: Justice Against Epistemicide*. New York: Routledge.

DelVecchio Good, Mary Jo, Sandra Teresa Hyde, Sarah Pinto, and Byron J. Good, eds. 2008. *Postcolonial Disorders*. Berkeley: University of California Press.

Dotson, Kristie. 2011. "Tracking Epistemic Violence, Tracking Practices of Silencing." *Hypatia* 26, no. 2: 236–57.

Dreby, Joanna. 2010. *Divided by Borders: Mexican Migrants and Their Children*. Berkeley: University of California Press.

Dzubow, Jason. 2022. "Affirmative Asylum Updates: Winners and Losers." *The Asylumist Blog*. April 6, 2022. https://www.asylumist.com/2022/04/06/affirmative-asylum-updates-winners-and-losers.

———. 2021. "Congress Addresses the Asylum Office Backlog." *The Asylumist Blog*. September 15, 2021. https://www.asylumist.com/2021/09/15/congress-addresses-the-asylum-office-backlog.

Edwards, Alice. 2005. "Human Rights, Refugees, and the Right 'to Enjoy' Asylum." *International Journal of Refugee Law* 17, no. 2: 293–330.

Eggerman, Mark, and Catherine Panter-Brick. 2010. "Suffering, Hope, And Entrapment: Resilience and Cultural Values in Afghanistan." *Social Science & Medicine, 71*, no. 1: 71–83.

Einolf, Christopher J. 2001. *The Mercy Factor: Refugees and American Asylum System*. Chicago: Ivan Dee.

El-Shaarawi, Nadia. 2021. "A Transit State: The Ambivalences of the Refugee Resettlement Process for Iraqis in Cairo." *American Ethnologist* 48, no. 4: 404–17.

———. 2016. "Life in Transit: Mental Health, Temporality, and Urban Displacement for Iraqi Refugees." In *Global Mental Health: Anthropological Perspectives*, edited by Brandon A. Kohrt and Emily Mendenhall, 73–86. New York: Routledge.

———. 2015. "Living an Uncertain Future: Temporality, Uncertainty, and Well-being Among Iraqi Refugees in Egypt." *Social Analysis* 59, no. 1: 38–56.

Erdal, Marta Bivand, and Ceri Oeppen. 2018. "Forced to Leave? The Discursive and Analytical Significance of Describing Migration as Forced and Voluntary." *Journal of Ethnic and Migration Studies* 44, no. 6: 981–98.

Erfani, Azadeh. 2022. "Asylum Seekers Have the Right to a Fair and Reliable Asylum Process. New Biden Rules Would Rush Them to their Deportation." *National Immigrant Justice Center* (blog). May 17, 2022. https://immigrantjustice.org/staff/blog/asylum-seekers-have-right-fair-and-reliable-asylum-process-new-biden-rules-would-rush.

Espiritu, Yên Lê 2014. *Body Counts: The Vietnam War and Militarized Refugees*. Berkeley: University of California Press.

Etzold, Benjamin, and Anne-Meike Fechter. 2022. "Unsettling Protracted Displacement: Connectivity and Mobility Beyond 'Limbo.'" *Journal of Ethnic and Migration Studies*. https://doi.org/10.1080/1369183X.2022.2090153.

Eule, Tobias G., Lisa Marie Borrelli, Annika Lindberg, and Anna Wyss. 2019. *Migrants before the Law: Contested Migration Control in Europe*. Cham, Switzerland: Palgrave Macmillan.

Fan, Stephen Shie-Wei. 1997. "Immigration Law and the Promise of Critical Race Theory: Opening the Academy to the Voices of Aliens and Immigrants." *Columbia Law Review* 97, no. 4: 1202–40.

Fanon, Frantz. 1967. *Black Skin, White Masks*. Translated by Charles Lam Markmann. New York: Grove Press.

Farmer, Paul. 2004. "An Anthropology of Structural Violence." *Current Anthropology* 45, no. 3: 305–25.

———. 1996. "On Suffering and Structural Violence: A View from Below." *Daedalus* 125, no. 1: 261–83.

Fassin, Didier. 2015. "Introduction: Governing Precariousness." In *At the Heart of the State: The Moral Worlds of Institutions*, edited by Didier Fassin, 1–14. London: Pluto Press.

———. 2011. "Policing Borders, Producing Boundaries. the Governmentality of Immigration in Dark Times." *Annual Review of Anthropology* 40: 213–26.

———. 2008. "The Humanitarian Politics of Testimony: Subjectification through Trauma in the Israeli-Palestinian Conflict." *Cultural Anthropology* 23, no 3: 531–58.

Fassin, Didier, and Estelle d'Halluin. 2007. "Critical Evidence: The Politics of Trauma in French Asylum Policies." *Ethos* 35, no. 3: 300–29.

———. 2005. "The Truth from the Body: Medical Certificates as Ultimate Evidence for Asylum Seekers." *American Anthropologist* 107, no. 4: 597–608.

Fassin, Didier, and Richard Rechtman. 2009. *Empire of Trauma: An Inquiry into the Condition of Victimhood*. Princeton, NJ: Princeton University Press.

Fassin, Didier, Matthew Wilhelm-Solomon, and Aurelia Segatti. 2017. "Asylum as a Form of Life: The Politics and Experience of Indeterminacy in South Africa." *Current Anthropology* 58, no. 2: 160–87.

Feldman, Ilana. 2016. "Reaction, Experimentation, and Refusal: Palestinian Refugees Confront the Future." *History and Anthropology* 27, no. 4: 411–29.

Fernandes, Jason. 2017. *Alternatives to Detention and the For-Profit Immigration System*. Washington, DC: Center for American Progress. https://www.americanprogress.org/article/alternatives-detention-profit-immigration-system.

Fiddian-Qasmiyeh, Elena, and Yousif M. Qasmiyeh. 2010. "Muslim Asylum-Seekers and Refugees: Negotiating Identity, Politics and Religion in the UK." *Journal of Refugee Studies* 23, no. 3: 294–314.

Fleay, Caroline, and Lisa Hartley. 2016. "'I Feel like a Beggar': Asylum Seekers Living in the Australian Community without the Right to Work." *Journal of International Migration and Integration* 17, no. 4: 1031–48.

Foner, Nancy. 2018. "Race in an Era of Mass Migration: Black Migrants in Europe and the United States." *Ethnic and Racial Studies* 41, no. 6: 1113–30.

Fricker, Miranda. 2007. *Epistemic Injustice: Power and the Ethics of Knowing.* Oxford: Oxford University Press.

Garcia, Angela. 2008. "The Elegiac Addict: History, Chronicity, and the Melancholic Subject." *Cultural Anthropology* 23, no. 4: 718–46.

Garner, Steve, 2007. "The European Union and the Racialization of Immigration, 1985–2006." *Race/Ethnicity: Multidisciplinary Global Contexts* 1, no. 1: 61–87.

Garro, Linda C. 1992. "Chronic Illness and the Construction of Narratives." In *Pain as Human Experience: An Anthropological Perspective,* edited by Mary-Jo DelVecchio Good, Paul E. Brodwin, Byron J. Good, and Arthur Kleinman, 100–37. Berkeley: University of California Press.

Garro, Linda C., and Cheryl Mattingly. 2000. "Narrative as Construct and Construction." In *Narrative and the Cultural Construction of Illness and Healing,* edited by Cheryl Mattingly and Linda Garro, 1–49. Berkeley: University of California Press.

Ghorashi, Halleh, Marije de Boer, and Floor ten Holder. 2018. "Unexpected Agency on the Threshold: Asylum Seekers Narrating from an Asylum Seeker Centre." *Current Sociology* 66, no. 3: 373–91.

Gibney, Matthew. 2004. *The Ethics and Politics of Asylum: Liberal Democracy and the Respose to Refugees.* Cambridge: Cambridge University Press.

Giordano, Cristiana. 2008. Practices of Translation and the Making of Migrant Subjectivities in Contemporary Italy. *American Ethnologist* 35, no. 4: 588–606.

Gill, Nicholas. 2018. "The Suppression of Welcome." *Fennia-International Journal of Geography* 196, no. 1: 88–98.

———. 2016. *Nothing Personal?: Geographies of Governing and Activism in the British Asylum System.* Hoboken, NJ: John Wiley & Sons.

———. 2009. "Longing for Stillness: The Forced Movement of Asylum Seekers." *M/C Journal* 12, no. 1. https://doi.org/10.5204/mcj.123.

Gill, Nicholas, and Anthony Good. 2019. *Asylum Determination in Europe: Ethnographic Perspectives.* Berlin: Springer Nature.

Good, Anothy. 2007. *Anthropology and Expertise in the Asylum Courts.* London: Routledge-Cavendish.

Good, Byron, Mary-Jo DelVecchio Good, Sandra Hyde, and Sarah Pinto. 2008. "Postcolonial Disorders: Reflections on Subjectivity in the Contemporary

World." In *Postcolonial Disorders,* edited by Mary-Jo DelVecchio Good, Sandra Teresa Hyde, Sarah Pinto, and Byron J. Good, 1–40. Berkeley: University of California Press.

Gonzales, Roberto G. 2015. *Lives in Limbo: Undocumented and Coming of Age in America.* Berkeley: University of California Press.

Goździak, Elżbieta M., and Izabella Main. 2020. "European Norms and Values and the Refugee Crisis: Issues and Challenges." In *Europe and the Refugee Response,* edited by Elżbieta Goździak, Izabella Main, and Brigitte Suter, 1–11. New York: Routledge.

Grace, Breanne L. 2019. "Family from Afar? Transnationalism and Refugee Extended Families after Resettlement." *Journal of Refugee Studies* 32, no. 1: 125–43.

Grace, Breanne L., Rajeev Bais, and Benjamin J. Roth. 2018. "The Violence of Uncertainty—Undermining Immigrant and Refugee Health." *New England Journal of Medicine* 379, no. 10: 904–5.

Griffiths, Melanie. 2017. "The Changing Politics of Time in the UK's Immigration System. In *Timespace and International Migration,* edited by Elizabeth Mavroudi, Ben Page, and Anastasia Christou, 48–60. Cheltenham, UK: Edward Elgar Publishing, Inc.

———. 2015. "'Here, Man Is Nothing!' Gender and Policy in an Asylum Context." *Men and Masculinities* 18, no. 4: 468–488.

———. 2014. "Out of Time: The Temporal Uncertainties of Refused Asylum Seekers and Immigration Detainees." *Journal of Ethnic and Migration Studies* 40, no. 12: 1991–2009.

Grosfoguel, R., and C. S. Georas. 2000. "'Coloniality of Power' and Racial Dynamics: Notes toward a Reinterpretation of Latino Caribbeans in New York City." *Identities* 7, no.1: 85–125.

Haas, Bridget M. 2021. "'Asylum is the Most Powerful Medicine': Navigating Therapeutic Interventions in Limbo." *Culture, Medicine, and Psychiatry* 45, no. 2: 193–217.

———. 2019. "Asylum Officers, Suspicion, and the Ambivalent Enactment of Technologies of Truth." In *Technologies of Suspicion and the Ethics of Obligation in Political Asylum,* edited by Bridget M. Haas and Amy Shuman, 105–28. Athens, OH: Ohio University Press.

———. 2017. "Citizens- in- Waiting, Deportees- in- Waiting: Power, Temporality, and Suffering in the US Asylum System." *Ethos* 45, no. 1: 75–97.

Haas, Bridget M., and Amy Shuman, eds. 2019. *Technologies of Suspicion and the Ethics of Obligation in Political Asylum.* Athens, OH: Ohio University Press.

Hage, Ghassan. 2009. "Waiting Out the Crisis: On Stuckedness and Governmentality." *Anthropological Theory* 5, no. 1: 463–75.

———. 2005. "A Not So Multi-Sited Ethnography of a Not So Imagined Community. *Anthropological Theory* 54: 463–75.

———. 2002. "The Differential Intensities of Social Reality: Migration, Participation, and Guilt." In *Arab-Australians Today: Citizenship and Belonging,* edited by Ghassan Hage, 192–205. Victoria, Australia: Melbourne University Press.

Hall, Brian J., and Miranda Olff. 2016. "Global Mental Health: Trauma and Adversity among Populations in Transition." *European Journal of Psychotraumatology* 7, no. 1, 31140. DOI: 10.3402/ejpt.v7.31140.

Hamlin, Rebecca. 2021. *Crossing: How We Label and React to People on the Move.* Stanford, CA: Stanford University Press.

Hasselberg, Ines. 2016. *Enduring Uncertainty.* New York: Berghahn Books.

Hathaway, James C. 2007. "Forced Migration Studies: Could We Agree to Just 'Date'?" *Journal of Refugee Studies* 20, no. 2: 349–69.

———. 1991. "Reconceiving Refugee Law as Human Rights Protection." *Journal of Refugee Studies* 4, no. 2: 113–31.

Herrera, Jack. 2021. "One Way Trump May Have Changed Immigration Forever." *Politico,* March 2, 2021. https://www.politico.com/news/magazine/2021/03/02/biden-immigration-trump-legacy-asylum-refugees-472008.

Hess, Julia Meredith, Brian L. Isakson, Suha Amer, Eric Ndaheba, Brandon Baca, and Jessica R. Goodkind. 2019. "Refugee Mental Health and Healing: Understanding the Impact of Policies of Rapid Economic Self-Sufficiency and the Importance of Meaningful Work." *Journal of International Migration and Integration* 20, no. 3: 769–86.

Heyman, J. M. 2013. "The Study of Illegality and Legality: Which Way Forward?" *Political and Legal Anthropology Review* 36, no. 2: 304–7.

———. 2009. "Trust, Privilege, and Discretion in the Governance of the US Borderlands with Mexico." *Canadian Journal of Law and Society/La Revue Canadienne Droit et Société* 24, no. 3: 367–90.

Heyman, J., J. Slack, and E. Guerra. 2018. "Bordering a 'Crisis': Central American Asylum Seekers and the Reproduction of Dominant Border Enforcement Practices." *Journal of the Southwest* 60, no. 4: 754–86.

High, Lucas. 2018. "Boulder's BI Incorporated has Earned More than Half-Billion Dollars from ICE Contracts." *The Denver Post.* July 16, 2018. https://www.denverpost.com/2018/07/16/boulder-bi-incorporated-ice-contracts.

Hill, Mike. 2012. "Ecologies of War." In *Telemorphosis: Theory in the Era of Climate Change,* edited by Tom Cohen, 239–269. Ann Arbor, MI: Open Humanities Press.

Hirsch, Shirin. 2019. "Racism,'Second Generation'Refugees and the Asylum System." *Identities* 26, no. 1: 88–106.

Hocking, Debbie C., Gerard A. Kennedy, and Suresh Sundram. 2015. "Mental Disorders in Asylum Seekers: The Role of the Refugee Determination

Process and Employment." *Journal of Nervous & Mental Disease* 203, no. 1: 28–32.

Holland, Dorothy, William Lachicotte, Debra Skinner, and Carole Cain. 1998. *Identity and Agency in Cultural Worlds.* Cambridge, MA: Harvard University Press.

Holland, Madeline. 2018. "Stories for Asylum: Narrative and Credibility in the United States' Political Asylum Application." *Refuge: Canada's Journal on Refugees/Refuge: revue canadienne sur les réfugiés* 34, no. 2: 85–93.

Holmes, Seth M. 2007. "'Oaxacans Like to Work Bent Over': The Naturalization of Social Suffering among Berry Farm Workers." *International Migration* 45, no. 3: 39–68.

Holmes, Seth M., and Heide Castañeda. 2016. "Representing the 'European Refugee Crisis' in Germany and Beyond." *American Ethnologist* 43, no.1: 12–24.

Horst, Cindy. 2006. *Transnational Nomads: How Somalis Cope with Refugee Life in the Dadaab Camp of Kenya.* New York: Berghahn Books.

Horton, Sarah B. 2020. "Introduction: Paper Trails: Migrants, Bureaucratic Inscription, and Legal Recognition." In *Paper Trails*, edited by Sarah B. Horton and Josiah Heyman, 1–26. Durham, NC: Duke University Press.

———. 2016. *They Leave Their Kidneys in The Fields: Illness, Injury, And Illegality Among US Farmworkers.* Berkeley: University of California Press.

———. 2009. "A Mother's Heart is Weighed Down With Stones: A Phenomenological Approach to the Experience of Transnational Motherhood." *Culture, Medicine, and Psychiatry* 33, no. 1: 21.

Human Rights First. 2021. *Protection Postponed: Asylum Office Backlogs Cause Suffering, Separate Families, and Undermine Integrati.* April 8, 2021. https://humanrightsfirst.org/library/protection-postponed-asylum-office-backlogs-cause-suffering-separate-families-and-undermine-integration.

Human Rights Watch. 2013. *"At Least Let Them Work": The Denial of Work Authorization and Assistance for Asylum Seekers in the United States.* New York: Human Rights Watch. https://www.hrw.org/report/2013/11/12/least-let-them-work/denial-work-authorization-and-assistance-asylum-seekers-united.

Huysmans, Jef. 2006. *The Politics of Insecurity: Fear, Migration and Asylum in the EU.* New York: Routledge.

Hyndman, Jennifer, and Wenona Giles. 2011. "Waiting for What? The Feminization of Asylum in Protracted Situations." *Gender, Place & Culture* 18, no. 3: 361–79.

Hyndman, Jennifer, and Alison Mountz. 2008. "Another Brick in the Wall? Neo-refoulement and the Externalization of Asylum by Australia and Europe 1." *Government and Opposition* 43, no. 2: 249–69.

Immigrant Law Center of Minnesota. 2018. *Refugees in Minnesota: Quick Facts.* March 27, 2018. https://www.ilcm.org/latest-news/refugees-in-minnesota-quick-facts/.

International Organization for Migration. n.d. Missing Migrants Project. Accessed February 7, 2021. https://missingmigrants.iom.int.

Jacobsen, Christine M., and Mary-Anne Karlsen. 2021. "Introduction: Unpacking the Temporalities of Irregular Migration." In *Waiting and the Temporalities of Irregular Migration*, edited by Christine M. Jacobsen, Mary-Anne Karlsen, and Shahram Khosravi, 1–19. London: Routledge.

Jacobsen, Christine M., Mary-Anne Karlsen, and Shahram Khosravi. 2021. *Waiting and the Temporalities of Irregular Migration.* London: Routledge.

Jacquemet, Marco. 2009. "Transcribing Refugees: The Entextualization of Asylum Seekers' Hearings in a Transidiomatic Environment." *Text & Talk* 29, no. 5: 525–46.

Jansen, Stef. 2015. *Yearnings in the Meantime: 'Normal Lives' and the State in a Sarajevo Apartment Complex.* New York: Berghahn Books.

———. 2013. "On Not Moving Well Enough: Temporal Reasoning in Sarajevo Yearnings for 'Normal Lives.'" *Current Anthropology* 55, supplement 9: S74–S84.

Jeffrey, Craig. 2010. *Timepass: Youth, Class, and the Politics of Waiting in India.* Stanford, CA: Stanford University Press.

Jenkins, Janis H. 2015. "Straining Psychic and Social Sinew: Trauma among Adolescent Psychiatric Patients in New Mexico." *Medical Anthropology Quarterly* 29, no. 1: 42–60.

———. 1998. "The Medical Anthropology of Political Violence: A Cultural and Feminist Agenda." *Medical Anthropology Quarterly* 12, no. 1: 122–31.

———. 1991. "A State Construction of Affect: Political Ethos and Mental Health among Salvadoran Women Refugees." *Culture, Medicine & Psychiatry* 15: 139–65.

Jubany, Olga. 2017. *Screening Asylum in a Culture of Disbelief: Truths, Denials and Skeptical Borders.* Cham, Switzerland: Palgrave MacMillan.

Kagan, Michael. 2003. "Is Truth in the Eye of the Beholder?: Objective Credibility Assessment in Refugee Status Determination." *Georgetown Immigration Law Journal* 17: 367–415.

Kaiser, Bonnie N., Emily E. Haroz, Brandon A. Kohrt, Paul A. Bolton, Judith K. Bass, and Devon Hinton. 2015. "'Thinking Too Much': A Systematic Review of a Common Idiom of Distress." *Social Science and Medicine* 147: 170–83.

Kallio, Kirsi Pauliina, Isabel Meier, and Jouni Häkli. 2020. "Radical Hope in Asylum Seeking: Political Agency Beyond Linear Temporality." *Journal of Ethnic and Migration Studies* 47, no.17: 4006–22.

Kapferer, Bruce. 1995. "Bureaucratic Erasure: Identity, Resistance and Violence–Aborigines and a Discourse of Autonomy in a North Queensland

Town." *In Worlds Apart: Modernity through the Prism of the Local,* edited by Daniel Miller, 69–90. London: Routledge.

Khosravi, Shahram. 2018. "Stolen Time." *Radical Philosophy* 2, no. 3: 38–41.

———. 2010. "The 'Illegal' Traveller: An Auto- Ethnography of Borders." *Social Anthropology* 15, no. 3: 321–34.

Kirmayer, Laurence J. 1992. "The Body's Insistence on Meaning: Metaphor as Presentation and Representation in Illness Experience." *Medical Anthropology Quarterly* 6, no. 4: 323–46.

Kleist, Nauja, and Stef Jansen. 2016. "Introduction: Hope Over Time—Crisis, Immobility and Future-making." *History and Anthropology* 27, no. 4: 373–92.

Kline, Nolan. 2017. "Pathogenic Policy: Immigrant Policing, Fear, and Parallel Medical Systems in the US South." *Medical Anthropology* 36, no. 4: 396–410.

Kobelinsky, Carolina. 2015. "Judging Intimacies in the French Court of Asylum." *PoLAR: Political and Legal Anthropology Review* 38, no. 2: 338–55.

———. 2010. *L'Accueil Des Demandeurs d'Asile: Une Ethnographie De l'Attente.* Paris: Editions du Cygne.

Konings, Piet, and Francis B. Nyamnjoh. 2019. "Anglophone Secessionist Movements in Cameroon." In *Secessionism in African Politics,* edited by Lotje de Vries, Pierre Englebert, and Mareike Schomerus, 59–89. Cham, Switzerland: Palgrave Macmillan.

———. 2004. "President Paul BIya and the 'Anglophone Problem' in Cameroon." In *The Leadership Challenge in Africa: Cameroon Under Paul Biya,* edited by John Mukum Mbaku and Joseph Takougang, 191–234. Trenton, NY: Africa World Press.

Koulish, Robert. 2013. "Entering the Risk Society: A Contested Terrain for Immigrant Enforcement." In *Social Control and Justice: Crimmigration in the Age of Fear,* edited by Maria Joao Guia, Maartje Van Der Woude and Joanne Van Der Leun., 61–86. The Hague, Netherlands: Eleven International.

Lanard, Noah. 2017. "Trump's Immigration Proposal Could Make it Radically Harder to Get Asylum." *Mother Jones.* October 11, 2017. https://www.motherjones.com/politics/2017/10/trumps-immigration-proposal-could-make-it-radically-harder-to-get-asylum.

Larchanché, Stéphanie. 2012. "Intangible Obstacles: Health Implications of Stigmatization, Structural Violence, and Fear Among Undocumented Immigrants in France." *Social Science & Medicine* 74, no. 6: 858–83.

Lawrance, Benjamin N. 2019. "From Witchcraft to Forced Marriage: Country of Origin Informaiton, Hermeneutics of Suspicion, and Magical African Refugee Claims." In *Technologies of Suspicion and the Ethics of Obligation in Political Asylum,* edited by Bridget M. Haas and Amy Shuman, 129–52. Athens, OH: Ohio University Press.

Lee, Stephen. 2019. "Family Separation as Slow Death." *Columbia Law Review* 119, no. 8: 2319–84.

Lewis, Hanna, Peter Dwyer, Stuart Hodgkison, and Louise Waite. 2014. *Precarious Lives: Forced Labour, Exploitation and Asylum*. Bristol, UK: Bristol University Press.

Li, Susan SY, Belinda J. Liddell, and Angela Nickerson. 2016. "The Relationship between Post-Migration Stress and Psychological Disorders in Refugees and Asylum Seekers." *Current Psychiatry Reports* 18, no. 9: 82.

Löbel, Lea-Maria. 2020. "Family Separation and Refugee Mental Health–A Network Perspective. *Social Networks* 61: 20–33.

Lopez, William D. 2019. *Separated: Family and Community in the Aftermath of an Immigration Raid*. Baltimore, MD: Johns Hopkins University Press.

Low, Setha M. 1994. "Embodied Metaphors: Nerves as Lived Experience." In *Embodiment and Experience: The Existential Ground of Culture and Self,* edited by Thomas J. Csordas, 139–62. Cambridge: Cambridge University Press.

Lucht, Hans. 2011. *Darkness Before Daybreak: African Migrants Living on the Margins in Southern Italy Today*. Berkeley: University of California Press.

Luhrmann, Tanya M. 2006. "Subjectivity." *Anthropological Theory* 6, no. 3: 345–61.

Lustig, Stuart L., Sarah Kureshi, Kevin L. Delucchi, Vincent Iacopino, and Samantha C. Morse. 2008. "Asylum Grant Rates Following Medical Evaluations of Maltreatment among Political Asylum Applicants in the United States." *Journal of Immigrant and Minority Health* 10, no. 1: 7–15.

Mahler, Sarah J. 2001. "Transnational Relationships: The Struggle to Communicate across Borders." *Identities Global Studies in Culture and Power* 7, no. 4: 583–619.

Malkki, Liisa. 1996. "Speechless Emissaries: Refugees, Humanitarianism, and Dehistoricization." *Cultural Anthropology* 11, no. 3: 377–404.

———. 1995. "Refugees and Exile: From Refugee Studies to the National Order of Things." *Annual Review of Anthropology* 24: 495–523.

———. 1992. "National Geographic: The Rooting of Peoples and the Territorialization of National Identity among Scholars and Refugees." *Cultural Anthropology* 7, no. 1: 24–44.

Martínez, Daniel E., Jeremy Slack, and Ricardo Martínez-Schuldt. 2018. "The Rise of Mass Deportation in the United States." In *The Handbook of Race, Ethnicity, Crime, and Justice*, edited by Ramiro Martinez, Jr., Meghan E. Hollis, and Jacob I. Stowell, 173–201. Oxford, UK: Wiley Blackwell.

Martinez-Aranda, Mirian G. 2022. "Extended Punishment: Criminalizing Immigrants through Surveillance Technology." *Journal of Ethnic and Migration Studies* 48, no. 1: 74–91.

Mattingly, Cheryl. 2010. *The Paradox of Hope: Journeys through a Clinical Borderland*. Berkeley: University of California Press.

Mayblin, Lucy. 2020. *Impoverishment and Asylum: Social Policy as Slow Violence*. London: Routledge.

———. 2017. *Asylum after Empire: Colonial Legacies in the Politics of Asylum Seeking*. London: Rowman & Littlefield.

———. 2016a. "Troubling the Exclusive Privileges of Citizenship: Mobile Solidarities, Asylum Seekers, and the Right to Work." *Citizenship Studies* 20, no. 2: 192–207.

———. 2016b. "Complexity Reduction and Policy Consensus: Asylum Seekers, the Right to Work, and the 'Pull Factor' Thesis in the UK Context. "*The British Journal of Politics and International Relations* 18, no. 4: 812–28.

Mayblin, Lucy, Mustafa Wake, and Mohsen Kazemi. 2020. "Necropolitics and the Slow Violence of the Everyday: Asylum Seeker Welfare in the Postcolonial Present." *Sociology* 54, no. 1: 107–23.

Mbembe, Achille. 2003. "Necropolitics." *Public Culture* 15, no. 1: 11–40.

McColl, Helen, Kwame McKenzie, and Kamaldeep Bhui. 2008. "Mental Healthcare of Asylum-seekers and Refugees. *Advances in Psychiatric Treatment* 14, no. 6: 452–59.

McGranahan, Carole. 2018. "Refusal as Political Practice: Citizenship, Sovereignty, and Tibetan Refugee Status."*American Ethnologist* 45, no. 3: 367–79.

McGuirk, Siobhán, and Adrienne Pine. 2020. *Asylum for Sale: Profit and Protest in the Migration Industry*. Oakland, CA: PM Press.

McKinnon, Sara L. 2009. "Citizenship and the Performance of Credibility: Audiencing Gender-based Asylum Seekers in U.S. Immigration Court." *Text and Performance Quarterly* 29, no. 3: 205–21.

McNevin, Anne, and Antje Missbach. 2018. "Luxury Limbo: Temporal Techniques of Border Control and the Humanitarianisation of Waiting. "*International Journal of Migration and Border Studies* 4, no. 1–2: 12–34.

Menjívar, Cecilia. 2006. "Liminal Legality: Salvadoran and Guatemalan Immigrants' Lives in the United States."*American Journal of Sociology* 111, no. 4: 999–1037.

Menjívar, Cecilia, and Leisy Abrego. 2012. "Legal Violence: Immigration Law and the Lives of Central American Immigrants." *American Journal of Sociology* 117, no. 5: 1380–1421.

Merry, Sally Engle, and Susan B. Coutin. 2014. "Technologies of Truth in the Anthropology of Conflict: AES/APLA Presidential Address, 2013." *American Ethnologist* 41, no. 1: 1–16.

Meyer, Maureen, and Adam Isacson. 2019. *The 'Wall' Before the Wall: Mexico's Crackdown on Migration at its Southern Border*. WOLA: Advocacy for Human Rights in the Americas. https://www.wola.org/analysis/mexico-southern-border-report.

Miller, Alexander, Julia Marie Hess, Deborah Bybee, and Jessica R. Goodkind. 2018. "Understanding the Mental Health Consequences of Family Separation for Refugees: Implications for Policy and Practice." *American Journal of Orthopsychiatry* 88, no. 1: 26.

Miller, Banks, Linda Camp Keith, and Jennifer S. Holmes, eds. 2015. *Immigration Judges and US Asylum Policy*. Philadelphia: University of Pennsylvania Press.

MN Department of Health. 2021. "Primary Refugee Arrival to Minnesota by Initial County of Resettlement and Country of Origin, 2019. https://www.health.state.mn.us/communities/rih/stats/19yrsum.pdf.

———. 2012. "Primary Refugee Arrival to Minnesota by Initial County of Resettlement and Country of Origin, 2011." https://www.health.state.mn.us/communities/rih/stats/11yrsum.pdf.

Moffette, D., and S. Vadasaria. 2016. "Uninhibited Violence: Race and the Securitization of Immigration." *Critical Studies on Security* 4, no. 3: 291–305.

Mountz, Alison. 2010. *Seeking Asylum: Human Smuggling and Bureaucracy at the Border*. Minneapolis: University of Minnesota Press.

Mountz, Alison, Richard Wright, Ines Miyares, and Adrian J. Bailey. 2002. "Lives in Limbo: Temporary Protected Status and Immigrant Identities." *Global Networks* 2, no. 4: 335–56.

Ní Raghallaigh, Muireann. 2014. "The Causes of Mistrust Amongst Asylum Seekers and Refugees: Insights from Research with Unaccompanied Asylum-Seeking Minors Living in the Republic of Ireland." *Journal of Refugee Studies* 27, no. 1: 82–100.

Nixon, Rob. 2011. *Slow Violence and the Environmentalism of the Poor*. Cambridge, MA: Harvard University Press.

Núñez, Guillermina, and Josiah Heyman. 2007. "Entrapment Processes and Immigrant Communities in a Time of Heightened Border Vigilance." *Human Organization* 66, no. 4: 354–365.

Nwati, Morgan Tebei. 2021. "The Anglophone Crisis: The Rise of Arms Trafficking and Smuggling, its Effects on the Two English Regions of Cameroon." *Advances in Applied Sociology* 11, no. 1: 1.

Nyers, Peter. 2015. "Migrant Citizenships and Autonomous Mobilities. *Migration, Mobility, & Displacement* 1, no. 1: 23–39.

———. 2006. *Rethinking Refugees: Beyond States of Emergency*. New York: Routledge.

Ong, Aihwa. 2003. *Buddha is Hiding: Refugees, Citizenship, the New America*. Berkeley: University of California Press.

———. 1996. "Cultural Citizenship as Subject-Making: Immigrants Negotiate Racial and Cultural Boundaries in the United States." *Current Anthropology* 37, no. 5: 737–62.

Ordóñez, Juan Thomas. 2008. "The State of Confusion: Reflections on Central American Asylum Seekers in the Bay Area." *Ethnography* 9, no. 1: 35–60.

Ortner, Sherry B. 2006. *Anthropology and Social Theory: Culture, Power, and the Acting Subject*. Durham, NC: Duke University Press.

Parla, Ayşe. 2019. *Precarious Hope: Migration and the Limits of Belonging in Turkey.* Stanford, CA: Stanford University Press.

Parish, Steven M. 2008. *Subjectivity and Suffering in American Culture.* New York: Palgrave MacMillan.

Paskey, Stephen. 2016. "Telling Refugee Stories: Trauma, Credibility, and the Adversarial Adjudication of Claims for Asylum." *Santa Clara Law Review* 56: 457–530.

Penn State Law, Immigrants' Rights Clinic and American Immigration Council's Legal Action Center. 2010. *Up Against the Asylum Clock: Fixing the Broken Employment Authorization Asylum Clock.* Center for Immigrants' Rights Clinic Publications. https://www.americanimmigrationcouncil.org /sites/default/files/other_litigation_documents/asylum_clock_paper.pdf.

Perdigon, Sylvain. "Comment on 'Asylum as a Form of Life: The Politics and Experience of Indeterminacy in South Africa.'" *Current Anthropology* 58, no. 2: 181–82.

Peteet, Julie. 2005. *Landscape of Hope and Despair.* Philadelphia: University of Pennsylvania Press.

Peutz, Nathalie, and Nicholas De Genova. 2010. "Introduction." In *The Deportation Regime: Sovereignty, Space, and the Freedom of Movement,* edited by N. De Genova and N. Peutz, 1–32. Durham, NC: Duke University Press.

Pierce, Sarah, and Jessica Bolter. 2020. *Dismantling and Reconstructing the US Immigration System: A Catalog of Changes Under the Trump Presidency.* New York: Migration Policy Institute. https://www.migrationpolicy.org /sites/default/files/publications/MPI_US-Immigration-Trump-Presidency-Final.pdf.

Polivy, Janet, and C. Peter Herman. 2002. "If at First You Don't Succeed: False Hopes of Self-Change." *American Psychologist* 57, no. 9: 677–89.

Price, Patricia L. 2010. "At the Crossroads: Critical Race Theory and Critical Geographies of Race." *Progress in Human Geography* 34, no. 2: 147–74.

Puumala, Eeva, Riitta Ylikomi, and Hanna-leena Ristimäki. 2017. "Giving an Account of Persecution: The Dynamic Formation of Asylum Narratives." *Journal of Refugee Studies* 31, no. 2: 197–215.

Quesada, James. 2012. "Illegalization and Embodied Vulnerability in Health." *Social Science and Medicine* 74, no. 6: 894–96.

Quijano, Anibel. 2000. "Coloniality of Power and Eurocentrism in Latin America." *International Sociology* 15, no. 2: 215–32.

———. 1992. "Colonialidad y modernidad/racionalidad." *Perú Indigena* 13.29: 11–20.

Rainbird, Sophia. 2014. "Asserting Existence: Agentive Narratives Arising from the Restraints of Seeking Asylum in East Anglia, Britain." *Ethos* 42, no. 4: 460–78.

Ramji-Nogales, Jaya, Andrew I. Schoenholtz, and Philip G. Schrag. 2011. *Refugee Roulette: Disparities in Asylum Adjudication and Proposals for Reform*. New York: NYU Press.

Ramsay, Georgina. 2020a. "Time and the Other in Crisis: How Anthropology Makes Its Displaced Object." *Anthropological Theory* 20, no. 4: 385–413.

———. 2020b. "Humanitarian Exploits: Ordinary Displacement and the Political Economy of the Global Refugee Regime. *Critique of Anthropology* 40, no. 1: 3–27.

———. 2017. *Impossible Refuge: The Control and Constraint of Refugee Futures*. London: Routledge.

Reardon, Gabriela. 2008. "Immigrants Fight Restrictions at Home." *City Limits*, September 8, 2008. https://citylimits.org/2008/09/08/immigrants-fight-restrictions-at-home.

Reiter, Keramet, and Susan Bibler Coutin. 2017. "Crossing Borders and Criminalizing Identity: The Disintegrated Subjects of Administrative Sanctions." *Law & Society Review* 51, no. 3: 567–601.

Rempell, Scott. 2009. "Credibility Assessments and the REAL ID Act's Amendments to Immigration Law." *Texas International Law Journal* 44: 185–232.

Robleda, Zubia Willman. 2020. "Re-inventing Everyday Life in the Asylum Centre: Everyday Tactics among Women Seeking Asylum in Norway." *Nordic Journal of Migration Research,* 10, no. 2: 82–95.

Rousseau, Cécile, François Crépeau, Patricia Foxen, and France Houle. 2002. "The Complexity of Determining Refugeehood: A Multidisciplinary Analysis of the Decision-making Process of the Canadian Immigration and Refugee Board." *Journal of Refugee Studies* 15, no. 1: 43–70.

Rousseau, Cécile, and Patricia Foxen. 2010. "Look Me in the Eye: Empathy and the Transmission of Trauma in the Refugee Determination Process." *Transcultural Psychiatry* 47, no. 1: 70–92.

Rousseau, Cécile, Marie-Claire Rufagari, Déogratias Bagilishya, and Toby Measham. 2004. "Remaking Family Life: Strategies for Re-Establishing Continuity among Congolese Refugees during the Family Reunification Process." *Social Science & Medicine* 59, no. 5: 1095–1108.

Rotter, Rebecca. 2016. "Waiting in the Asylum Determination Process: Just an Empty Interlude?" *Time & Society* 25, no. 1: 80–101.

Rozakou, Katerina. 2020. "The Violence of Accelerated Time: Waiting and Hasting during 'the Long Summer of Migration'in Greece." In *Waiting and the Temporalities of Irregular Migration,* edited by Christine M. Jacobsen, Mary-Anne Karlsen, and Shahram Khosravi, 23–39. London: Routledge.

Rutgers School of Law-Newark Immigrant Rights Clinic in conjuction with American Friends Service Committee. 2012. *Freed but Not Freed: A Report Examining the Current Use of Alternatives to Immigration Detention.*

Newark: Rutgers School of Law. http://*www.law.newark.rutgers.edu/irc-publications*.

Salina Gross, Corina. 2004. "Struggling with the Imaginaries of Trauma and Trust: The Refugee Experience in Switzerland." *Culture, Medicine, and Psychiatry* 28: 151–67.

Sanchez, Gabriella, and Mary Romero. 2010. "Critical Race Theory in the US Sociology of Immigration." *Sociology Compass* 4, no. 9: 779–88.

Sargent, Carolyn, and Stéphanie Larchanché. 2011. "Transnational Migration and Global Health: the Production and Management of Risk, Illness, and Access to Care. *Annual Review of Anthropology* 40: 345–61.

Scheel, S., and Vicki Squire. 2014. "Forced Migrants as Illegal Migrants." *The Oxford Handbook of Refugee and Forced Migration Studies,* edited by Elena Fiddian-Qasmiyeh, Gil Loescher, Katy Long, and Nando Sigona, 188–99. Oxford, UK: Oxford University Press.

Scheper-Hughes, Nancy. 1992. *Death Without Weeping: The Violence of Everyday Violence in Brazil.* Berkeley: University of California Press.

Scheper-Hughes, Nancy, and Philippe Bourgois. 2004a. "Introduction: Making Sense of Violence." In *Violence in War and Peace: An Anthology,* edited by Nancy Scheper-Hughes and Philippe Bourgois, 1–27. Malden, MA: Blackwell Publishing.

———. 2004b. "Comment on 'An Anthropology of Structural Violence.'" *Current Anthropology* 45, no. 3: 317–18.

Schoenholtz, Andrew. 2005. "Refugee Protection in the United States Post-September 11th." *Columbia Human Rights Law Review* 36, no. 2: 323–64.

Schuster, Liza. 2018. "Fatal Flaws in the UK Asylum Decision-Making System: An Analysis of Home Office Refusal Letters." *Journal of Ethnic and Migration Studies* 46, no. 7: 1371–87.

Scott, Penelope. 2018. "'It's Like Fighting for Survival': How Rejected Black African Asylum Seekers Experience Living Conditions in an Eastern German State." *Journal of Immigrant & Refugee Studies* 16, no. 4: 372–90.

Shuman, Amy, and Carol Bohmer. 2012. "The Stigmatized Vernacular: Political Asylum and the Politics of Visibility/Recognition." *Journal of Folklore Research* 49, no. 2: 199–226.

Silbey, Susan S. 2005. "After Legal Consciousness." *Annual Review of Law and Social Sciences* 1: 323–68.

Silove, Derrick, Zachary Steel, Ina Susljik, Naomi Frommer, et al. 2007. "The Impact of the Refugee Decision on the Trajectory of PTSD, Anxiety, and Depressive Symptoms among Asylum Seekers: A Longitudinal Study." *American Journal of Disaster Medicine* 2, no. 6: 321–29.

Singer, Audrey, Susan W. Hardwick, and Caroline B. Brettell. 2008. "Twenty-First Century Gateways: Immigrants in Suburban America." Washington, DC: Migration Policy Institute.

Slack, Jeremy., Daniel E. Martínez, Alison Elizabeth Lee, and Scott Whiteford. 2016. "The Geography of Border Militarization: Violence, Death and Health in Mexico and the United States." *Journal of Latin American Geography* 15, no. 1: 7–32.

Smit, Ria, and Pragna Rugunanan. 2014. "From Precarious Lives to Precarious Work: The Dilemma Facing Refugees in Gauteng, South Africa." *South African Review of Sociology* 45, no. 2: 4–26.

Solórzano, Daniel G., and Tara J. Yosso. 2002. "Critical Race Methodology: Counter-Storytelling as an Analytical Framework for Education Research." *Qualitative Inquiry* 8, no. 1: 23–44.

Sorgoni, Barbara. 2019. "The Location of Truth: Bodies and Voices in the Italian Asylum Procedure." *PoLAR: Political and Legal Anthropology Review* 42, no. 1: 161–76.

Spivak, Gayatri Chakravorty. 1988. "Can the Subaltern Speak?" In *Marxism and the Interpretation of Culture,* edited by Cary Nelson and Lawrence Grossberg, 271–313. Urbana-Champaign: University of Illinois Press.

Squire, Vicki. 2009. *The Exclusionary Politics of Asylum*. London: Palgrave Macmillan.

Staples, James, and Tom Widger. 2012. "Situating Suicide as an Anthropological Problem: Ethnographic Approaches to Understanding Self-Harm and Self-Inflicted Death." *Culture, Medicine, and Psychiatry* 36: 183–293.

Statz, Michelle. 2018. *Lawyering an Uncertain Cause: Immigration Advocacy and Chinese Youth in the US*. Nashville, TN: Vanderbilt University Press.

Stephen, Lynn. 2018. "Creating Preemptive Suspects: National Security, Border Defense, and Immigration Policy, 1980-Present." *Latin American Perspectives* 45, no. 6: 7–25.

Stoler, Ann L. 2013. *Imperial Debris: On Ruins and Ruination*. Durham, NC: Duke University Press.

Stuesse, Angela, and Mathew Coleman. 2014. "Automobility, Immobility, Altermobility: Surviving and Resisting the Intensification of Immigrant Policing." *City & Society* 26, no. 1: 51–72.

Sullivan, Eileen. 2022. "Biden Administration Prepares Sweeping Changes to Asylum Process." *The New York Times*. March 24, 2022. https://www.nytimes.com/2022/03/24/us/politics/us-asylum-changes.html.

Summerfield, Derek. 2012. "Afterword: Against 'Global Mental Health.'" *Transcultural Psychiatry* 49, no. 3–4: 519–30.

Talavera, Victor, Guillermina Gina Núñez-Mchiri, and Josiah Heyman. 2010. "Deportation in the US-Mexico Borderlands: Anticipation, Experience, and Memory." In *The Deportation Regime*, edited by Nicholas De Genova and Nathalie Peutz, 166–95. Durham, NC: Duke University Press.

Tang, Eric. 2015. *Unsettled: Cambodian Refugees in the New York City Hyperghetto*. Philadelphia, PA: Temple University Press.

Tazreiter, Claudia. 2004. *Asylum Seekers and the State: The Politics of Protection in a Security-Conscious World.* Burlington, VT: Ashgate.

Tazzioli, Martina, Glenda Garelli, and Nicholas De Genova. 2018. Autonomy of Asylum?: The Autonomy of Migration Undoing the Refugee Crisis Script. *South Atlantic Quarterly* 117, no. 2: 239–65.

Tazzioli, Martina, and William Walters. 2016. "The Sight of Migration: Governmentality, Visibility and Europe's Contested Borders. *Global Society* 30, no. 3: 445–64.

Terretta, Meredith. 2015. "Fraudulent Asylum Seeking as Transnational Mobilization." In *African Asylum at a Crossroads,* edited by Iris Berger, Tricia Redeker Hepner, Benjamin N. Lawrence, Joanna T. Tague, and Meredith Terretta, 58–74. Athens: Ohio University Press.

Thomas, Robert. 2006. "Assessing the Credibility of Asylum Claims: EU and UK Approaches Examined." *European Journal of Migration and Law* 8: 79–96.

Thomson, Marnie J. 2012. "Black Boxes of Bureaucracy: Transparency and Opacity in the Resettlement Process of Congolese Refugees." *PoLAR: Political and Legal Anthropology Review* 35, no. 2: 186–205.

Ticktin, Miriam. 2011. *Casualties of Care: Immigration and the Politics of Humanitarianism in France.* Berkeley: University of California Press.

———. 2006. "Where Ethics and Politics Meet: The Violence of Humanitarianism in France." *American Ethnologist* 33, no. 1: 33–49.

Toosi, Nahal, Ted Hesson, and Sarah Frostenson. 2018. "Foreign Visas Plunge Under Trump." *Politico.* April 3, 2018. https://www.politico.com/interactives/2018/trump-travel-ban-visas-decline.

Tuckett, Anna. 2018. *Rules, Paper, Status: Migrants and Precarious Bureaucracy in Contemporary Italy.* Stanford, CA: Stanford University Press.

Turnbull, Sarah. 2016. "'Stuck in the Middle': Waiting and Uncertainty in Immigration Detention." *Time & Society* 25, no. 1: 61–79.

Turner, Stuart. 2016. "Staying Out of Place: The Being and Becoming of Burundian Refugees in the Camp and the City." *Conflict and Society* 2, no. 1: 37–51.

Tormey, Anwen. 2007. "'Everyone with Eyes Can See the Problem': Moral Citizens and the Space of Irish Nationhood." *International Migration* 45, no. 3: 69–98.

Transactional Records Access Clearinghouse (TRAC) Immigration. n.d. "Immigration Court Backlog Tool." Accessed September 25, 2022. https://trac.syr.edu/phptools/immigration/court_backlog.

Transactional Records Access Clearinghouse (TRAC) Immigration. 2021. "Immigration Court Asylum Backlog." November 30, 2021. https://trac.syr.edu/phptools/immigration/asylumbl.

Transactional Records Access Clearinghouse (TRAC) Immigration. 2012. Judge-by-Judge Asylum Decisions in Immigration Courts FY 2007–2012. https://trac.syr.edu/immigration/reports/306/include/denialrates.html.

Tyler, Imogen. 2006. "'Welcome to Britain': The Cultural Politics of Asylum." *European Journal of Cultural Studies* 9, no. 2: 158–202.

US Citizenship and Immigration Services (USCIS). n.d. "Case Processing Times." Accessed November 29, 2019. https://egov.uscis.gov/processing-times.

US Citizenship and Immigration Services (USCIS), Asylum Division. 2016. *Affirmative Asylum Procedures Manual.* May 2016. *https://www.uscis.gov /sites/default/files/document/guides/AAPM-2016.pdf.*

US Department of Justice, Executive Office for Immigration Review. March 4, 2012. *FY2011 Statistical Yearbook. https://www.justice.gov/sites/default /files/eoir/legacy/2012/02/21/fy11syb.pdf*

Utržan, Damir S., and Andrea K. Northwood. 2017. "Broken Promises and Lost Dreams: Navigating Asylum in the United States." *Journal of Marital and Family Therapy* 43, no. 1: 3–15.

van der Kist, Jasper, and Damian Rosset. 2020. "Knowledge and Legitimacy in Asylum Decision-Making: The Politics of Country of Origin Information." *Citizenship Studies* 24, no. 5: 663–79.

Vaughan-Williams, Nick, and Maria Pisani. 2020. "Migrating Borders, Bordering Lives: Everyday Geographies of Ontological Security and Insecurity in Malta." *Social & Cultural Geography* 21, no. 5: 651–73.

Viruell-Fuentes, Edna A. 2007. "Beyond Acculturation: Immigration, Discrimination, and Health Research among Mexicans in the United States." *Social Science & Medicine,* 65: 1524–1535.

Viruell-Fuentes, Edna A., Patricia Y. Miranda, and Sawsan Abdulrahim. 2012. "More Than Culture: Structural Racism, Intersectionality Theory, And Immigrant Health." *Social Science & Medicine* 75, no. 12: 2099–2106.

Vogt, Wendy A. 2018. *Lives in Transit: Violence and Intimacy on the Migrant Journey.* Berkeley: University of California Press.

Waite, Louise. 2017. "Asylum Seekers and the Labour Market: Spaces of Discomfort and Hostility." *Social Policy and Society* 16, no. 4: 669–79.

Watters, Charles. 2019. "Geographies of Aspiration and the Politics of Suspicion in the Context of Border Control." In *Technologies of Suspicion and the Ethics of Obligation in Political Asylum,* edited by Bridget M. Haas and Amy Shuman, 47–60. Athens: Ohio University Press.

———. 2007. "Refugees at Europe's Borders: The Moral Economy of Care." *Transcultural Psychiatry* 44, no. 3: 394–417.

———. 2001a. "Avenues of Access and the Moral Economy of Legitimacy." *Anthropology Today* 17, no. 2: 22–23.

———. 2001b. "Emerging Paradigms in the Mental Health Care of Refugees." *Social Science & Medicine* 52: 1709–1718.

Walker, Eliot. "Asylees in Wonderland: A New Procedural Perspective on America's Asylum System." *Northwestern Journal of Law and Social Policy* 2, no. 1: 1–29.

Weber, Leanne. 2013. *Policing Non-Citizens.* New York: Routledge.

Weiss, Gail, Ann V. Murphy, and Gayle Salamon, eds. 2019. *50 Concepts for a Critical Phenomenology.* Chicago: Northwestern University Press.

Welander, Marta, and Leonie Ansems De Vries. 2016. "Refugees, Displacement, and the European 'Politics of Exhaustion.'" *OpenDemocracy.* September 19, 2016. https://www.opendemocracy.net/en/mediterranean-journeys-in-hope/refugees-displacement-and-europ.

Welch, Michael, and Liza Schuster. 2008. "American and British Constructions of Asylum Seekers: Moral Panic, Detention, and Human Rights." In *Keep Out the Other: A Critical Introduction to Immigration Enforcement Today,* edited by David C. Brotherton and Philip Kretsedemas, 138–59. New York: Columbia University Press.

Whyte, Zachary. 2011. "Enter the Myopticon: Uncertain Surveillance in the Danish Asylum System." *Anthropology Today* 27, no. 3: 18–21.

Willen, Sarah S. 2019. *Fighting for Dignity: Migrant Lives at Israel's Margins.* Philadelphia: University of Pennsylvania Press.

———. 2012. "Migration, 'Illegality,' and Health: Mapping Embodied Vulnerability and Debating Health-Related Deservingness. *Social Science & Medicine* 74, no. 6: 805–11.

———. 2010. "Citizens, 'Real' Others, and 'Other' Others: The Biopolitics of Otherness and the Deportation of Unauthorized Migrant Workers from Tel Aviv, Israel." In *The Deportation Regime: Sovereignty, Space and the Freedom of Movement,* edited by Nicholas P. De Genova and Nathalie Peutz, 262–94. Durham, NC: Duke University Press.

———. 2007. "Toward a Critical Phenomenology of 'Illegality': State Power, Criminalization, and Abjectivity Among Undocumented Migrant Workers in Tel Aviv, Israel." *International Migration* 45, no. 3: 8–38.

Wise, A. 2006. *Exile and Return among East Timorese.* Philadelphia: University of Pennsylvania Press.

Wise, Amanda, and Selvaraj Velayutham.,2017. "Transnational Affect and Emotion in Migration Research." *International Journal of Sociology* 47, no. 2: 116–30.

Yarris, Kristin. 2017. *Care Across Generations.* Stanford, CA: Stanford University Press.

———. 2011. "The Pain of 'Thinking Too Much': Dolor de Cerebro and the Embodiment of Social Hardship among Nicaraguan Women." *Ethos* 39, no. 2: 226–48.

Yarris, Kristin, and Heide Castañeda. 2015. "Discourses of Displacement and Deservingness: Interrogating Distinctions between 'Economic' and 'Forced' Migration." *International Migration* 53, no. 3: 64–69.

Zarowsky, Christina. 2004. "Writing Trauma: Emotion, Ethnography, and the Politics of Suffering among Somali Returnees in Ethiopia." *Culture, Medicine and Psychiatry* 28, no. 2: 189–209.

Zetter, Roger. 2007. "More Labels, Fewer Refugees: Remaking the Refugee Label in an Era of Globalization." *Journal of Refugee Studies* 20, no. 2: 172–92.

Zigon, Jarrett. 2018. "Hope and Waiting in Post-Soviet Moscow." In *Ethnographies of Waiting: Doubt, Hope, and Uncertainty,* edited by Manpreet Janeja and Andreas Bandak, 65–86. London: Bloomsbury Academic.

———. 2009. "Hope Dies Last: Two Aspects of Hope in Contemporary Moscow." *Anthropological Theory* 9, no. 3: 253–71.

Index

Founded in 1893,
UNIVERSITY OF CALIFORNIA PRESS
publishes bold, progressive books and journals
on topics in the arts, humanities, social sciences,
and natural sciences—with a focus on social
justice issues—that inspire thought and action
among readers worldwide.

The UC PRESS FOUNDATION
raises funds to uphold the press's vital role
as an independent, nonprofit publisher, and
receives philanthropic support from a wide
range of individuals and institutions—and from
committed readers like you. To learn more, visit
ucpress.edu/supportus.